Mojo

and

ALSO BY JEZ BUTTERWORTH
AVAILABLE FROM TCG

Jerusalem

Mojo
and Other Plays

JEZ BUTTERWORTH

THEATRE COMMUNICATIONS GROUP

NEW YORK

2012

Contents

An Interview with Jez Butterworth

The playwright talked to Nick Hern on the eve of the reopening of *Jerusalem* in the West End in October 2011.

Can we start when you're twenty-five, which is when you write Mojo? *Do you want to say how that came about?*

I left London and moved to Pewsey in Wiltshire, which ended up being the fictional model for Flintock in *Jerusalem*. It was a dreamlike experience: I left London with the unrealistic dream of writing a play which spoke to people. And that's kind of what happened.

It was very odd – to spend this period of utter penury through the winter out in the countryside, writing every day and every night, no television, no car, only a bicycle…

But Mojo *is a very urban play. Where did that come from?*

The actual initial impetus for the play was a conversation I had with Malcolm McLaren. He was talking about Soho and the wonderful collision between early rock and roll and gangland violence. It wasn't something I knew anything about, but there was something about the collision between these two things that sparked something. Who knows where plays come from, but in this case it came from Malcolm.

What I *didn't* want it to be was about gangsters. I wanted it to be about people who *think* they are – or who possibly *know* – gangsters, but aren't. Because they're a bunch of children, everyone in the play: it's like a school playground game really. Sweets and Potts aren't gangsters. Skinny's not a gangster. Nobody in it is, really. Baby's just a lost soul… It was always taken as a gangland play, but it's not at all.

So you sent it to the Royal Court?

My agent at the time, Nick Marston, sent the play to the Bush, and Dominic Dromgoole [then artistic director of the Bush] mentioned it by mistake in conversation with Stephen Daldry [then artistic director of the Royal Court], and Stephen Daldry just poached it.

So the play was virtually fast-tracked onto the stage? It was, as you say, a dream come true.

I finished the play in January. In February I was sitting in an office at the Royal Court with Stephen and Ian Rickson.

He'd been brought in to direct it?

Ian wanted to do it and to do it on the main stage. I went through a process of rewriting it for a week and then they decided they were going to stick it on the main stage. I moved back to London on May 1st, on May 2nd I won the George Devine Award, and we started rehearsing a month later. And a month after that it was a sell-out.

So no wonder in the photo on the front of this book, which is you outside the Royal Court at that period, you're looking a bit…

…shell-shocked.

Exactly: shell-shocked!

And then me and the Royal Court kind of parted company… I directed a film of *Mojo* the next year. And lost touch with Ian, partly, I think, because Ian had wanted to do it. I don't think I was very sensitive about it at the time. It was a good long while before I set foot back in the Royal Court.

And you were writing a large number of screenplays during this absence from the theatre?

Yes, lots of screenplays – lots of which didn't get made, lots of which were working on other people's things. I realised by the time I was thirty-three, thirty-four that I'd taken a wrong turning. Some dreadful cocktail of fear and being paid just enough money meant that I had completely wheel-clamped my creative desire to go in any direction that was going to satisfy me. And I had to own up to that. So it was around that point that I moved back to the countryside.

Was there a Road to Damascus moment?

There was a moment in 2003/2004 when the music I was trying to listen to didn't sound as good: troubling rather than nourishing. I'd started lying to myself about something to do with my nature and what I want, and I've got to go and find it out. And so the next year or so was a fairly fearless swan-dive into a place where I felt I could write a line that was true and resonated with my own heart rather than being the right length and suiting someone else's needs.

I do understand that: you were psychoanalysing yourself in a sense...

On a lot of long walks by rivers with a dog we'd just bought, where I started thinking about what I wanted to do with my work. I realised I was properly marooned and needed to do something about it. *The Winterling* was the first play I wrote out in Devon, where I was living. It's pretty much a cross-section of what was going on with me at the time. I'd started to keep, slaughter and butcher animals. And that play is very much a visceral, animal-like experience. Really it's about the question – it strikes me now – as to whether there is any mercy in the world. Of course there is: we're the only ones that have it. But it's a question of where it gets exercised in the course of that play. There's an act of mercy at the end of that play, which is the first thing that happens in it that a bear wouldn't be capable of doing.

You wrote it at top speed because of this gap that had opened up in the programme for the Royal Court's fiftieth anniversary year?

I sat down to write one play and another one came out. I was left alone in the cottage that we lived in and it was the night that Harold Pinter did his Nobel Prize speech, called 'Art, Truth and Politics'. And I watched it. I knew Harold – I'd directed him in the film of *Mojo* – but I hadn't seen him for ages. And in the first part of that speech, he tells you how to write a play – in the first ten minutes: he just takes you through it. It was like being reminded how to write a play. You'll remember Harold was extremely ill, too ill to go and collect the award: it was like he was going to die any day. So I decided to sit down and write using entirely his technique. And try to speak like him. *The Winterling* sounds a lot like Harold Pinter.

It really does.

Everybody said that – except Harold. I wish to God I'd dedicated the play to him, because then it would have been obvious what it was I was up to: it was really an exercise in homage and also a wish to try to get close to him.

Close to him as a person or…?

Close to him as a creative force. To try to stand in his shoes. I saw the play again the other day for the first time and I was surprised by how much I liked it. I expected to find that it was a stuffed bird, but it's not at all. It flies. I don't give a fuck how much it sounds like Harold; it's not easy to sound like Harold. If you're going to do any kind of apprenticeship – and I still consider myself in one – it's a great experience to… Everybody does it: there's a point where you sing in someone else's voice before you sing in your own. There's this thing that critics get up to here where it's almost as if they're trying to work out who you copied your homework off. Voice is the hardest thing to grasp. But the critics' attitude to writers is: 'Let's stamp the shit out of them when they're on a journey to finding their voice.' Were I a different person, I could have been destroyed by the response to that play.

You said you were too busy to see the play more than once. That was because your film career was carrying on in tandem? But not so very long after that you seemed to be returning to the theatre more frequently. Did you deliberately wind down your film commitments?

I did, yes. Around 2007 I started to change my ideas about what I wanted to use the theatre for. It wasn't just a mysterious process that you threw yourself at in a short space of time. I suddenly realised that it was of foremost importance to me that I'd always written for actors not audiences. I love the idea that an actor gets to spend a month – or two if you're lucky – with your work, your words, and thinks about it in a way that an audience isn't privileged to. It becomes a part of the actor's life. And I realised the whole process is about evoking anxieties that we share, anxieties that you can bring to light and deal with in the theatre. It hit me like a bolt of lightning: that's what it's for; this is a church. If I get this right, and I try hard enough, and I'm brave enough about it, I'm going to be able to access something which is going to be of importance to the actors first of all, and then to the audience.

With Parlour Song *and then* Jerusalem *appearing on stage here in the UK in the same year, it seemed that some floodgate had been opened. What happened? Did you write them in parallel? Is the one related to the other?*

One takes place in a wood and the other takes place in a new estate that's been built on the site of a wood. Ned in *Parlour Song* says: 'There's been a wood; it was here for a thousand years. Now it's gone: we're here.' And then in *Jerusalem* there's the idea that the wood is going to be erased and replaced by housing estates. And though they're set in different parts of England, those two ideas speak to each other. Rooster Byron in *Jerusalem* and Ned in *Parlour Song* couldn't be more opposite. One is utterly defiant, courageous and free-spirited, the other is occluded, scared, closed, neurotic and shutting everything out – throughout. Albeit they're both in states of delusion and denial, they're opposite ends of the scale.

So did they come together in your mind?

Not consciously, but then at this point very little is conscious in terms of what it is I'm trying to do. I've found a way of disengaging consciously altogether from the process and of following a path, almost like following a trail of breadcrumbs through a wood, of goosebump experiences. I'm just using it as a compass: if the next bit creates goosebumps in some way, I'll go there and I don't ask why.

Harold Pinter used to talk about writing down snatches of dialogue or even just images which then went nowhere. Do you have false starts, or are you able to follow your compass accurately?

Jerusalem was a false start in as much as I wrote a first draft in 2004 and wholly disliked the first stab. The play was obviously big in scope, and I simply was unable to corral its effects into any kind of satisfying whole. Whether this was because, on a basic level, I hadn't composed for that many instruments before, or whether it was because I was afraid to really say what the play wanted to say, I will never know. But I returned to it in the spring of 2009, by which time, as I've described, my whole approach to my work had fundamentally changed. And it just came.

Apart from that, I don't have many half-written things. If I sit down to do it, I'll do it. I tend to end up with very few notes, usually a small amount that I will have lost along the way. It's almost like a performance, I suppose, where you sit down and set yourself an unfeasible time limit, usually dictated by a deadline, so it's got to happen. It's that feel of an actor walking on stage. What a neurologist might call 'performance arousal' occurs, where your brain sets itself up along different lines under pressure.

In 2007 I became friends with Harold Pinter and had lots of lunches with him and conversations with him about writing. In the two years before he died I saw him a lot and went to visit him. The conversations that we would have made it clear to me what it was I wanted to do professionally for the rest of my life, if I can. The things that Harold was saying were so extraordinarily profound and so meaningful to me that there was to be no fear from now on. There was going to be no place for that at all. In July 2007 he said something to me that was absolutely the ignition and spur to my decision to dedicate myself to playwriting.

Can you put it into words?

I'm never going to tell anyone.

That was 2007.

After *The Winterling,* before *Parlour Song* and *Jerusalem.*

Did Parlour Song *start with a specific image? Did you, for instance, turn into a particular housing estate and think, 'God, how deadly'?*

I grew up on a new-build estate. We moved in a good five years after the houses were built on green-belt land on the edge of the countryside. *Birthday Girl* [a film written and directed by Jez, starring Nicole Kidman, in 2001] deals with that as well: he's got suburbs out the front and wilderness out the back. I knew that world. I knew it really clearly. It wasn't something I needed to research. We grew up in a house where the house next door was a mirror image.

Both Parlour Song *and* Jerusalem *came about from following the breadcrumbs and getting goose pimples?*

Yes.

I have the impression that the pre-rehearsal draft of Jerusalem *that I read was a good deal longer than what appeared on stage. Do you get it all down and then look at what you've got?*

I was producing a film in New York at the time by day, *Fair Game,* and writing *Jerusalem* by night. There's an idea that this play took eight years to write, but actually it took about nine weeks over eight years: three weeks, four weeks and two weeks. The last bit was in New York, literally moonlighting, trying to get it finished at the very last minute. So we went into rehearsal with it not completed, which is, by the way, my dream state to enter any rehearsal. Ian was wonderful about it, even though I know he'd much rather have his annotated script before he goes into rehearsal.

So would the Royal Court, presumably.

They were brilliant about it too. We were a week into rehearsal, and Ian and I were saying, 'We need another actor.' And they were fine. 'And it's going to be three hours and fifteen minutes long.' And the Royal Court were absolutely fine. Dominic [Cooke, artistic director] is a big, big reason why this play ended up being what it is.

Tell me, finally, about the two short plays in this volume.

I've had a fifteen-year affair going on with the Atlantic Theater in New York. I did *Mojo* there in 1997, which was after Ian directed it at Steppenwolf. I met Neil Pepe, who's been the Atlantic's artistic director for a good twenty years, and we just hit it off. They've put on three of my plays and two shorts. And again, they will call up and say, 'We've got the twentieth anniversary coming up, can you write a one-act?' So I'll bang something out. Those sort of call-to-arms have always sparked me off. *Parlour Song*, for instance, started at the Atlantic, because they had a slot. The two one-acts were both essentially occasional pieces for different events.

There was no theme suggested to you?

None whatsoever, no. The last one, *The Naked Eye,* came about because I'd met Zosia Mamet, who's David Mamet's daughter and a wonderful actor, and I wanted to write something specifically for her. That was as far as it went in terms of a theme.

And Leavings, *the one about the dog, obviously has links to* The Winterling.

The Winterling was written incredibly quickly. I literally put that down and started writing *Leavings*. And oddly enough it starts exactly the same way. My neighbour had come round in floods of tears: her husband had left a brace of duck which he'd forgotten about on the seat of their Land Rover. She'd opened the door and they'd leapt out: one of them was dead and the other wasn't. They were a mating pair, so one was tied to the dead partner. And it just struck me... Anyone who's struggling with any kind of grief with the death of someone... So a lot of that was just the putting together of things that had happened to me immediately that week. It was an odd state to be in – very creative.

It was as though you had that handful of breadcrumbs.

Two handfuls.

Before we finish, is there anything else you want to say about this period that you feel should go on record?

The most important thing in my career so far, without a shadow of a doubt, has been Ian Rickson. His sense of what it is I'm trying to do has never faltered. To watch him in rehearsal... He'll go in with one set of ideas – he's running the Royal Court and coping with the politics – then, twenty minutes into rehearsal, he's changed completely, he's become a different creature: I don't think he knows it. He's become this intuitive blob that can put stuff together the way it should be put together. He directs not like a conductor but like a composer: this goes here, that goes there, so beautifully put-together. He's fearless in what he does and doesn't want to have in it. It's been a terrific working relationship. It's had fits and starts, and we often go off in a huff with each other. But I love working with him, and if I could spend my entire life fruitfully collaborating with Ian, it would be wonderful.

Mojo
and Other Plays

MOJO

Mojo was first performed at the Royal Court Theatre Downstairs in Sloane Square, London, on 14 July 1995, with the following cast:

SILVER JOHNNY	Hans Matheson
SWEETS	Matt Bardock
POTTS	Andy Serkis
BABY	Tom Hollander
SKINNY	Aidan Gillen
MICKEY	David Westhead

Director	Ian Rickson
Designer	Ultz
Lighting Designers	Ultz and Mark Ridler
Sound Designer	Paul Arditti
Composer	Stephen Warbeck

The production transferred to the Royal Court Theatre Downstairs in St Martin's Lane, London, on 10 October 1996, with the following cast:

SILVER JOHNNY	Daniel Newman
SWEETS	Callum Dixon
POTTS	Neil Stuke
BABY	Paul Reynolds
SKINNY	Darren Tighe
MICKEY	Simon Kunz

4

Characters

in order of appearance

SILVER JOHNNY, *seventeen*

SWEETS, *early twenties*

POTTS, *early twenties*

BABY, *twenties*

SKINNY, *early twenties*

MICKEY, *thirties*

Act One takes place upstairs at Ezra's Atlantic in Dean Street, Soho, July 1958.

Act Two takes place downstairs in the club and starts around 6 p.m. on the same day.

ACT ONE

Scene One

Upstairs at the Atlantic. SILVER JOHNNY *stands alone. We hear the drums, the thudding bass, the screams from the club below.* SILVER JOHNNY *does steps by himself, tight, menacing, explosive, like a boxer in the seconds before a fight. A low distorted voice announces the act, the girls scream, but he keeps them waiting. The music rises, faster, louder. It reaches its height,* SILVER JOHNNY *stands at the top of the steel staircase. When the moment comes, he vaults into the stairwell and vanishes, enveloped by sound.*

The drums pound on in the blackout. Suddenly they stop and the next second we are back upstairs at the Atlantic, after the show. SWEETS *and* POTTS *are sitting at a table. There is a pot of tea on the table with three pretty cups, on a tray. The door to the back room is shut.*

SWEETS. Is that brewed?

POTTS. Four minutes.

SWEETS. You want a pill?

POTTS. My piss is black.

SWEETS. It's the white ones. Don't eat no more of the white ones. (*Pause.*) So where is he sitting?

POTTS. Who?

SWEETS. Mr Ross.

POTTS. He's on the couch.

SWEETS. Right.

POTTS. Mr Ross is on the couch.

SWEETS. Good. How is he?

POTTS. What?

SWEETS. Good mood, bad mood, quiet, jolly, upfront, offhand. Paint me a picture.

POTTS. Tan suit. No tie. Penny loafers. No tassle.

SWEETS. Uh-huh. Right. Does he look flush?

POTTS. He's Mr Ross.

SWEETS. Absolutely.

POTTS. He's a flush man.

SWEETS. Naturally.

POTTS. Ten-guinea Baltimore loafers. Suit sweat a year for you couldn't buy. Shirt undone. Tanned like a darkie. Yes he looks flush.

SWEETS. Ten-guinea Baltimores? Fuck me briefly.

POTTS. Penny. No tassle.

SWEETS. They're *talking about it* aren't they… (*Pause.*) Okay. Okay. So where's Ezra?

POTTS. Ezra's at the desk, but he's not in his chair. He's round here to one side.

SWEETS. The Mr Ross side or the miles-away side?

POTTS. Round here to the side on the poochy stool.

SWEETS. Poochy stool. Good.

POTTS. Sit behind the desk it's like I'm the man. Like I'm trying to big you out. Sit round the side on the poochy stool, Hey Presto, we're all a circle.

SWEETS. Okay. Okay. So where's the kid?

POTTS. Couch.

SWEETS. Couch. Good.

POTTS. On the couch with Mr Ross.

SWEETS. Exactly. Let him see the merchandise.

They sit there, waiting for the tea to brew.

You know Beryl? She goes to me tonight, she goes, 'When Silver Johnny sings the song my pussyhair stands up.'

POTTS. Relax.

SWEETS. I know. I know. Her pussyhair.

POTTS. We just sit here.

SWEETS. I know. Her fucking minge. Her fur. *It stands up*.

POTTS. I see these girls. It's voodoo. Shaking it like they hate it. Like they hate themselves for it.

SWEETS. In the alley. 'Get it out,' she says. 'Get it out I'll play a tune on it…'

POTTS. One day he's asking his mum can he cross the road the next he's got grown women queueing up to suck his winkle.

SWEETS. Seventeen. Child.

POTTS. These girls. They shit when he sings.

SWEETS. Exactly. (*Beat.*) What?

POTTS. Mickey knows. They shit. He seen it.

SWEETS. They what?

POTTS. It's a sex act. It's sexual.

SWEETS. Hold it. Hold it. Stop. Wait. (*Beat.*) They *shit*?

POTTS. All over.

Beat.

SWEETS. What does that mean?

POTTS. Means they have no control in front of a shiny-suited child. Sad fucking world. The end. I'm going to use this as a rule for life: 'Anything makes polite young ladies come their cocoa in public is worth taking a look at.'

SWEETS. Good rule.

POTTS. Great rule.

SWEETS. There's got to be rules and that's a rule.

POTTS. What time is it? Okay. Good. Sweets. Listen. (*Beat.*) When he announces it –

SWEETS. Hey –

POTTS. When Ezra –

SWEETS. Hey. Hey –

POTTS. If he takes you aside… (I know. I know. But listen) –

SWEETS. Could be me could be you. Could be me could be you.

POTTS. Exactly. I'm planning. I'm… listen. He takes you aside tells you takes me aside, it's not important. For me there's no difference.

SWEETS. It's exactly the same thing. Me or you. Exactly.

POTTS. Exactly. Good. The important thing is *whichever way it comes*, when he announces it, when it *happens*, act 'Surprised and Happy'.

SWEETS. Surprised and Good. Good.

POTTS. Happy and Good. Good. The end. That's four minutes. (*Stands and picks up the tea tray.*) What?

SWEETS. Absolutely. What? Nothing.

POTTS. I'll be straight back.

SWEETS. Right. Good luck.

POTTS. Relax.

SWEETS. I am relaxed. I'm talking.

> POTTS *takes the tea into the back room. He closes the door.* SWEETS *lights a cigarette.* POTTS *returns.*
>
> So?

POTTS. So what?

SWEETS. So what happened?

POTTS. Nothing.

SWEETS. Right.

POTTS. They're drinking the tea.

SWEETS. Right. Good. What about the Campari? Has the kid drunk his Campari?

POTTS. He's sipping it.

SWEETS. Good.

POTTS. It's casual.

SWEETS. Good sign.

POTTS. You know? Loose.

SWEETS. Excellent. Excellent sign.

POTTS. Ezra's still on the poochy stool. But he's moved it. He's tugged it over in snug next to Sam.

SWEETS. Hold it. Hold it. Stop. Who?

POTTS. What?

SWEETS. You said Sam.

POTTS. Indeed.

SWEETS. Who's Sam?

POTTS. Mr Ross.

SWEETS. Oh.

POTTS. Sam is Mr Ross.

SWEETS. Oh right.

POTTS. Sam Ross. That's his name.

SWEETS. Since when?

POTTS. Everyone calls him Sam. His mum named him Sam.

SWEETS. Lah-di-dah.

POTTS. Listen. Sam Ross is here next to Ezra he's got his legs crossed and he's letting his loafer hang off his foot like this. It's bobbing there.

SWEETS. Don't.

POTTS. Right next to Ezra's leg.

SWEETS. Stop.

POTTS. Eyes wide like this. Both of 'em. Like long-lost puppies.

SWEETS. Fuck me. They're talking about it aren't they.

POTTS. And remember: Sam Ross came to us.

SWEETS. He did. (*Beat.*) What's the kid doing?

POTTS. Nothing. Sitting in between looking pretty.

SWEETS. Good.

POTTS. He ain't saying nothing. Just sitting there looking foxy.

SWEETS. Good. The kid's doing good.

POTTS. He knows why he's there. He's paid to warble and look pretty. He ain't paid to give it large in the back room.

SWEETS. Has he got the jacket on?

POTTS. Who?

SWEETS. The kid. Has he got the Silver Jacket on?

POTTS. He's took it off. It's on the table.

SWEETS. Hang on. Hang on. He's took it off?

POTTS. It's on the table.

SWEETS. Hang on. Hang on. What the fuck is he doing?

POTTS. What?

SWEETS. What the fuck is going on?

POTTS. What's up?

SWEETS. He's supposed to wear the Silver Jacket. He's Silver Johnny. Silver Johnny, Silver Jacket.

POTTS. Sweets –

SWEETS. Silver Johnny, Silver Suit. That's the whole point.

POTTS. I know.

SWEETS. Ezra buys the Silver Jacket he should wear it.

POTTS. It's hot in there.

SWEETS. I don't give a fuck if it's hot. Mr Ross deserves the full benefit. He's not called Shirtsleeves Johnny is he. He was called Shirtsleeves Johnny it would be perfect.

POTTS. It's laid-back. It's a jackets-off atmosphere. He's right to take the jacket off. It's good.

SWEETS. I'm not happy. (*Pause.*) Has he got the trousers on?

POTTS. What?

SWEETS. Has he got the silver trousers on?

POTTS. Of course he fucking has.

SWEETS. Well that's something.

POTTS. Fuck do you think they're doing in there? He's gonna sit there in just his pants?

SWEETS. I know. I'm just excited.

POTTS. He's got his trousers on.

SWEETS. I know. Relax.

POTTS. You relax.

SWEETS. I am relaxed. I'm talking.

POTTS. Exactly. (*Pause*.) Ezra done this. (*Winks*.)

SWEETS. At you?

POTTS. Ezra don't forget. I mean who fucking discovered the kid? I did.

SWEETS. Right.

POTTS. Fact. One solid-gold forgotten fact. Ask Mickey. Up Camden. Luigi's.

SWEETS. Luigi who fucks dogs.

POTTS. Yes. No. Luigi with the daughter. Parkway. With the Italian flag up behind the. The thing behind the.

SWEETS. With the daughter. Does the liver and onions.

POTTS. That's him. I'm up doing all the Camden jukes. Three weeks running Luigi's light on his pennies. Every machine in Parkway is pulling in eight nine quid a week, Luigi's it's one bag, two, three quid if you're lucky. So I say stop having a chuckle, inky pinky blah blah blah you're gonna get a kidney punched out.

SWEETS. Only fucking language they speak.

POTTS. So he's gone, listen, he's gone, 'No one's playing the juke.'

SWEETS. Yeah right.

POTTS. He says. Nobody's playing it.

SWEETS. Like we're in Outer Russia.

POTTS. Like it's the *Moon*. Outer Russia. Exactly. He says
they're doing it themself. He says they've got a kid comes in
here, gets up in the corner, does it himself. The fucking shake
rattle roll himself. I mean. Camden kids?

SWEETS. Micks.

POTTS. Do me a favour.

SWEETS. Micks and Paddies.

POTTS. Do me a good clean turn.

SWEETS. Micks and Paddies and wops who fuck dogs.

POTTS. He says, 'Come back tonight, you'll see.' So I come
back tonight. And I take Ezra, Mickey we're gonna scalp him
take the rig back he's told us a fib. (*Pause.*) Lo and behold.

SWEETS. No.

POTTS. In the corner, all the moves. Doing 'Sixty Minute Man'.
Everyone watching. In the corner. A *child*. (*Pause.*) That's
what happened. I'm not whining. I'm not bleating. You know,
am I supposed to get back in the van start doing sums? 'I want
X-Y-Z. Twenty, thirty, forty per cent.'

SWEETS. You're not some fuckin' vulture.

POTTS. I'm not some fucking *doorboy*. I want what's due. I want
what's fucking mine.

Beat.

Enter BABY. *He stands there for a bit.*

BABY. Drinking wine spo-deeodee,
Drinking wine spo-deeodee,
Drinking wine spo-deeodee,
Dancing on a Saturday night.

POTTS. Oh watcha Baby…

SWEETS. Watcha Babes. How you getting on?

POTTS. How's it going down there? Anyone left?

BABY. Hello Sweets. What a night eh?

SWEETS. Yeah…

POTTS. How you feeling Babes?

BABY. Well Sid, actually I feel great.

POTTS. Yeah? You look awful.

SWEETS. Go and put your feet up. You look like a corpse.

BABY. Yeah. Well let's play then. Bring a crate up, relax, few disks… Let's get it started.

POTTS. Yeah. Actually. We'll get it started later…

BABY. Oh. What's up?

POTTS. Nothing.

SWEETS. Nothing at all. No. (*Pause.*) It's just they're having a bit of a meeting.

POTTS. No they're not.

SWEETS. Exactly.

BABY. What's going on then?

POTTS. Nothing. They're just relaxing.

BABY. What? In there?

POTTS. Something like that. It's nothing. Best keep the noise down.

BABY. Say no more Sidney. (*Laughs.*) Ssshhh!

SWEETS. Exactly. Sssh.

BABY. Look at that. We forgot the cake.

SWEETS. Yeah. That was my fault. I was supposed to take it down at the last song, pass it around. Completely forgot.

BABY. Look at that cake. That is a brilliant cake. You better hide it Sweets. Or you'll be in hot water.

SWEETS. Yeah I will. I'm gonna hide it.

BABY. Well. All right. I'm gonna go downstairs now.

POTTS. Brilliant.

BABY. Have a spruce-up drink.

POTTS. Good idea.

BABY. Just to spruce me up a bit. You want to join me?

POTTS. Yeah. We'll be right down.

BABY. Sweets?

SWEETS. Yeah. I'm gonna be straight down.

BABY. All right. I'm going down now.

POTTS. Okay. See you in a bit mate. Play a game later.

BABY. Drinking wine spo-dee-o-dee. My piss is black.

SWEETS. It's the white ones. Don't eat no more of the white ones.

BABY. The white ones. (*Laughs.*) Spo-dee-o-dee. Sssshh!

   Exit BABY.

SWEETS. Do you think he knows?

POTTS. What do you think?

SWEETS. Ezra wouldn't tell him.

POTTS. He couldn't find the gents' in this place without asking.

SWEETS. Ezra wouldn't tell him. Ezra wouldn't trust him.

POTTS. Ezra wouldn't trust him to run a tub. He doesn't know.

SWEETS. If you don't know you don't know.

POTTS. Good. Good. The end. Sweets. I heard 'fifty-fifty'.

   Pause.

SWEETS. Okay. Say that again.

POTTS. I don't know.

SWEETS. Okay. Just that little last bit again.

POTTS. I don't know.

SWEETS. You heard fifty-fifty. You said you heard fifty-fifty.

POTTS. I don't know. Don't turn it into nothing. Don't knit a
   blanket out of it.

SWEETS. Okay. Stop. Sid. Think. Was it Sam? Did Sam say it?

POTTS. Tricky. With the smoke, I'm pouring tea bent double I heard those words. That word. 'Fifty.' Twice. Fifty. Fifty. Five-O. And the single word 'America'.

They look at each other.

SWEETS. Okay. Okay. Okay. All we know –

POTTS. All we know is 'Fish are jumping, and the cotton is high'.

SWEETS. Fish are jumping. Precisely.

POTTS. Good. The end. Talk about something else.

SWEETS. Exactly. Good. Great night.

POTTS. Great night. Exactly. We're fucking made.

SWEETS. My life makes sense.

POTTS. Go upstairs see if there's an angel pissing down the chimney.

SWEETS. My whole fucking life makes sense. (*Pause.*) Hold it. Hold it. We've not been told.

POTTS. Makes no difference.

SWEETS. Have you been told?

POTTS. Have you been told?

SWEETS. No.

POTTS. Makes no difference. Go to the museum.

SWEETS. Right. What?

POTTS. Go down take a look at any picture Napoleon. Go take a butcher's at the Emperor Half the World. And you'll see it. You'll see. They got a lot of blokes *standing around*. Doers. Finders. Advisors. Acquaintances. Watchers. An *entourage*.

SWEETS. Big fuckers in fur boots. On the payroll.

POTTS. Napoleon's chums. And they're all there. Sticking around. Having a natter. Cleaning rifles. Chatting to cherubs. Waiting. Waiting for the deal to come off.

SWEETS. They weren't there they wouldn't have fuckin' painted them.

POTTS. Just 'cos now he's got a big horse don't mean he don't need chums. He's got big, they've put him on the big pony, his mates go – 'Maybe Napoleon don't want us around no more. Cramping him up. Holding him back.' 'Cos one thing Sweets. They've put you in sealskin boots told you you're Emperor, that's when you need mates. 'Cos one day they're gonna lift you back out, stand you in the snow watch your fucking toes drop off.

SWEETS. Listen. Okay. All we know –

POTTS. All we know is 'Fish are jumping, and the cotton is high'.

SWEETS. 'Fish are jumping.' Exactly.

POTTS. 'It's a Nice Day' and 'Oh look the fish are jumping, and will you look how high that cotton's got.' Good. Good. The end. They're going back to his.

SWEETS. Tonight?

POTTS. Billiards.They're going to Sam's house for billiards.

SWEETS. Clover.

POTTS. Knee-deep. Thrashing around in it. God spoke to me last night Sweets.

SWEETS. Doesn't surprise me an ounce.

POTTS. God, said to me, 'Do not be troubled Sidney for your ship is coming in. Yours is the racy big cock-shaped one over there going faster than the rest so just keep your mouth shut and wait.'

SWEETS. Doesn't surprise me an ounce.

POTTS. He's gone 'Keep your mouth shut, unless your nose is in the trough, then open your mouth, and chew like fuck. That's all there is chum.'

SWEETS. You know what God said to me last night? He goes, 'Sweets, There's no God, do what you will, good luck, end of message.'

POTTS. The way I see it it goes like this: Fuck God.

SWEETS. Precisely. Fuck him on a cloud.

POTTS. Fuck God if you know the king. Do you know what I mean? Fuck God if you only know someone knows someone knows the king. Because if you know someone knows someone knows the king, and you wait long enough sooner or later you're gonna get a sweet taste of the king's cock.

SWEETS. Good rule.

POTTS. Great rule.

SWEETS. There's got to be rules and that's a rule.

POTTS. He's got dyed hair.

SWEETS. Who?

POTTS. Sam Ross has got dyed hair.

SWEETS. You're kidding.

POTTS. He's took his hat off wham! Bright-yellow dyed hair. Not blond or nothing. Yellow. Like a banana.

SWEETS. I never thought I'd know that. I never thought I'd know that detail.

POTTS. Sweets. Sweets. The shoes. The motherfucking *shoes* on the man.

SWEETS. Buckskin. Hand-stitched.

POTTS. Baby buckskin. Baby fucking hand-stitched buckskin.

SWEETS. Baby fuckin' buckskin hand-stitched by elves.

POTTS. Baby fucking buckskin.

SWEETS. Baby what? Who *knows*? (*Laughs.*) Eh? Who fucking *knows*?

POTTS. Something rare. Something rare and soft. Something young, can hardly walk, kill it, turn it inside out –

SWEETS. Unborn pony.

POTTS. That's the one. Still attached. Still in the –

SWEETS. Still in its mother's womb.

POTTS. Asleep in the fucking exactly. Wake it up, rip it out, lah-di-dah, pair of shoes. Bom. It's over. I'm going out.

SWEETS. You don't like it? Who cares? I'm fucking paying.

Feet on the steps.

POTTS. Don't say nothing. Fish are jumping.

SWEETS. The cotton is high.

Enter SKINNY *with a broom. He is seething, furious.*

SKINNY (*shouts*). You cheap fucking sweaty fucking…
fucking… Jew… fucking… (*Pause. Lights a cigarette.*)

SWEETS. All right Skinny? What's up?

SKINNY. Nothing. (*Pause.*) I'm leaving. I've had enough. I'm
telling Ezra. I'm going to get a proper job. I'm going to work
in a bank.

SWEETS. Oh yeah? Something gone wrong.

SKINNY. You know the one in the dress with the thing up the
back? We're having a chat, she's up for it, and Baby swans up,
stands in here, close, and he does the thing with the… Says the
thing about bad breath. The thing about that I've got bad
breath. About my breath being bad. I get fifteen minutes free
time, yeah, enjoy the night before the coats start leaving and
he gives it the breath.

Pause.

I'm tickets at the door seven Saturdays in a row. Seven
straight. 'Skinny, you're on the door.' 'Skinny you're on
coats.' The juke's fucked, who finds a spanner greases up his
new shirt? 'Skinny chum, mop this pile of sick up for two and
six an hour.' Yeah? Meanwhile, right, what's he doing? What's
he doing? Oh look, he's at the bar. Oh look, he's leaning on the
fucking bar. Is that Alan Ladd? No. I don't think so.

POTTS. Come here.

He does.

Breathe.

He does.

Skinny, your breath smells beautiful.

SKINNY. Thank you.

POTTS. It smells like English roses.

SKINNY. What? Thank you. Thank you.

POTTS. It's a pleasure.

SKINNY. Start of the night about five people in here, he comes up behind me on the door squeezes my bollocks. Not playful. Really gripping. And you know when you're not crying but water comes to your eyes. (*Pause.*) Fucking night. What you doing up here?

POTTS. Nothing.

SKINNY. Fucking weekend. Where's Ezra?

SWEETS. He ain't here. He's gone home.

SKINNY. It's all right, you just sit up here have a natter.

SWEETS. They all cleared off?

SKINNY. That darkie's still down there dancing on his own.

POTTS. Chuck him out.

SKINNY. You playing a game later?

SWEETS. Dunno.

POTTS. We'll see.

SKINNY. Is Baby playing? Because I'm not playing if Baby's playing.

SWEETS. Skin. Pop up the Half-Wops, get us all a frothy coffee, come back, then we'll all play.

SKINNY. Okay. I'll go and get a coffee. I've had enough of all this. I'm going to get hurt. I might want to have children one day.

Pause.

POTTS. Go up the Half-Wops, come back, we'll play.

SKINNY. Fucking weekend. My piss is black.

SWEETS. It's the white ones. Don't eat no more of the white ones.

Blackout. Drumming.

Scene Two

Upstairs at the Atlantic. SKINNY *is tied with his hands around the back of a jukebox, his pants round his ankles.* BABY, *naked from the waist up, wild, is wielding an old navy cutlass and screaming at* SKINNY *that he is going to die. The others are all appealing to* BABY *to stop, but* BABY *swings the cutlass around, pointing it at each of them in turn.* SWEETS *gets up on the desk, still shouting as* BABY *pushes the point against* SKINNY*'s cheek. Enter* MICKEY.

SWEETS *is the first to spot* MICKEY *in the doorway. He calls to* BABY *over and over, and after the music ends it is a full ten seconds before the din subsides and* SWEETS *is just calling 'Baby' over and over, his eyes shut. Having won* BABY*'s attention,* SWEETS *indicates to the door.*

BABY. Oh. Hi Mickey.

SKINNY. Mickey. Christ. Thank Christ.

> BABY *puts the cutlass down.* MICKEY *walks to the blinds and opens them. Bright sunlight pours into the smoke-filled room.* MICKEY *opens the window. Sounds from the street.*

POTTS. Gonna be another corker Mickey. Look at all that sunshine.

SWEETS. Mickey mate. How hard is this eh? I try to tell him. I be like a dad.

> MICKEY *just stands there.*

POTTS. How's your head cold Mickey?

SWEETS. Mickey, how's your head chum? You feeling better chum? Bit more like it eh?

MICKEY. Everybody having a good time?

POTTS. Looks bad doesn't it?

SWEETS. Looks dreadful. Tell me how bad it looks. Tell me.

POTTS. Last night Mickey! You should have *been* there.

SWEETS. You missed a *night*. Like everyone's birthday at once. Place looks like a palace.

POTTS. One word. Sequins.

SWEETS. I'm going to say one word now and it's just been said… The fucking sequins.

POTTS. Sequin after sequin after sequin. Sequins on the walls. Sequins on the ceiling. Sequins round the bar.

SWEETS. Looks like Little Richard walked in and exploded.

POTTS. I was saying only just now, wasn't I Sweets. *Underwater* theme. 'Ezra's *Atlantic*'. See, we noticed. The whole joint sparkles like the Briny Deep. Like Neptune's cove.

SKINNY. Hold it. Hold It. I say 'Fuck the Decor'. I say back to the issue of Me Being Tortured.

SWEETS. Look, this sprung from, you know, from circumstances. Game of cards. Few drinks. Few laughs. Few pills.

POTTS. Great pills. Sweet's pills.

SWEETS. M'mum's pills. Slimming pills.

POTTS. You have to wolf hundreds but in the end…

SWEETS. So. Few drinks. Few laughs. Few pills…

POTTS. Then lots of pills.

SWEETS. Our big mistake.

POTTS. Giant Mistake. Turned sour see. Big up then a big dipper down. What's the word? Emotional.

SWEETS. Emotional. That's Mum. Thin as piss but so emotional.

POTTS. You're up then 'bing' – (what's the word?) 'Jivey.'

SWEETS. 'Antsy.' Antsy in the pantsy.

POTTS. Puts the big gorilla monkey on your back. So. Few pills. Pale Ale. Big hand, it's all tense, Skin here whips the King of Spades out his sock.

SWEETS. Clean out his loafer.

SKINNY. I swear. It fell on the floor.

POTTS. I miss it, Sweets missed it, Baby sees it, he's got Queens-over-eights. Nine fucking guineas lying panting on the table.

SWEETS. And the rest is history.

POTTS. Exactly.The rest mostly speaks for itself. So.

SWEETS. So. That's what happened. That's what happened up until now.

POTTS. Hold it. Hold it. (*Beat*.) My heart's stopped.

SWEETS. Breathe.

POTTS. I can't breathe. My heart's stopped.

SWEETS. Are you sweating?

POTTS. I got no pulse.

SWEETS. Take a white one.

POTTS. I already had a white one.

SWEETS. Have your feet gone dead?

POTTS. Check.

SWEETS. Prickly face?

POTTS. Check.

SWEETS. Pits pouring sweat?

POTTS. Check.

SWEETS. Take a white one.

POTTS. You said –

SWEETS. It's up to you. Take a white one or die.

POTTS. What about black piss?

SWEETS. You want to be dead or you want black piss?

POTTS *takes one*.

Put your arms above your head and pant like a dog.

POTTS *holds his arms above his head. He pants. Pause*.

SKINNY. Mickey. What we were talking about in the van.

POTTS. Bingo. I'm back.

SWEETS. Welcome home. You should get a rush.

POTTS. I'm getting a rush.

SWEETS. Euphoria. Your body's glad it's not dead.

POTTS. She's going like a choo-choo…

SWEETS. You're glad to be alive.

POTTS. Great to be me. Great to be me. This is a fucking great time to be me. I'm all right.

SWEETS. Great night. Great night.

POTTS. I'm better than all right. I'm fantastic. Great night. Great night. Hey Mickey. Mickey. Guess what? I saw this bloke sick up in his bird's mouth.

SWEETS. I saw that.

SKINNY. Mickey. Enough. Remember what we spoke about in the van. And this isn't for me. It's for you. Fuck me. For you.

BABY. This is advice you're about to get Mickey.

SKINNY. Advice? Are you Italian now? No. You're not. You're a Jew. *Be* one.

BABY. He's pulling them out his shoes, I'll just lie down and take it eh?

SKINNY. It fell on the ground. It falls on the ground you pick it up.

POTTS. Baby. I think you have something to say to Mickey.

SWEETS. Yeah, c'mon Babes and we can all get on with our fuckin' lives.

Pause.

BABY. Uh, Skinny. (*Laughs.*) What are you staring at?

POTTS. Charming. Charming. Baby –

SKINNY. Fuck off.

BABY. What, are you giving me the eye? Are you giving me the evil eye?

SKINNY. You nothing fucking piece of dog's plop.

SWEETS. Baby –

BABY. Because (excuse me Mickey). Because if you're giving me the evil eye you're doing it wrong.

SKINNY. I fuck your mother and she shouts your name.

BABY. Because you look like you love me. You look like you want to put your cock in my ear. Look away. Look away.

SKINNY. Fuck off. I'm not playing.

SWEETS. Drop it Baby. We're all a bit honky-tonk.

BABY. Lookin' like you want to put your cock in my ear. Look away. Look at the floor.

SKINNY. Big man. Big man.

BABY. Look at the floor. Don't look at me. Look –

SKINNY. I'm going to get hurt here Mickey.

POTTS. Oh this is helping. This is fucking perfect for a tired man with head cold to come back to work to.

BABY. Sweets boy, put on something slow and evil. Mickey looks like he wants to dance.

SKINNY. This is it. Mickey. You see? It's *time…*

    BABY *starts to leave.*

    … Watch this. Watch this.

MICKEY. Baby…

    BABY *stops.*

    Where you going?

BABY. Well, Mickey, you know I thought I'd pop out and get a toffee apple.

    Pause.

SKINNY. A toffee apple… What does that mean? For me it means Mickey you take it up the bum with a toffee apple you let me walk out of here. I don't see how it could possibly refer to anything else.

    Pause.

MICKEY. Go out the front. Don't go out the back.

SKINNY. Brilliant.

MICKEY. Lock the door.

BABY. I don't have my key.

MICKEY. Where is your key?

BABY. I lost it. Dancing.

MICKEY. Don't go out the back.

BABY. How's your head cold Mickey? You feeling all right?

MICKEY. Did you hear me? Don't go out the back.

BABY. Oh. Mickey, I forgot to say. I love the sequins. They make the whole night sparkle.

Exit BABY. *They untie* SKINNY.

POTTS. Hard-man act.

SWEETS. Nutter act.

POTTS. Complete fucking bollocks.

SWEETS. Giving it the stare. Complete fucking bollocks.

POTTS. You only do that when it's bullcrap.

SKINNY. Mickey, with the key bit. Did you hear? He lost it dancing… Eh? And some people get trusted with keys some don't – You watch. Now we'll get the till nicked and we'll all stand around wondering how they got in. I get kicked in the shins, get my nuts squeezed. Now do something or don't do something but it's time to do something Mickey. It's time to do something.

MICKEY (*low*). Shut your fucking gob all right? Shut your fucking gob.

MICKEY *snaps the blinds shut.*

SKINNY. I'm sorry? Are you talking to me?

MICKEY. What time did you leave?

POTTS. Whassup Mickey?

MICKEY. Shut up. What happened here last night?

SKINNY. That's fucking charming.

SWEETS. Relax Mickey. It all went like a clock.

POTTS. Look, Mickey you know what he's like, he's talks a lot. Chat. I'll make sure this don't happen again.

MICKEY. Fuck all this. You stupid cunt. We're finished.

SWEETS. It's not that bad. Take a minute to clear up.

POTTS. What's up Mickey.

MICKEY. What's up? What's up? Ezra's dead.

Everything stops.

SWEETS. Something… uh… (*Pause.*) Something happen Mickey?

MICKEY. Yeah. Yes. Something happened.

Pause.

POTTS. He's fucking *what*?

SWEETS. You said that Mickey. You said he's dead.

Pause.

MICKEY (*trembling, quiet*). Jesus fucking Christ.

Silence. Then, all at once.

OMNES. Oh Jesus. Jesus, Jesus fucking Christ.

Pause.

Jesus. Jesus Christ.

Pause.

SWEETS. What's happened Mickey?

MICKEY. I don't know.

Pause.

SWEETS. Okay. Can I ask you something? We're all going you know… going… bit honky-tonk, and and and and and things are pretty going pretty fast here now to be honest and I feel you know I got my fucking heart flutters and everything –

SKINNY. Okay. Okay. Take it back. Take it back to before.

MICKEY. I got a call.

SKINNY. Are you sure?

MICKEY. I got… Of course I'm fucking sure.

SKINNY. Why didn't you fucking say?

MICKEY. It's… Why the fuck do you think? You're all sitting here going sixteen million –

POTTS. Mickey –

MICKEY. You're all… You fucking prick.

SKINNY. I'm sorry.

MICKEY. You're all doing six million miles an hour yap yap yap. You bunch of fucking children. Don't give me any mouth.

Silence.

SWEETS *puts his hands on his knees. He dry vomits.* POTTS *bends over and sticks his fingers down his throat.*

SWEETS. I got no sick.

POTTS. Put your… Stick your fingers down your throat. Tickle that thing at the back.

SWEETS Got to… hang on.

POTTS. Tickle that bit that hangs down… the fuckin'…

SWEETS. I got no sick. I'll… just be a minute. Just get back on the flat.

SWEETS *and* POTTS *try to vomit. Nothing happens. Silence.*

SKINNY. What did they say Mickey? When they rung.

Pause.

MICKEY. They said 'You're finished.'

SKINNY. 'You're finished.'

MICKEY. They said 'You're finished' and 'Look in the bins'.

SKINNY. Okay. Okay. Okay. Okay. Okay. We're fucked.

Pause.

SWEETS. Jesus.

POTTS. Jesus Christ.

SWEETS. They say we're finished I believe them.

SKINNY. How do you know?

SWEETS. He got rung up this morning.

SKINNY. Yes. I know. Who by?

MICKEY. Alec Guinness. How the fuck should I know?

SKINNY. Mickey, who –

POTTS. How does he know? Eh? How does he know?

SKINNY. Mickey. Who off?

POTTS. People... Fuck me gently... *People Ezra knows.*

SKINNY. Did they say who they was?

POTTS. No. No. Listen. (*Laughs.*) They don't tell you. They tell you it gives it away you catch them it makes it easy...

SKINNY. I'm not addressing you.

POTTS. Please. Please? Can I... Please... Someone he don't know isn't going to walk up do him for *fun*. He's not a fuckin' he's not some *slug*. He's not a fucking *spider* crawling across the floor.

SKINNY. Hey bullcrap, slow down. Open a window, take deep breaths. Relax, have a bubble bath. I'm talking to Mickey.

SWEETS. Warm milk. I need some warm milk.

Pause.

POTTS. All right. All right. All right. Stupid question Mickey... and good. Let's ask questions. Stupid, brilliant, we don't know till it's asked. Exactly. Right. Good. *Are you sure?*

MICKEY. Am I sure what?

POTTS. I don't know. It's early. That he's dead. Good question. Eh? Mickey. Eh?

SWEETS. Good question.

POTTS. Eh? Eh? My question and it *is* a question is are you sure?

MICKEY. He's out there.

Pause.

POTTS. Out where? Out the back?

SKINNY. Fucking hell. Now?

SWEETS. Fucking hell.

POTTS. It's a joke. It's Mickey's joke. It's Mickey's morning joke.

SWEETS. Out where?

SKINNY. Don't you listen? By the bins. That's what they said.
'You're finished' and 'Look by the bins'.

SWEETS. You said 'by the bins'. Mickey said 'in the bins'.

POTTS. By the bins in the bins. Is that the issue here? If it's 'by'
are we safe? If it's 'by' is there a deal?

SKINNY. Mickey. Okay okay. Indulge me. Please. Are you sure?
Are you ten times out of ten sure that he's passed away?

MICKEY. He's fucking cut in half. He's in two bins.

Pause.

SKINNY. You hear that? Is it clear now? He is dead because they
fucking cut him in half. So yes, he's fucking passed away.
Allow Mickey to *know*. So. So. (*Pause.*) Sweet Fucking Hell
Jesus and Mary.

POTTS. Fucking Nora. Fucking hell.

SWEETS. Suffering Jesus. They sawed him in half.

SKINNY. Poor fucking man.

SWEETS. You sweat your life away…

SKINNY. Poor fucking man.

SWEETS. Into a *bucket*…

SKINNY. Poor fucking man. Poor fucking man.

Silence.

MICKEY. Fucking mess…

SKINNY. Poor fucking man.

SWEETS. Wake up have breakfast. They saw you in half.

MICKEY. Hideous fuckin' mess…

SKINNY. Poor fucking man. Poor fucking man.

Silence.

POTTS. Sit down Mickey.

SWEETS. Sit down.

MICKEY. I'm all right.

Silence.

SWEETS. Who's got a pill? Get a pill here for Mickey. Or a glass of warm milk.

POTTS. Mickey –

MICKEY. I don't want a pill.

SWEETS. We need a blanket. Shall I put some music on? Soft music?

POTTS. You fucking prick. Yeah, and we'll all have a slow dance till the coppers get here.

SWEETS. I don't know. I'm not someone's mum.

POTTS. Jeeesus.

SWEETS. Fuck off. I'm not someone's mother. I'm not Mickey's mum.

SKINNY. I said. I said. You make a stink you attract the big lights.

POTTS. It's done.

SKINNY. Make a stink you attract big lights. Make a stink you attract big lights.

Pause.

POTTS. What the fuck does that mean?

SKINNY. You know… Fuck off. You know what it means.

POTTS. Make a… What the fuck can that possibly mean?

SKINNY. Fuck off Sidney Potts.

SWEETS. Mickey. Mickey. Mickey. Let's talk… Listen… Listen.
  Mickey. Listen to me now. Okay. Okay? Mickey. Charlie *Dodds*.

SKINNY. We'll… Mickey –

SWEETS. Please. Please. Couple of pistols just to make me feel
  better. Please. Listen, please, as a precaut – Listen…
  Mickey… Mickey… Please. Just in case. In a drawer.
  Something. A safety net…

SKINNY. Mickey listen…

SWEETS. One or two. Just one or two pistols. You know? One or
  two in a drawer in a jacket. All we've got's an old cutlass.
  Let's at least try and make it fair sides.

SKINNY. We're gonna make this worse. We're gonna make this
  worse.

SWEETS (*overlapping*). Just *something* down here just so it ain't
  the fucking – just so it ain't the fucking Alamo.

SKINNY (*overlapping*). Sweets. Sweets. Sweets. Sweets. Sweets.
  Sweets. Sweets. Sweets. Sweets. Fuckin' *ease down* mate. Lie
  down. Lie down take deep breaths.

SWEETS. I'm fine.

SKINNY. Lie down.

SWEETS. I'm fine. I'm going to die.

MICKEY. Where's the kid?

POTTS. Sorry?

Pause.

SKINNY. Fuck the kid. This –

POTTS. Mickey –

SKINNY. Excuse me Mickey. But really. *Fuck* the kid.

MICKEY. Where is he? Where's the kid?

POTTS. Mickey –

SKINNY. This isn't about the kid. Mickey –

MICKEY. Is my question.

SKINNY. This isn't about Silver Johnny.

MICKEY. Am I Satan? Am I suddenly Satan? Am I Devil? Excuse me but I've been *robbed*. I've just had everything *taken away*. My fucking plans. My fucking everything. (*To* SKINNY.) Now I want some fucking answers. Now. Where is he Sidney?

POTTS. I don't know. Well I'm not in charge am I...

MICKEY. Did he leave?

POTTS. He'll be round his mum's. He'll be having a nap.

MICKEY. No one saw him leave?

POTTS. Sorry. It's dark down there. Maybe you want the full story you should have been here. I don't know.

SKINNY. Hold it. Hold it. Mickey wasn't here. We were here. You were fucking here. You were here too so stop slinging shit.

MICKEY. Right. Right. All of you. Listen to me. Listen. What time did the kid come off?

SKINNY. Eleven. Sung 'Boogie Woogie Flu' came off.

MICKEY. Eleven.

SWEETS. Just before. I didn't see.

MICKEY. And Ezra left?

POTTS. Yes.

MICKEY. Right. Right. Who with?

POTTS. No one.

MICKEY. He left on his own?

POTTS. Entirely on his own.

MICKEY. Skinny, did you see him leave?

SKINNY. I was handing out the fucking coats for a change.

MICKEY. Right. Then you all came up here. It's. (*Pause.*) So I get called at eight say. That's five hours. And no one heard nothing.

POTTS. What like.

MICKEY. What like? What like? Like someone sawing your boss in two outside the fucking window.

POTTS. We didn't hear nothing. We had the juke on.

SKINNY. You have to listen... Mickey, these are the people you got here. They fuckin' –

POTTS. I like the juke on.

SKINNY. They get it all day long they've got to listen to it all night.

POTTS. I like the juke on. You put on a quiet platter you don't expect to have to listen out for untold carnage in your fuckin' back alley.

SKINNY. You live in a dream world.

POTTS. So now I did it. I did it. It's all my fault Charlie Chan. You caught me straight off. I popped out to stretch my legs, bumped into Ezra, strolled around the back, and sawed him in two. Why don't we all kill each –

SKINNY. Listen you fuck –

POTTS. Yeah. Kill each other now make it fucking simple.

SKINNY. No one stuck a fucking cutlass up your nose for breakfast did they? *You're* jumpy?

POTTS. Look at him getting on Mickey's side.

SKINNY. There are no sides. There's just our side and *them*.

POTTS. They just sawed one of us in two. I don't think I want to *be* on our side.

Pause.

SKINNY. Mickey, what do you think. Do you think we're finished?

Silence. MICKEY *takes his tie off and puts it on the desk.*

SWEETS. Mickey. There was something.

POTTS. Sweets –

SWEETS. He was talk – (*To* POTTS.) What?

POTTS. Can I speak to you? Please can I speak to you please. Aside for a tick. Please. Excuse me, Sweets please.

SWEETS. What?

POTTS. Can I speak to you?

SWEETS. What?

POTTS (*quietly*). Do we know about this Sweets? I don't think we know about this.

SWEETS. They said. It's finished.

POTTS. Fish are jumping Sweets. Fish are still jumping.

SWEETS. It's *now*.

POTTS. We spoke about this. And it's not over. It's not over necessarily. You see?

SKINNY. Is this some game between you two?

POTTS. Sweets. My advice, please, and I've thought about this, is 'Shut the uck up'.

MICKEY. Tell me Sweets.

SWEETS. Um. (*Pause.*) I think maybe Mr Ross was here.

Pause.

MICKEY. Where?

SWEETS. Last night. We thought perhaps Mr Ross was here last night.

MICKEY. Look at me. Look at me.

POTTS. Mickey –

MICKEY. Shut up. Shut your mouth.

SWEETS. We thought you'd been told.

MICKEY. Did you see him?

SWEETS. Well not exactly.

MICKEY. Hang on. What do you mean 'not exactly'. What the fuck does that mean?

SWEETS. Sid did.

Everyone looks at POTTS.

POTTS. Okay. Okay. Okay. It's simple. Mickey. If you'll just give me thirty seconds and don't say anything because you don't want to get angry, I don't want to get angry, none of us does, we're all good ol' boys and all that so let's take it easy. Okay? Right. Now. It goes like this: What Sweets just said. It's a lie.

SWEETS. Sid.

SKINNY. What's going on?

POTTS. It's bollocks. It's not true.

SWEETS. Oh. Sid?

POTTS. That's – What? What?

SWEETS. It's just they said we're finished.

Pause.

POTTS. Shut up. *Mickey*. It's simple. What Sweets has said is not true. He *thinks* it's true but actually it's *not*. You see?

MICKEY. No Sidney. No I don't.

POTTS. Okay. Please. Please. Can I finish. Please? I know. I *know,* but. Hold on. Hold on. Exactly. Relax Mickey and I'll say.

SKINNY. I don't believe this.

POTTS. Hang on. Hang on. Mickey. Listen. This is my point. There was a chap here. But it weren't Mr Ross.

SWEETS. Sam.

SKINNY. What?

SWEETS. That's his name. Sam Ross.

SKINNY. Oh for fuck's sake Sid.

POTTS. We don't know it was him. We – don't… excuse… Mickey. Some bloke called Sam. Could be Sam Spade. Sam Cooke. Sam Davis Junior.

Excuse me. Excuse me. I cannot put my hand on my heart and say yes I saw him. Because I've never clapped eyes on the man in my life, I'm working all night I'm full of pills, people coming and going. Faces. Saturday night. I'm like who's this, who's this, drink more, smoke more. Busy busy busy. Really can't say.

SKINNY. I don't fucking believe this.

MICKEY. What did he look like?

POTTS. Normal. Everyday.

MICKEY. Sweets, what did he look like?

SWEETS. I didn't see him.

MICKEY. What was he wearing?

POTTS. Usual. Trousers. Shirt. Jacket. Menswear.

SWEETS. And uh... Sid...

POTTS. What? What the fuck are you going to say now? What the fuck else might you possibly... hold on... Hold on. Shut up. What might you possibly wish to add?

SWEETS. Well... About the fifty-fifty.

POTTS (*to* MICKEY). I don't know what he's talking about.

SWEETS. About them saying fifty-fifty.

POTTS. I didn't say that.

SWEETS. Oh. Right. I thought you did.

POTTS. That's not what I said. Mickey. I thought they *might* have. I thought they might have said fifty-fifty. I was excited. All right. I was excited and a bit honky-tonk. It's not my business who comes here who doesn't. I take the tickets on the door and then I help clean up after. I drive –

SKINNY. Sid –

POTTS. I – Hang on. Hang on, because I... Some days I drive the van and I fix the machines. I don't front the place up. I hear a little rumour and I pass it on. That's me. I'm a cunt. Everyone knows it. So what? Doesn't make me Al Capone.

MICKEY. Sweets. Listen. Did he have yellow hair? (*Pause.*) I'm asking you. Did he have bright yellow hair?

Pause. MICKEY *walks up to* POTTS *and slaps his face.*

SWEETS. Oh fuck... Oh fucking Nora. We're dead.

SKINNY. What?

MICKEY. Is it locked downstairs?

SKINNY. Oh mothering Christ.

SWEETS. They're coming for us. Mr Ross is coming for us.

MICKEY. What did I tell you? Look at me. What did I fucking tell you?

SWEETS. He had about three blokes with him earlier. They're all coming for us. Mickey. They had a meeting. They all came up here for a meeting.

MICKEY. Shut up. Now listen to me. Shut up.

SWEETS. They had a meeting. In there.

MICKEY. How many of them was there?

SWEETS. I don't know. He was with some others but they went home.

MICKEY. How many?

SWEETS. Three or four. Two with tattoos. One thinks he's all fashionable. Maybe a couple more. I couldn't tell.

MICKEY. Sidney, tell me what you saw.

POTTS. Fuck off.

SKINNY. Tell him Sidney. What happened.

POTTS. Fucking handing out the cuffs. Getting all cuffy when I'm over here trying my best. Fuck off.

SWEETS. Give over Sid, we're all bang in this now.

POTTS. Really helps that. I'm feeling really relaxed now.

SKINNY. We should have stuck to the jukeboxes. A good business. A safe business. A business you don't get sawn in half by Sam Ross.

SWEETS. Why don't you go and sing somewhere else?

SKINNY. When we were doing the jukes I can't recall any of us getting sawn in half. It's fucking when you when you include people. Look where it gets you. And I know you agree with me Mickey because I've heard you and Ezra in there.

MICKEY. Are you listening? Did they leave with Silver Johnny?

POTTS. Hold it. *Hold* it. It was fucking *busy*, we work here, it's the middle of the night it's packed and you're too ill to be here, I'm supposed to leave the party, leave the night in the middle of everything seek you out to report back some half piece of information ain't even our lookout. Sorry, I'm not doing my job, next time I'll know.Who made you Prime Minister anyway? I get my wage off Ezra and he's dead. I don't answer to you, and no one else here does either. You have head cold. You weren't there so you don't know. You're walking in at the end.

Re-enter BABY.

BABY (*sings*). They call it a teenage crush,
    They can't believe it's real.
    They call it a teenage crush,
    They don't know how I feel.

Pause.

SWEETS. Baby...

SKINNY. Mickey. Mickey... Mickey... Fuckin' hell. You know. Fucking hell.

MICKEY. Shut up.

SKINNY. You know? Fuckin' hell.

MICKEY. Shut up. All right? Shut up.

    BABY *produces five toffee apples from behind his back.*

BABY (*sings*). They've forgotten when they were young.
    And the way they yearned to be free.
    All they say is the young generation
    Is not what they used to be.

He gives each person a toffee apple.

    This is just for now. Tonight Skinny Luke I'm gonna buy you a drink apologise. I'm gonna buy Mickey a drink apologise. I'm gonna apologise to everyone.

SKINNY. Mickey... Baby...

MICKEY. It's all right. Baby, I call... I got a call this morning. Somebody's murdered your dad.

BABY *stands still. He puts his toffee apple down on*
MICKEY*'s desk, walks around the desk and sits in the chair.*
They watch him.

BABY. Guess what I just saw. (*Pause.*) Out there. Go on. Guess.

MICKEY. Baby –

BABY. Have a guess. Out there on Dean Street. Have a guess.

Silence.

SWEETS (*quietly*). Some girl?

Pause.

BABY. Wrong. Mickey?

MICKEY. I don't know.

BABY. Guess.

MICKEY. Baby –

BABY. Sidney? Have a guess.

POTTS. I don't know.

BABY. Have a guess. Have a guess.

POTTS. Tony Curtis. Give up.

BABY. Guess. No. Guess.

POTTS. Henry the Eighth?

BABY *laughs at this. Pause.*

BABY. There's a *Buick* parked out there. A Buick in Dean Street.
Right outside the Bath House. It's brilliant. (*Pause.*) Makes it
look like Las Vegas. (*With a soft G. Pause.*) Tonna kids
hanging off it pretending they're… they're in a film. (*Pause.*)
What's happening to this town? A Buick.

Silence.

MICKEY (*to* SKINNY). Is it locked downstairs?

SKINNY. I'll check.

MICKEY. Go and check. Check the back and the front and check
the windows. Check everything then come back up here.

SKINNY. I will. Mickey –

MICKEY. Check the windows check the doors. What?

Do that and come back up. Don't go outside.

SKINNY. Right. (*Pause*.) Baby, look, I'm sorry about before, I had the card in my sock. I'm sorry. I'm not... with the pills...

Pause.

BABY (*to* SKINNY). Why didn't you say so earlier? I've just spent fivepence on presents.

SKINNY. What? Yes.

BABY. Toffee apples. Fivepence.

SKINNY. I know.

BABY. You cost me fivepence. Penny each. Five of us. Fivepence. You've just said sorry. You owe me fivepence for toffee apples.

MICKEY. Okay look –

BABY. It's your fault (hang on). It's your fault pay for the toffee apples.

SKINNY. I don't have it.

BABY. Borrow it off someone.

MICKEY. Baby don't mess around.

BABY. I think things should be fair round here now, or we'll all start wondering if we're getting done fairly. We don't want any hard feeling what with everything else do we. *Do* we?

MICKEY. No...

BABY (*to* SKINNY). Then pay me. Pay me. *Pay me*.

Pause.

SKINNY. Mickey can I borrow fivepence?

MICKEY. Okay. Okay. Let's do this first. Because this is quite jolly. Are you having fun?

MICKEY *finds the money and makes to give it to* BABY.

BABY. Ah ah. Not to me. To Luke.

MICKEY. Just take the money. Take the money.

Pause. He does, and puts it in his pocket.

BABY. I accept your apology Luke.

MICKEY. Check it's all locked up come back up.

SKINNY. I've got to talk to you Mickey.

MICKEY. Just do it. (*To* POTTS.) Bring the bins in.

SWEETS. Right. Mickey, I'm sorry. It's the pills. Warm milk we'll be fine.

MICKEY. Bring the bins up. Don't go out the front.

POTTS. Shall I help him?

MICKEY. Yeah. And give us a minute. Don't go out the front.

POTTS. Right. (*Pause.*) I'm sorry Baby.

Pause.

BABY. Fucking night eh Sid?

POTTS. Yeah. Yeah. Fucking night.

Exit SKINNY, SWEETS *and* POTTS. BABY *sits in Ezra's chair.* MICKEY *watches him. He picks up the cutlass and carries it into Ezra's back office. He re-emerges.*

BABY. You seen Luke's trousers?

MICKEY. What?

BABY. I go all the way to Monkeytown buy myself some stay-like-it twelve-pleats. I walk around in them one week. Lo and behold Luke walks in here this morning it's like I'm looking in a mirror. And the red plims. Where's he got that idea from? Fucking twelve-pleats and red plims.

MICKEY. Baby –

BABY. What? He copies my walk. I look over there, there's another me.

MICKEY. It's because he likes you.

BABY. It's because he likes me. Oh I know. He loves me. You know that smoke-ring thing I used to do.

Pause.

MICKEY. You need a sleep? (*Pause*.) When did you last sleep? Eh? (*Pause*.) Sid said someone was here last night.

BABY. Hold it. Hold it. If we're gonna talk business I don't feel right. If we're gonna uh… I'm not dressed right.

BABY *takes* MICKEY'*s tie, puts it on.*

MICKEY. Okay. We'll do… Fine. We'll do this later.

BABY. But it's working day. And I'm a working man.

MICKEY. Are you going to be *funny* about this?

BABY. I'm all ears.

MICKEY. You're all ears. You're all ears.

BABY. I'm all ears.

Pause.

MICKEY. Do you know who Sam Ross is?

BABY. Who?

MICKEY. Sam Ross. I know you know who he is.

BABY *sits there.* MICKEY *stands up.*

We'll do this later.

BABY (*overlapping*). Yes.

MICKEY *looks at* BABY. *He sits back down.*

MICKEY. Ross was here about the kid. He been after a part of the kid.

BABY. Oh yes? Which part?

MICKEY. He… Listen. Ross wanted to do a deal with your dad.

BABY. Over John?

MICKEY. Over… yes… Over Silver Johnny.

BABY. No one told me.

MICKEY. I know you knew.

BABY. No one told me.

MICKEY. I know you knew. Even Sweets knew.

BABY. No one told me. This is fun. Two businessmen enjoying the morning.

Pause.

MICKEY. He was… Ross was saying he could get us into the halls, into the… into the cinemas. The money was going up. But…

BABY. But what?

MICKEY. Your dad weren't going to swap the kid for anything.

BABY. That's touching isn't it? (*Pause.*) We can do this later Mickey. If it's too upsetting.

MICKEY. Ross has got the kid. I don't know what the fuck has happened, I don't want any of this.

BABY. Mickey, I just drink the beer, have a laugh, kiss the girls and make them cry. Don't ask me.

MICKEY. They're going to come here…

BABY (*overlapping*). I wish I was more like *you* Mickey. I wish I was less like me, and more like you.

Pause.

MICKEY. *Listen to me.* They're going to come here.

BABY. They're going to come here.

MICKEY. Yes. I think they are.

BABY. Yes. I think they are.

MICKEY. If… listen.

BABY. If… Listen.

MICKEY. Baby –

BABY. Baby –

Pause.

MICKEY. You think you're in a book.

BABY. I am. I'm Spiderman.

Re-enter SWEETS *and* POTTS.

SWEETS. Mickey. I've just…

MICKEY. What?

SWEETS. Sorry. It's just I've just had a thought.

MICKEY. What?

SWEETS. Well it's just this. What about Ezra's Sunday Parlez-Vous?

MICKEY. What?

SWEETS. The Sunday… Ezra's Sunday Parlez-Vous. Everyone's gonna wonder why we're shut…

POTTS. What time is it?

SWEETS. Eleven. Says noon on the ticket.

POTTS. He's right.

SWEETS. There'll be a queue.

POTTS. I sold about a twenty tickets last night alone.

MICKEY. Listen.

POTTS. It's going to be very popular. We'll have a queue round the block in twenty minutes.

MICKEY. Listen. Listen. Fuck the Sunday Parlez-Vous. I'll… *fuck* the Sunday Parlez-Vous. I'll worry about that.

SWEETS. Yeah but Mickey, there's going to be a queue outside in ten minutes.

BABY. It's a problem Mickey. What are you going to do?

MICKEY. I worry about that. We'll put a sign on the door say we're decorating –

BABY. We just decorated…

MICKEY. I don't fucking care. We're doing it again.

Enter SKINNY.

SKINNY. It's all locked. There some kids hanging around out the front.

POTTS. It's the Par… Mickey. What did I just say? Eh? It's the Parlez-Vous.

SKINNY. What? Fuck.

POTTS. What did I just say?

SKINNY. Fuck. Is it Sunday?

POTTS. You watch. They'll flock.

SWEETS. Everyone was on about it last night.

POTTS. You watch.

SWEETS. That Sylvia, with all those mates. Knows those Mick builders.

POTTS. Who's suggestion was it? Eh? Turn Sunday, a dead day in the week, make it something. Who thought up the name. The continental feel. Who was it?

MICKEY. Sidney. Please.

POTTS. I'm just pointing it out.

MICKEY. I know. Just… Just keep the door locked they'll fuck off. Shut up. Just keep out of sight they'll all fuck off.

BABY. Skinny you look fantastic.

SKINNY. Sorry?

BABY. You look like a prince. Can I ask you a question? Where d'you get those trousers?

SKINNY. What? Oh…

MICKEY. Leave the trousers.

BABY. Aren't they lovely? With the pleats. Little turn-up. (*Looks down at his own and feigns shock.*) Well well. Small world.

SKINNY. Mickey –

BABY. Now I ask myself, where would you get a fashionable idea like that from?

SKINNY. Baby I never knew you had a pair. Mickey, I never knew he had a pair.

BABY. It's lucky that or people might think you were copying me. People might think you loved me or something.

SKINNY. I bought them over Monkeytown. I saved up.

BABY. You're a fucking liar Skinny Luke.

MICKEY. Baby go downstairs.

BABY. I'm gonna… Excuse me Mickey… I'm gonna let you wear them so long as you kiss mine.

SKINNY. What?

BABY. I promise. I won't cause a fuss, if you just come over here and kiss my pegs.

SKINNY. Fuck off. Mickey –

BABY. Kiss my pegs.

POTTS. Here we go.

BABY. Kiss my pegs.

SKINNY. Fuck off.

BABY. I know why you say all those things about me. It's because you love me so much. Mickey says.

MICKEY. Baby, leave him alone.

BABY. It's because you're fighting with yourself. I know what I do to you Skinny Luke. Now show me. Kiss my pegs. Kiss them. (*Throws a chair at* SKINNY.) Look at the floor. Look at the floor.

SKINNY. Great fucking game. Great fucking game. Great fucking game.

BABY. Look at the… Look at the floor. I'll close your fuckin' eyes. Kiss my pegs.

SKINNY. Fuck off.

BABY. Kiss my pegs. Kiss my pegs.

SKINNY. Fuck off. Mickey –

BABY. Kiss my pegs. Kiss my pegs.

POTTS. Kiss his fucking pegs.

SKINNY. Throwing chairs Mickey. That's a new one. That's an escalation. What did I tell you about the pattern. Insults, spitting, squeezing, threatening. Throwing chairs. I'm going to end up dead Mickey. You watch.

MICKEY. All right. Calm it down.

SKINNY. I've had enough.

MICKEY. Skin listen. Go over Charlie Dodds'.

SKINNY. I've had enough.

MICKEY. Shut up and listen. Go over Charlie Dodds'.

SKINNY. Right.

MICKEY. Do you know where he is?

SKINNY. Who?

MICKEY. Charlie Dodds'. Does the guns. Do you know –

SKINNY. Yeah. Yes. Old Compton up the top.

MICKEY. Get the best he's got. Go there come back. Don't talk to no one. Don't get stopped.

SKINNY. Right.

MICKEY. Stuff it up your shirt down your trousers. Don't get fuckin' pinched.

SKINNY. What if I bump into someone?

MICKEY (*handing over money*). Act.

SKINNY. Right. And I'll get some sandwiches.

MICKEY. Listen. For fuck's sakes. Are you listening to me? Just go Charlie Dodds' come back here. Go now.

SKINNY. Right. I've got to talk to you Mickey.

MICKEY. Do it now then come back here.

SKINNY. Good. Good. I've… We'll talk Mickey. I might want to have children one day.

Exit SKINNY.

SWEETS. This is it. This is it. We're all going to die here.

MICKEY. We're not going to die. We're going to stay here, we'll be all right.

SWEETS. I'm scared Mickey.

MICKEY. It's all right. Go out the back get those old mattresses.

POTTS. Are we staying here?

MICKEY. Just get them.

SWEETS. Are you sure Mickey? That we're going to be all right?

MICKEY. Yes. I am. I'm sure it's all right.

BABY *gets up to leave.*

Where are you going? Baby.

BABY. I fancied a sandwich.

MICKEY. Stay here.

BABY. I'm hungry.

MICKEY. Stay here. Do you want to still be a part of this or not?

BABY. Do I want to be a part of this...? This is brilliant!

MICKEY. Because you are a part...

BABY. Is this an... an *invitation*...?

MICKEY. You're supposed to be a part...

BABY. Am I being asked? Am I being courted?

MICKEY. Look. I don't care what you do long term, I don't mind. But for a couple days I need you here.

BABY. What for?

MICKEY. Because you're his son. It goes Ezra you me to the outside.

BABY. That's why I've been here? Decoration. Like the sequins.

MICKEY. They're going to come here. If not Ross, anyone wants this place. Now to the outside you're the son, so you're the man.

BABY. So why did they call you? (*Pause.*) Somebody decides to kill my daddy, do they call me tell me? No Mickey. They give you the call. (*Pause.*) You see what I mean Mickey? You got the call.

Re-enter SKINNY.

SKINNY. Mickey.

MICKEY. What the fuck is it? I sent you to do a job.

SKINNY. It's just I found this on the doorstep.

SKINNY *holds out a box, big enough to hold a football, gift-wrapped with a silver ribbon. He puts it on the floor in front of them all.*

POTTS. I know what that is. I know what that is.

SWEETS. What?

POTTS. I know what that is.

SWEETS. What is it?

SKINNY. Fucking hell.

POTTS. Oh no.

SKINNY. Fucking hell. Fucking hell.

POTTS. It's the kid. It's the fucking kid's head.

SKINNY. Oh Jesus.

POTTS. Look at it. What do you think it is. It's the kid's head isn't it?

SWEETS. Oh Jesus.

POTTS. It's the kid's head. It's the fucking kid's nut isn't it. Well isn't it?

MICKEY. Shut up.

POTTS. Look at it. Perfect size. It's his nut.

MICKEY. Shut up.

SWEETS. Look. It's his fucking head. It's his fucking head in a box.

POTTS. How heavy is it? Heavy. I bet it's about a couple of stone. If it's a couple of stone it's his nut. One two stone it's the nipper's nut without much doubt.

MICKEY. Shut up.

POTTS. Oh my Jesus. They cut his head off.

MICKEY. Calm down.

POTTS. They're going to kill us all.

SWEETS. My God.

POTTS. It's over.

MICKEY. Shut up. All of you. Shut up.

SKINNY. Just say if it is because I don't want to see. Just nod if it is.

POTTS. We're finished. We're finished.

BABY *goes to the box. He unties the ribbon and opens it. He stares into it, standing over it. He pulls out a silver jacket, folded up. He unfolds it and looks at it. He holds it up for the others to see. Puts it on.*

He goes to the jukebox, jingles his pockets, finds a penny, drops it in the slot, presses a number and a tune begins.

Rock 'n' roll plays loud in the office. All eyes are on BABY. *He ties the silver ribbon round his head and begins to dance. He starts slowly, menacingly, quick steps, tight, arrogant. As the song builds he moves faster and faster until it has become a noise. The sound grows, the drums getting louder, the instruments in discord, the beat intensifies until it reaches fever pitch, a wall of sound. It grinds deafeningly as* BABY *gets closer and closer to* MICKEY, *until he is right in his face. At its peak, everything stops except the drumming, with* BABY *frozen, staring into* MICKEY's *eyes. They are staring at each other. The drumming halts. Tableau.*

Blackout. End of Act One.

ACT TWO

Scene One

Downstairs at the Atlantic. Sequins everywhere. A staircase up to the office at the back with a chain across, 'Private'.

An enormous banner across the back reads 'Ezra's Atlantic Salutes Young People'.

BABY *is out cold at a table, wearing the silver jacket.*

MICKEY *talks on the telephone.*

MICKEY. I want Camberwell 7212. (*Pause.*) Hello? (*Pause.*) It's Mickey. I want to speak to Mr Ross. To Sam Ross. Yes. Yes I'll wait.

Enter SWEETS. MICKEY *puts the phone down.* SWEETS *walks back out and re-enters dragging a dustbin, followed by* POTTS, *also dragging a dustbin.*

MICKEY. Is the back locked?

POTTS. I've put the bolt on.

MICKEY. That bolt's too weak. A kid could break it in. Where's Skinny?

SWEETS. He's not back.

POTTS. Look. It's gone six.

SWEETS. Count on it Mickey. He's fucked it up.

POTTS. You sent the wrong bloke. Probably had his collar felt five pistols down his pants.

SWEETS. Who you calling Mickey?

MICKEY. A band for next week. Tell me when he wakes up. (*Heads towards office.*)

SWEETS. Mickey. Can I have a quick word?

MICKEY. What?

SWEETS. Had a little idea.

MICKEY. What is it Sweets?

SWEETS. Quick little tetty over here…

MICKEY *waits*.

Can I? Good. Lovely. (*Pause*.) You know that business earlier with Sid. I know he's sorry. It was the pills.

MICKEY. Forget it. None of us is ourself.

SWEETS. Couple of days we'll all be us again, go for a drink crack jokes about it, eh?

MICKEY. What was your idea?

SWEETS. What?

MICKEY. You said you had an idea.

SWEETS. Good. I've come up with a plan and it makes sense to me in my head, but before you answer, mull it over for half a minute, live with it a tick then see if I'm wrong. Okay? So: (*Pause*.) I say we all do a runner.

Pause.

MICKEY. Sweets –

SWEETS. Mull it over Mickey.

MICKEY. Is that it?

SWEETS. Sounds obvious but the best ones always do. We've had a shock lah-di-dah who says we all of us put it behind us jump on a train. All of us, as a team, train down Margate splash in the sea.

Pause.

MICKEY. Baby wakes up let me know.

SWEETS. Give it half a minute watch it grow on you. The cool sea breeze. Cure-all. Works wonders for head cold. What?

MICKEY. We've got no lease on this place. We've got no deed.

SWEETS. Right…

MICKEY. It gets out about Ezra anyone who wants this place can walk in make themselves at home.

SWEETS. Uh-huh.

MICKEY. So we go down Margate, lark around, come back find it's gone. Then we've lost it all.

SWEETS. Absolutely.

MICKEY. So we're gonna stay here sweat out the weekend. See what happens, hopefully Monday it's still ours. After that, I don't know.

SWEETS. Horse sense. Twenty-four carat.

MICKEY. You see?

SWEETS. Mickey, go in there, close the door, lie down, let the dirt drop out your fingernails. Any news we'll give you the holler.

POTTS. There's a hole in your plan Mickey.

MICKEY. Oh yeah Sidney. Tell me.

POTTS. This. What if Mr Ross comes back? (*Pause.*) Eh? Sam Ross gets his strength back comes here finds we hung around. What next?

MICKEY. Then I don't know.

Pause.

SWEETS. You don't know?

MICKEY. No.

SWEETS. Think about my plan Mickey. It's got something. Sun. Donkeys. Kiss-Me-Quick...

MICKEY. Nothing's keeping you here Sweets. You want a piece of what's left, okay; you want to go out in the sun get an ice cream, go to Margate you're welcome. Train goes from Victoria.

Pause.

SWEETS. Mickey come over here and piss all down my leg. How far do we go back? Don't... How far do we go back?

MICKEY. I know.

SWEETS. I walked in the old warehouse can I have a job I'll work for fuck-all. Come over here and piss all down my leg.

MICKEY. I'm proud of you Sweets.

POTTS. Mickey. Do you think he's going to come for us?

MICKEY. You've met him Sidney. You tell me.

MICKEY *goes up the staircase.*

POTTS. What?

SWEETS. What? Nothing.

POTTS. I thought you said something.

SWEETS. No. Me? No.

POTTS. Handing out the cuffs. Fucking getting cuffy. I didn't start all this.

SWEETS. He's as shook up as any.

POTTS. My ears still ringing.

SWEETS. I know. Wake up tomorrow you'll be right as rain.

POTTS. We're not waking up tomorrow. You heard what he said. He hasn't got a plan. What if I cuffed him. That'd be it wouldn't it? But no. I'll just stand there line up let you all have a swing. (*Pause.*) He tries it again I'm gonna start thumping back. And hard as I can.

SWEETS. Relax Sid. Have some cake.

POTTS. Who fucking discovered the kid?

SWEETS. Right.

POTTS. Fact. One solid-gold forgotten fact.

Pause. BABY *stirs in his sleep.*

SWEETS. Poor bastard.

POTTS. I shouldn't worry about him too long Sweets.

SWEETS. Don't you feel a pang for him?

POTTS. I've got my own plate of shit to eat today thank you. I don't even know this hurts him.

SWEETS. Big heart Sid. Course it hurts him.

POTTS. Mickey first says it to him, 'Sorry Baby but your dad's been done.' What does he do? He gives it the Buick. Some sketch about a car in the street. (What he's already told you and me the day before, the same fucking words.) Now chop my old man up see if I stand around swapping car models.

SWEETS. Yeah but there's dads and dads. You're thinking of a *dad*. Like in a book. Fucking figure of something.

POTTS. Yes but –

SWEETS. Not some bloke waits for you come home home from school stuffs his hands down your pants. Not one has you biting the sheets and then don't tell your mum.

POTTS. Don't get me wrong. I like him. I'm not saying I'd run back in and save him the building catches fire but he's a mate. He's one of my best mates isn't he? But he's a cunt. Oh. He's had it tough. Oh. His dad did the funny on him. Well that's all the past isn't it. Fucker's dead. He ought to draw a line now. Start afresh. But he won't. I know he won't. The trouble with his type is they think the world owes them a big kiss and a trip down the zoo. (*Pause.*) Have you got any pills?

SWEETS. I've run out.

POTTS. Thank Christ for that.

Enter SKINNY.

SKINNY. Relax. Panic over. You sweat for nothing and suddenly it's okay. Sweets you are a genius. This is your town. (*Removes a Derringer purse-pistol.*) Can you see that? Can you just *make that out*?

SWEETS. Christ.

SKINNY. A Derringer.

POTTS. Marvellous…

SKINNY. An antique…

POTTS. Sweets…

SKINNY. A collector's item. A curiosity.

SWEETS. Where d'you get that?

SKINNY. They crash in here it turns sour I'll gun them all down.

POTTS. Brilliant.

SKINNY. Mow 'em all down go up the Nellie Dean.

POTTS. Marvellous.

SKINNY. Five quid for the week off Charlie Dodds. Our private angel over Old Compton Street.

POTTS. Fuck. It's a sign.

SKINNY. It is. It's a sign. It says 'We are the men with the small gun'.

SWEETS. Did you say you was with me?

SKINNY. Yeah. Yeah. Yes. Yeah. 'Sweets Who?'

Beat.

SWEETS. Cunt.

POTTS. That's a big hole in the plan then.

SWEETS. My brother had two Webleys off him last March.

SKINNY. Bow and arrow we've got the set.

SWEETS. Colin did. Pair a Webleys.

SKINNY. Have you bolted the back?

POTTS. What's the point? A kid could break in. Hang on. How did you get in?

SKINNY. Mickey gave me the key.

POTTS. When?

SKINNY. Last night. When he said I was in charge. I'm going to go and check the back. Come back find you all dead.

Exit SKINNY. *Pause.*

POTTS. Did you know that?

SWEETS. I had no idea.

Pause.

POTTS. Do you believe him?

SWEETS. He's got the key.

Pause.

POTTS. This, Sweets, is very bad for us.

SWEETS. What the fuck is going on?

POTTS. He's got the... Mickey gave him the key.

SWEETS. Big mistake. Mickey's made a big mistake there.

POTTS. I'm disappointed. I'm disappointed in Mickey.

SWEETS. It explains a lot. The whole... the –

POTTS. Minute we turn our backs – 'Mickey can I help you with this.' 'Mickey let me shake the *drips* off.' Before, right, before it's this is wrong with the club, that's wrong with the club, and and and as soon as soon as there's aggro he runs under the fucking shawl.

SWEETS. Don't waste any time do you Missy...

POTTS. You watch, they'll share a fucking mattress tonight. And with the... with the Charlie Dodds. Who suggested that eh? Who suggested it?

SWEETS. Me.

Beat.

POTTS. Exactly. And who gets packed off. Who gets trusted? You and me? Now... Now he'll walk in here and he'll want us all to kneel down kiss his crack.

SWEETS. With all the ordering us about with the mattresses. Like it's a Scout camp...

POTTS. Getting into it. This isn't a fuckin' fresh-air fortnight. This is real.

SWEETS. Thinking he's in the trenches –

POTTS. Giving it the Uncle Tommy –

SWEETS. The fucking Uncle Tommy –

POTTS. We're gonna get the Uncle Tommy. We're gonna get the Uncle Tommy. (*Pause.*) Fucking mess we're in.

Re-enter SKINNY.

SKINNY. Where's Mickey?

POTTS. See?

SKINNY. Where is he. (What?)

POTTS. Never you mind love.

SKINNY. What?

SWEETS. He's upstairs.

POTTS. He's got his head cold.

SWEETS. He's got his head cold doesn't want bothering. What's it like out there?

SKINNY. Beautiful. Sunny. There's a few kids out there. Stupid bastards are queueing up.

SWEETS. Yeah. tell 'em the show's round Mr Ross's tonight.

SKINNY (*re: the bins*). This him then?

POTTS. Yeah.Yeah that's him.

SKINNY. Fucking hell. (*Pause.*) You had a look?

POTTS. You haven't got the stomach.

SKINNY. A quid.

POTTS. Done.

SKINNY. Here. Half a crown and a Bazooka Joe.

POTTS. Done.

They shake. SKINNY *readies himself. He can't do it.*

Shitter.

SKINNY. It's harder than you think. (*Gives* POTTS *half a crown and the Bazooka Joe.*) I don't fucking like this.

POTTS. Don't you feel bad about it? What with it all happening on your first night in charge. Not a pretty start, is it?

SKINNY. Fuck off.

POTTS. Saps your confidence though I bet. As a leader.

SKINNY. I'm not listening to you.

Pause.

SWEETS. Poor man. One minute he's up on the stage.
Introducing. Doing all the introducing. In his blue suit. His
best blue suit. His little joke at the start.

Pause.

SKINNY. We should have stuck to the machines.

POTTS. Here we go. What was that Skipper?

SKINNY. What? Ezra never saw straight again the day the kid
walked in here. Buying him silver suits. Wearing tight trousers
himself. I mean an old man wearing tight trousers. It's asking
for trouble.

SWEETS. That's true.

SKINNY. Eh? Thinking I am in love all's well in the world.
Thinks if he combs his hair puts on tight trousers it's All Hail
the Prince of Clothes.

POTTS. You're all heart Skin.

SKINNY. Just because some old man wants to fuck children for a
hobby don't mean we all have to die in his good name.

SWEETS. He was always level to us weren't he Sid.

POTTS. Treated me fair. Played the gent.

SWEETS. Poor man. I'll miss him. (*Pause.*) All right. Here's a
good bet. Which half's his legs and which half's his head?

POTTS. Ten bob says left one's his head.

SWEETS. I reckon left.

SKINNY. Yeah you've picked 'em up.

POTTS. Yeah but we haven't looked.

SKINNY. Null bet. Null bet.

POTTS. Jeeez. Nice to be trusted.

SWEETS. You should be a bit more trusting.

SKINNY. I watch my back all right.

SWEETS. You should be a bit more trusting my son.

SKINNY. I watch my back all right.

Pause.

POTTS. You get any sandwiches?

SKINNY. Mickey gave me a fiver. I spent it on a small gun.

SWEETS. Eat the cake.

POTTS. I've eaten the cake.

SWEETS. Eat the cake. It's got… It's the same as bread.

POTTS. I eat any more of the cake I'm going to die. I'm going to turn blue die of cake poisoning.

SWEETS. It's the same as bread.

POTTS. The cherries. They're wax. They taste like wax.

SKINNY. Chuck a bit over then. (Blue icing…)

POTTS (*to* SWEETS). Look at this…

SKINNY. What.

POTTS. Am I the cake-fetcher?

SKINNY. I'm asking you – Just gimme a piece.

POTTS. Am I your cake-fetcher?

SKINNY. No. No. You're not. Absolutely. You jumpy cunt. I thought we were mates.

POTTS. Would you get *me* a piece of cake?

SKINNY. Mates. Friendship. You know?

POTTS. Would you fetch me cake?

SKINNY. I thought we were mates.

POTTS. We're business friends.

SWEETS. I'll get you some. You want some of the cake?

SKINNY. Grow up.

SWEETS. I'm sorry?

SKINNY. No.

SWEETS. What did you say?

POTTS. He said 'Grow up'.

SKINNY. I don't want to play.

POTTS. He said 'Grow up'.

SKINNY. I don't want to play that's all.

POTTS (*to* SWEETS). You see?

SKINNY. What?

SWEETS. Fucking Victor Mature.

POTTS. Fucking coming-of-age party.

SKINNY. You two live in a dreamworld.

POTTS. Whereas you have a long flowing beard.

SKINNY. A world of your own.

POTTS. You have the long whiskers of wisdom.

SKINNY. You know nothing about the real world. My Uncle
    Tommy was in the RAF, yeah, and when they were pinned
    down, and some, say someone said, 'Here Tom, Tommy, fetch
    me a bit of cake or a cuppa tea' you did it because of team spirit.

POTTS (*to* SWEETS). With the Uncle Tommy…

SWEETS (*to* POTTS). Do you hear that?

POTTS (*to* SWEETS). What did I say… ?

SKINNY. What?

POTTS (*to* SWEETS). Fuckin' Uncle Tommy who won the war
    on his own.

SKINNY. It's true… they helped each other out. Someone says
    'Can I have a cup of tea' –

POTTS. Uncle Tommy and his Halifax bomber. Uncle Tommy
    who shot down Hitler. Uncle Tommy who pinned down the
    Bosch single-handed at the Somme.

SKINNY. He fought in both World Wars.

POTTS. Here we go. And they're off.

SKINNY. What? Fuck off. He fought in both World Wars. He said he was older than he was in the First and younger than he was in the Second.

SWEETS. And he had four brothers and they all died in action at the Somme.

POTTS. Shame.

SWEETS. Four older brothers mind.

POTTS. I bet they did it on purpose. I bet they did it on purpose to get away from Uncle Tommy.

SWEETS. Fucking... Skin, give Uncle Tommy a call get him round here and when Sam Ross gets here he can kill him for us.

SKINNY. I'm not listening to you. I asked you for a piece of cake. You just have no understanding of history. Those people died for you.

POTTS. Are you still here Sunshine. Why don't you fuck off and join up.

SWEETS. Join up fight the gyppos. Take your little gun. See if they'll have you.

SKINNY. You have no understanding of history.

Pause.

SWEETS. There's toffee apples.

POTTS. I know there's toffee apples. Stop fucking toffee-appling me.

SWEETS. They're good.

POTTS. Fucking mess we're in.

Pause.

SWEETS. Anyway, why's he called your Uncle Tommy when he's shacked up with your mum?

SKINNY. Fuck off. I'm not listening.

SWEETS. Eh? Sid. *Uncle.*

POTTS. Fucking friendly uncle.

SKINNY. I'm not listening.

Pause.

POTTS. Fucking mess we're in.

Enter MICKEY *from the upstairs.*

MICKEY. What did Charlie say?

SKINNY. Mickey. I'm sorry. He only had this.

POTTS. Might as well give Sam Ross a Chinese burn as pop him with that. Waste of Sam's time.

SWEETS. He's got more. I know he's got more.

POTTS. Mickey, sorry but you sent the wrong bloke.

SKINNY. He doesn't even know you.

POTTS. That's nice Skin. Mickey gives you a job, you walk around in the sunshine, fuck it up, come back point the stinky finger at Sweets.

SWEETS. It's got a lovely bone handle.

MICKEY. Give it here. (*Takes the gun.*) All right. Don't worry. We've still got the cutlass.

SWEETS. Where is it?

MICKEY. It's up there.

SWEETS. Shouldn't we have it out here? Handy.

MICKEY. Leave it. Have you eaten?

POTTS. Mickey, it's about the cake. I can't actually eat any more or I'm going to sick up.

SWEETS. It's the same as bread.

POTTS. We need some supplies. You're in charge. What next?

SKINNY. Mickey, can I have a word?

MICKEY. What about? (Eat the cake.)

POTTS. Sorry. It makes me gag.

SWEETS. There's toffee apples.

SKINNY. Mickey –

POTTS. Fucking leave it with the toffee apples.

MICKEY. For tonight it's the cake. We'll get something else in the morning.

SWEETS. Mickey, what do you suppose he's doing right now?

MICKEY. Who?

SWEETS. Silver Johnny.

MICKEY. I don't know. He's with Sam Ross.

POTTS. He's on a plane to Acapulco with Sam Ross. He's sitting in a bubble bath. I know he is. Right now up to his scrawny neck. Eating a goose off a floating platter.

MICKEY. He's got a big fat smile across his face I can tell you that much.

SWEETS. Do you know what I think? I think he's had all his teeth covered in silver, and he's got silver-plated hair and nails, silver feet and silver pubes and he's singing at the Washington Bowl with loads of famous people watching.

Pause.

SKINNY. Mickey?

MICKEY. What?

SKINNY. Can I have a quick word? It's private.

MICKEY. What is?

SKINNY. The quick word. Can we go up there?

MICKEY. Okay. Go up.

SKINNY *goes up the stairs.*

Tell me when he wakes up.

Exit MICKEY *up the stairs.*

POTTS. Stick a pin in me.

SWEETS. If I hadn't seen it…

POTTS. Did I fall asleep miss the wedding?

SWEETS. Bad for morale that. Very bad.

POTTS. You know he can stand in the corner down here clicking his fingers being big with the twelve-year-olds waving like he don't drive the van. He drives the van and I say he should drive the van.

SWEETS. Standing at the bar like he don't drive the van.

POTTS. In the corner with the twelve-year-olds...

SWEETS. And... and... and... With the fuckin' –

POTTS. The fucking American.

SWEETS. With the American accent.

POTTS. Honestly. It's sad.

SWEETS. To girls. In this stupid American accent.

POTTS. He sounds Welsh.

SWEETS. Getting snug.

POTTS. Cuddling up to Mickey... this is wrong that's wrong. With his fucking bunch of keys.

SWEETS. ... Fucking bad breath –

POTTS. Fucking bad-breath van-boy. Fucking bad-breath van-boy with chat.

BABY *suddenly sits up. He sits there, not moving.*

Here we go.

SWEETS. Hello Colonel. How's that?

POTTS. Bit more like it eh?

SWEETS. Now that feels a lot better don't it.

POTTS. Sweets, get Baby a glass of water.

SWEETS. How you feeling Baby-o. Ready for the party?

Pause. BABY *sits there.*

BABY. What time is it?

POTTS. What? It's the evening.

SWEETS. July. Lovely long evening.

POTTS. Still hot. Long shadows down Dean Street I bet.

SWEETS. Lovely out. Must be.

POTTS. Boiling hot. Skin said.

BABY. Yeah? (*Pause.*) I miss anything?

POTTS. Yeah. There was a wedding.

SWEETS. Yeah. Mickey and Skinny got hitched.

POTTS. Whirlwind romance. Very touching.

SWEETS. That's the cake over there. Potts was best man and I sung the carol.

BABY. Where's is he?

SWEETS. Mickey? He's up there mate.

POTTS. Up there with the lucky lady.

SWEETS. He's up there bumming him off right now.

POTTS. Yeah. He's bumming off his bad-breath van-boy bride. So. Mickey don't love us any more. That's what's happened. That's all you missed.

Pause.

BABY. You know it *is* a hot evening. I can smell it on the breeze.

POTTS. Yeah.

BABY. Yes. I can smell it. Like when you're a kid and you wake up and it's summer.

SWEETS. Typical eh? Rains all July, then the day they chop your boss up you go into hiding, wouldn't you know, a scorcher.

POTTS. Shut it Sweets.

SWEETS. Absolutely. Sorry Babes.

POTTS. It's the cake. He's eaten nothing but cake for ten hours.

SWEETS. It's the blue icing.

POTTS. Relax.

Pause.

BABY. So who wants to go up the pictures?

POTTS. That'd be the one wouldn't it. Normal Sunday have a cold lemon go up the Curzon.

SWEETS. Fuck about after up St James.

POTTS. Maybe head down Monkeytown. Hang out.

SWEETS. Town's your oyster.

BABY. What about it? Quick flick. Eh? Quick Bob Mitchum.

POTTS. Yeah. Sorry Babes. Can't.

SWEETS. Love to Babes. Not allowed.

BABY. Come on. Who wants to go and see a Wild West?

POTTS. I personally would love to. But Mickey's decided it. We're all stopped here.

BABY. Who says?

POTTS. Mickey says.

BABY. Mickey says.

   Pause.

   There's probably kids outside.

SWEETS. Skin said there's a few.

BABY. Shall we get them in. Open the bar?

SWEETS. We can't mate. Love to. Can't.

BABY. Oh. (*Pause.*) Sidney, quick film?

POTTS. All right Baby. Stop pulling my cock.

BABY. What?

POTTS. You know we ain't going out, having a party, doing a conga, nothing. We're staying here. Why? Because of what's in those bins. Blunt as it is, I've had nothing but sorrow and birthday cake since sun-up, so stop the Music Hall. All right love?

SWEETS. Relax Sid.

POTTS. I'm relaxed. I'm talking.

BABY. This him?

He lifts the lid off one. He looks. He puts it down. He lifts the lid off the other. He looks, then puts it down.

Sweets?

SWEETS. Yes Babes?

BABY. I think I'll have that glass of water now please.

SWEETS. I'll just get you one.

Exit SWEETS.

POTTS. Fucking weekend. You feeling all right?

BABY. Tell the truth I'm a bit tired.

POTTS. Yeah?

BABY. Yeah. Feel… tired like when you see old people and they look tired. You know what I mean?

POTTS. You'll pick up. It's the shock. (*Pause.*) You shouldn't have done that.

BABY. What?

POTTS. Had a look. You'll only have a bad dream now. I remember when I was four I saw this dog get ripped up by these pikeys. They had it tied up on a swing and they had these pinking shears and a rake. (*Pause.*) Carried that little doggie round in my head for weeks.

BABY. Yeah. Maybe I'll have a bad dream or something.

Pause.

POTTS. You should hear what Skinny was saying about you Babes.

Pause.

BABY. About me?

POTTS. What?

BABY. You just said.

POTTS. Yeah. He was saying stuff to Mickey. About you.

BABY. What about me?

POTTS. How now's the time to brush you off.

BABY. Did he say that?

POTTS. Fucking bad breath… He opens his mouth something uncouth plops out.

BABY. What did he say then?

POTTS. He saying to Mickey he reckons we should brush you off. That 'blah blah pissing on we don't need the Jew no more'.

BABY. Ah… He doesn't mean that.

POTTS. He said it. Something like it…

BABY. He doesn't mean that. He only says that because he loves me.

POTTS. Yeah? They're up there right now. Luke and Mickey. He's fucking got his feet nicely under the table.

BABY. I take no notice. I know it's just because he wants to walk like me. You all right Sid?

POTTS. Me? Tops.

BABY. You look white.

POTTS. It's the pills. I'm crampy. My stomach's all shrunk.

BABY. Your tummy? Does it hurt?

POTTS. It's like a lump of stone.

BABY. You had a sleep?

POTTS. What? No. I can't.

BABY. You should have a sleep Sid. I'll keep watch.

POTTS. Go downstairs stick your head under the tap. Clear your thoughts. (*Pause*.) I'm fucking shitting myself Baby.

BABY. Ah I shouldn't worry. Mickey's got it all under control.

POTTS. He ain't even got a plan. Besides, they made him God I missed it. Fucking getting cuffy with me.

BABY. He hit you?

POTTS. Right on my eardrum. It's ringing.

BABY. Mickey hit you? Did he hurt you?

POTTS. What? Not bad. But it knocks you back you get a cuff.

BABY. I'll say. That's not like him.

Re-enter SWEETS.

SWEETS. Here you go. Nice chilly drink.

POTTS. You run it for a bit? The nippers climb up there slash in the tank. Always run it count to six.

BABY. Thank you Sweets.

BABY *drinks the water.*

SWEETS. You ever seen him before?

BABY. Who?

SWEETS. Mr Ross.

POTTS. Fucker's a legend South of the River.

SWEETS. Last year. Last year, when the Billy thing. Billy the…

POTTS. The Billy thing.

SWEETS. The fuckin' Billy thing. The fucking Billy the Bass.

POTTS. The double bass –

SWEETS. The double Billy thing. The stand-up bass player. Getting his own –

POTTS. Says he wants –

SWEETS. About his own manager. Shows up one night he's got his own manager along. He's the *bass player*. What happens? Eh? I'll tell you what happens.

POTTS. To the manager. This is the Hyde Park –

SWEETS. They find him lying in Hyde Park. I'll tell you what happens. They find him lying in Hyde Park.

POTTS. (…fuckin'…)

SWEETS. They find him *twitching* in the park.

POTTS. (…fuckin'…)

SWEETS. They've woken him up driven up the Hyde, staked the fucker out and and and and and –

POTTS. The lawn –

SWEETS. … and drove a lawnmower over him. Over his face. Drove a lawnmower over his face.

POTTS. Fuckin' hell.

SWEETS. Over his face.

POTTS. Fuckin' hell.

SWEETS. Lawnmower. Over his face.

POTTS. Fuckin' hell.

SWEETS. The bloke's a vegetable.

POTTS. He's chopped liver.

SWEETS. His face is chopped liver.

POTTS. (… a pool of its former glory…)

SWEETS. A mockery of its former self. Then they've had breakfast, gone round the bass player's and they've cut his thumb off.

POTTS (*simultaneous with 'cut'*). Cut his fucking thumb off.

SWEETS. Lah-di-dah – they've cut his fucking thumb off. Round his mum's. In front of his mum. Him in his jimmy-jams.

POTTS. (Pyjamas.) Thereby depriving him of his livelihood.

SWEETS. Thereby depriving him of his *thumb*. The livelihood speaks for itself.

POTTS. You do that and it can speak for itself.

SWEETS. Then exactly.

POTTS. Good.

BABY. I don't know him no. But I'd like to meet him.

POTTS. Yeah? Well it looks like you're going to get the chance my son.

SWEETS. I know one thing. He comes back here I'm over the roofs and in Stepney before he's had time to get his saw out again.

Re-enter SKINNY *and* MICKEY.

POTTS. So what's he like?

SKINNY. What?

POTTS. You ought to brush your teeth more.

SKINNY. What?

POTTS. Me? Nothing. What's that smell?

SKINNY. What are you talking about?

POTTS. Mickey, can I say something. As it's all up in the air, I'm
a bit jumpy, Sweets is a bit jumpy, can we have the little
councils down here in the open. Not up there with the cutlass. I
mean I love you both but I'm a bit scatty with the pills and I
might get the hump kill you both in your sleep. I'm not saying
you're planning nothing but my mind might be damaged. You
never know.

Pause.

MICKEY. You all right Baby?

BABY. I'm fine thank you Michael.

MICKEY. You feel better?

BABY. Sweets here got me a nice drink of water.

SWEETS. He's looking the part now.

BABY. Mickey, can I have a word with you?

MICKEY. What?

BABY. In private.

MICKEY. What do you want to say?

BABY. It's not for everyone to hear. It's like… (*Laughs.*) It's
private.

MICKEY. Baby –

BABY. Seriously, I want a word.

MICKEY. Anything you want to say, say it to us all.

POTTS. Hang on. Hang on. Do I have to point out the fucking
obvious here?

SKINNY. What?

POTTS. Giving me the what? Mickey. *Come on.*

MICKEY. What's your problem Sidney?

POTTS. Why don't I tell you. I get a thump in the head Skinny gets a massage upstairs.

SWEETS. Let's all take a step back.

POTTS. You should hear the stuff he says when you're not here.

SKINNY. I do not.

POTTS. 'Mickey should have done this...Mickey fucked this up, Mickey knew all about the deal did nothing.'

SKINNY. Mickey I did not.

POTTS. He did. He said you knew all about Sam wanting the kid and you done nothing.

SKINNY. He's lying Mickey.

MICKEY. Sid, relax.

POTTS. I'm not happy Mickey. My ear's still ringing.

MICKEY. I'm... Listen. Relax. I'm sorry I hit you.

POTTS. I've got some things I could say. I've got some ideas.

MICKEY. I know.

POTTS. I'm not happy Mickey.

MICKEY. Just relax Sidney. Everyone knows you're here.

BABY. Mickey, I want to say sorry. (*Pause*.) Uhhh. (*Pause*.) All right. I think... Well. (*Laughs*.) I know I don't do much to run things, in the past. And I haven't like... Well, I've decided to buck myself up. Make improvements. Because I want to stay round here, and I think if we're going to uhh... Well, that's it.

MICKEY. It's still too early for –

BABY. No. I'm serious. I've thought about it.

MICKEY. I'm pleased.

BABY. I know what you must think. But you know, there's nothing like someone cutting your dad in two for clearing the mind. (*Pause*.) I do think that, what with my making improvements, I should be allowed to be more of a help to you

Mickey. As if we were going to run things together. I mean, obviously you're in charge, but we could like run the club together. Like I could tell people that we run it together. Do you know what I mean?

MICKEY. I'm glad you've thought about it. We need you here, like I said.

BABY. I know. And I know why and I understand. I'm happy with that. I mean, where else would I go eh? Where else would I have this much fun?

MICKEY. Baby, I'm going to make you a deal. You don't dance me around, you leave Skinny Luke alone, then you help out a bit more then in a week we'll talk. That's all I'm gonna say.

BABY. I want to try.

MICKEY. You do that, you leave Skinny to get on with it, we're in business. Yes?

BABY. Okay.

MICKEY. You start squeezing his nuts I've got a problem. Because he's a good little worker, and he's telling me now he's walking out of here you give him any more niggle.

BABY. You said that.

SKINNY. I've just had enough Baby. I want us to get along.

BABY. Skinny, I'm sorry. I'm not going to squeeze your nuts any more.

SKINNY. It's just it really hurts. I might want kids one day.

BABY. I'm sorry.

MICKEY. Right. What time is it?

POTTS. It's sunset. Getting cooler.

MICKEY. All right listen. Skinny, bring up the other mattresses. Bring up some of the painting covers and stuff, make some blankets and things.

SKINNY. Right.

MICKEY. You two, take some full beer barrels from in there, push them up against the back door.

SWEETS. Right.

MICKEY. Baby, give them a hand.

BABY. Okay. Uh. Mickey.

MICKEY. What?

BABY. What are you going to do?

MICKEY. I'm making a call.

BABY. Right. I've had an idea.

MICKEY. What's the problem?

BABY. I think maybe you should give them a hand.

MICKEY. Sorry.

BABY. I think you should. With the barrels.

MICKEY. That didn't last long then did it?

BABY. No. No. Hang on. It's just… What are you going to do?

MICKEY. I told you.

BABY. What was it again?

MICKEY. I'm going to make a fucking telephone call.

BABY. Who to?

MICKEY. What do you mean 'Who to'?

BABY. Just who might you have to call?

MICKEY. I've got to call a band.

BABY. Which band?

MICKEY. What do you mean what… a band that was gonna play here Tuesday lunchtime.

BABY. Right.

MICKEY. An oldies' band.

BABY. I'll tell you what Mickey. You help them. I'll make the call.

MICKEY. I'm sorry?

SKINNY. Mickey –

MICKEY. It's all right. What do you want to prove Baby?

BABY. Nothing. I just think you should carry the barrels. Pushing them up against the door. It's a good idea.

MICKEY. You want to make a big deal out of the first fucking thing we do?

BABY. No. No. I just think we should start like it's all fair, and you should help with the barrels.

MICKEY. I've asked you to.

BABY. And I've asked you to.

MICKEY. Have you finished being hilarious? Because if you have I've got a phone call to make.

BABY. What's the number?

MICKEY. Fuck off.

BABY. Tell me. Tell me the number. What's the big deal? It's only a phone call. Don't you trust me to make a phone call?

SWEETS. Baby –

BABY. What? Mickey, listen, if Ezra asked you to carry the barrels, what would you do?

SWEETS. Me and Sid can manage the barrels. You put your feet up.

BABY. Mickey. You know? If Ezra asked you what would you do? Because the other day Ezra asked you to stick five thousand sequins all over here and you crawled round on your hands and knees all day. You did. I saw you.

POTTS. Babes that ain't going to help.

BABY. What? I don't see the problem.

MICKEY. It's all right Sid.

BABY. What's the difference now? Just imagine I'm Ezra.

Pause.

MICKEY. All right Baby. You're the boss. Tell me what you want me to do. Why don't you tell us all what we're going to do?

Pause.

BABY. Are you serious?

MICKEY. I'm waiting. Tell us all your plan.

BABY (*laughs*). All right. Who wants to go and find the blowjob?

POTTS. Don't fuck around Baby.

BABY. I'm serious. Why don't we all chip up Sam Ross's let him know how we feel. Let him know we're not happy and all. I reckon we ought put up a bit of a struggle. What do you reckon Sweets? All chip up at Sam Ross's door ask for him back. (*Pause.*) Skinny. Fancy it? That's not very Dunkirk of you. I bet your Uncle Tommy would be game.

SKINNY. Baby, just do this and it will make Mickey happy.

BABY. What?

SKINNY. What?

MICKEY. Go upstairs Skin.

SKINNY. What did I say?

MICKEY. Just go upstairs.

SKINNY. What did I say? What... Mickey? What did I say?

Pause.

BABY (*quietly*). Kiss my pegs.

SKINNY. Fuck off.

BABY. Kiss my pegs.

SKINNY. Fuck off. Mickey –

BABY. Do it. Kiss my pegs.

SKINNY. Two minutes. Two minutes and we're off again.

BABY. Kiss my pegs. Kiss my pegs.

POTTS. Baby.

BABY. Kiss my pegs.

Skinny. What did I say?

POTTS. Kiss his pegs.

SWEETS. Kiss his fucking pegs...

BABY. Do it. Do it. Do it.

MICKEY. Baby, why do you do this. Go upstairs cool off.

BABY (*to* SKINNY). Fucking get rid of me you cunt...

MICKEY. Go upstairs.

> BABY *stops. He goes upstairs.*

SKINNY. That's it. I'm off.

MICKEY. Skinny –

SKINNY. I've had it Mickey. I'm going to get hurt I stay here.

SWEETS. Just wait down here. He's in shock.

SKINNY. Fuck shock. He's a nutter.

POTTS. It's an act. He's a bullcrap. Go up there, punch him in the face, he'll turn into Little Bo Peep.

MICKEY. Skinny. Stay down here.

> *But* BABY *is coming back down out with the cutlass.*

POTTS. Here we go.

SWEETS. Oh for fuck's sake Baby. Who do you think you are?

SKINNY. Now I'm going to get hurt. Now he's going to kill me.

POTTS. He's not going to kill no one. It's bullcrap.

SWEETS. Don't shame yourself up Baby. Put the sword down. Look. Just stand there. Million pounds says he doesn't.

SKINNY. Sorry but that's not enough.

POTTS. We can do this again or we shift the barrels. That bolt won't hold.

BABY. Kiss my pegs.

SKINNY. All right. I'll do it.

POTTS. No you won't.

BABY. Do it.

POTTS. Tell him to fuck off.

SKINNY. Fuck off. I'll do it.

MICKEY. Baby. Get out.

BABY. I'm sorry?

Pause.

MICKEY. I'm sorry for you, but I don't want you around here any more.

Pause. BABY *is taken aback. He laughs.*

BABY. That's not very nice.

MICKEY. Just go.

BABY. I see.

MICKEY. I hope you do. I hope you do. I'm sorry, but I want you to leave.

Pause.

BABY. Now?

MICKEY. Yes. Now.

BABY. Right now. This second.

MICKEY. Yes.

Pause.

BABY. Uh, Mickey.

MICKEY. I'm not listening to you Baby. You've fucked around here for too long. I'm sorry.

BABY. I've always liked you Mickey...

MICKEY. Leave.

Pause.

BABY. Oh. Mickey. You've... You're so... You're a very decisive person aren't you. I mean, you've always been a bit of a dark one, a bit of a Mrs Mopp for my dad and now... Well, you're showing qualities aren't you. You surprise me.

MICKEY. I'm sorry. I'm not going to ask you again.

Pause.

BABY. Mickey. (*Pause.*) Watch what you say to me.

MICKEY. I don't think I have to. I don't think any of us do.

BABY. This is my dad's place. And there's… I'm his son. There must be deeds, and it passes on to me.

MICKEY. There's no deeds. You'd ever opened a drawer here you might know that.

BABY (*quietly*). Well.

Pause.

Be-bop-a-lula she's my baby, be-bop-a-lula I don't mean maybe…

Pause.

Be-bop-a-lula, she-hee-hee's my babuh, mah babuh. Mah Babah.

Very long pause. On and on. BABY *stands around. He lifts the cutlass and holds it over* MICKEY.

MICKEY. I don't believe you Baby.

BABY *stands there. In the end he lowers the cutlass.*

Now fuck off. And don't come back.

BABY *stands there. He leaves. Pause.*

SWEETS. Jesus.

POTTS. Mickey –

MICKEY. Put the barrels against the back door.

SWEETS. What? Right. Come on Sid.

Exit SWEETS *and* POTTS.

SKINNY. Mickey –

MICKEY. Skin, get the sheets.

SKINNY. Right. Thank you Mickey.

MICKEY. Get the sheets.

SKINNY. It's really got to me. I've been sleeping bad.

MICKEY. Use all the ones don't have paint on them. You can tear them up into… well, you know.

SKINNY. Leave it to me Mickey.

MICKEY. And check all the doors and windows. You finish that, help the others.

SKINNY. Right. Mickey. Where are we sleeping tonight?

MICKEY. You can sleep down here.

SKINNY. Good. Good. I just thought we could sleep up there with... all together. I just thought it would be better if we were all together.

MICKEY. Okay. Take the mattress up.

SKINNY. Is that all right?

MICKEY. Take them upstairs. Yes.

SKINNY. Thank you Mickey. I'll sleep better.

MICKEY. I've got to make a call.

SKINNY. Okay. Thank you Mickey.

MICKEY. Do the sheets.

Exit SKINNY. MICKEY *is alone. Enter* POTTS, *holding a large bowl with a cloth over it.*

POTTS. Mickey old son? I made you this.

MICKEY. What is it?

POTTS. For your head cold.

Beat.

MICKEY. Right.

POTTS. It's hot from the steamer. Strictly you need friar's balsam but I've bunged in a couple gills of crème de menthe. It's all spearmint or something. All does the trick on your pipes.

He sets it down.

MICKEY. I'm fine. Do the barrels.

POTTS. It doesn't hurt or nothing. You stick your head over, breathe it all in, fixes you up in minutes. Come here.

MICKEY. I'm all right.

POTTS. Nonsense Mickey, come here.

MICKEY *goes to the table and sits down.*

MICKEY. What do I do?

POTTS. You just breathe. You just put your head over it and breathe. Short while you'll feel like a baby. You'll be clear as rain.

MICKEY *puts the cloth over his head and breathes.*

I'm going to do the barrels now. You just stay there Mickey. All right? (*Pause.*) Just breathe Mickey.

Exit POTTS, *leaving* MICKEY *alone, breathing in the steam.*

Blackout.

Scene Two

Downstairs at the Atlantic. Hanging upside down in the middle of the room, gagged, is a young man, wearing silver trousers and a pink shirt. This is SILVER JOHNNY.

Perched on a bar stool opposite is BABY, *wearing the silver jacket and drinking beer. There are empty beer cans on the bar. The shotgun is across his knees.*

BABY. . . . I was about nine, bit younger, and my dad tells me we're driving to the country for the day.

He's got this half-share in this caff at the time, and it was doing really badly, so he was always really busy working day and night, so like, this was totally out of the blue.

So I got in his van with him, and we drive off and I notice that in the front of the cab there's this bag of sharp knives. And like, a saw and a big meat cleaver.

And I thought 'This is it. He's going to kill me. He's going to take me off and kill me once and for all.' And I sat there in silence all the way to Wales and I knew that day I was about to die.

So we drive till it goes dark, and Dad pulls the van into this field. And he switches off the lights. And we sit there in silence. And there's all these cows in the field, watching us. And suddenly Dad slams his foot down and we ram this fucking great cow clean over the top of the van. And it tears off the bonnet and makes a great dent in the top, but it was dead all right. See we'd gone all the way to Wales to rustle us a cow. For the caff.

Now a dead cow weighs half a ton. So you've got to cut it up there and then. And I was so relieved I had tears in my eyes. And we hacked that cow to pieces, sawing, chopping, ripping, with all the other cows standing around in the dark, watching.

Then when we'd finished, we got back in the cab and drove back to town. Covered in blood.

Pause.

Do you know why I'm called Baby?

Pause.

Take out the papers and the trash,
Or you don't get no spending cash;
If you don't la la la la la,
You ain't gonna rock 'n' roll no more
Yakety yak, don't talk back.

Pause. He drinks. Pause. He laughs.

Yakety yak don't talk back.

He laughs, he gets up and walks around.

Yakety yak don't talk back.

BABY *laughs. He moves the chair to right in front of* SILVER JOHNNY *and sits down.*

So, like… (*Pause.*) So like when you met Little Richard, what were you gonna say? (*Pause.*) 'Evening Richard… I…' (*Pause.*) 'Evening Little. Can I call you Little?' 'Sure, if I can call you Silver.' (*Pause.*) Seriously, you must have had some pretty nifty plans. What did you have planned? Were you going to go to Niagara Falls. Just you, Sam and the majestic spray.

Pause. BABY *clicks his fingers along to a tune in his head. He stops. He drinks. Pause.*

Do you think I'm good-looking? Seriously… No come on, I mean… Do you think I'm quite good-looking?

SILVER JOHNNY *nods helpfully.*

Seriously. Am I, like… Am I would you say rugged or striking? (*Pause.*) Hold on. Am I rugged?

SILVER JOHNNY *shakes his head.*

I'm not. Am I striking?

SILVER JOHNNY *nods.*

I am… You think so.

BABY *finishes his drink, crumples up the can and puts it in the pocket of the silver jacket. He searches through the other pockets of the jacket. He finds a guitar pick.*

What this? Is it a… guitar pick? Plectrum. Is it a plectrum?

SILVER JOHNNY *nods.*

Do you play the guitar? I didn't know you could play guitar. Can you play it? Seriously?

SILVER JOHNNY *shakes his head.*

Then what have you got this for?

SILVER JOHNNY *doesn't respond.*

What am going to do with you blowjob? Eh? What am I gonna do with you? (*Pause.*) What am I going to do with you?

Enter SWEETS *with the Derringer.*

SWEETS. Who is it? Who's there?

BABY. Who's that?

SWEETS. I've got a gun. Don't move.

BABY (*quietly*). Sweets. My man. You should be asleep.

SWEETS *is halfway down the stairs. It is dark and he can't see* SILVER JOHNNY.

SWEETS. Oh. Watcha Baby. We thought you'd gone.

BABY. Ah… you know… I thought I'd drop by.

SWEETS. Right. How are you?

BABY. I thought I'd pop back in. (Fine, yeah).

SWEETS. What time is it?

BABY. No idea. Must be… You been asleep?

SWEETS. Yeah… we're all…

BABY. Must be nearly morning. It was getting light out.

SWEETS. Yeah?

BABY. Gonna be another beautiful day. What you doing up so bright and early?

SWEETS. Oh. I'm supposed to be on watch.

BABY. What for. Baddies?

SWEETS. Yeah. Something like that.

BABY (*pointing to Derringer*). The fuck is that?

SWEETS. This? It's a… You know Charlie Dodds?

BABY. Yeah…

SWEETS. It's off him.

BABY. Give it here.

SWEETS. It's shit.

BABY. Give it here.

SWEETS. Wouldn't scare a kid.

BABY. It looks like a Turkish Delight.

SWEETS. Yeah. (*Pause.*) Baby, can I ask you a question?

BABY (*points it at* SWEETS). Fire away.

SWEETS. Right. Um… How did you get in here?

BABY (*stops*). I came down the chimney. Like Father Christmas.

SWEETS. Right. Right. We never thought of that.

BABY. No. No. You know my key. The one I lost dancing.

SWEETS. Yeah.

BABY. Yeah? Well, I never lost it dancing. It was in my shirt pocket all that time.

SWEETS. Right. Right.

BABY. I found it. I had it all the time. In here.

Beat.

SWEETS. Yeah actually, because I've been writing you a letter.

BABY. *You* have?

SWEETS. Yeah. Sounds a bit daft saying it like that.

BABY. What does it say?

SWEETS. Well, I've only just started it. It's just you know all that stuff Mickey said. Well I, for one and I think certainly Sid, right… Anyway. Just to say I don't really agree with Mickey on that one. I think he's wrong.

BABY. Thank you.

SWEETS. Because we've always been mates.

BABY. We have. Yeah.

SWEETS. And, you know Mickey's like chucked you out. Yeah. Well, as far as I'm concerned we should still go for drinks and stuff. I mean, who knows what's round the corner? And I bet Mickey changes his mind. Between you me and the lamp post.

BABY. Yeah?

SWEETS. What? Yeah. Yeah. Who knows? Who knows eh? What the fuck…

BABY. Yeah… Thing is Sweets, that's really nice and all, but the thing is I've always thought you were a bit of a tosser.

Pause.

SWEETS. What? Oh.

BABY. Yeah. I've always had you down as a right nasty little cunt underneath. Like, all sweetness and light to your face, and then as nasty as can be in the real world. Also, you're not very bright, and I think you only hang around Sid all the time because you want his cock up your arse. (*Pause.*) You know? To be frank.

SWEETS. Right. Well. What the fuck eh? (*Pause.*) I don't you know…

BABY. Don't what?

SWEETS. He's just a mate. (*Pause. The penny drops.*) You rotten bastard.

BABY. Aaaaahhhh!

SWEETS. You dirty shit.

BABY. I got you sunshine.

SWEETS. You dirty bastard. You had me there.

BABY. Your face.

SWEETS. I was thinking, 'What? What's he on about.'

BABY. You should have seen your face.

SWEETS. You dirty bastard. I twigged though.

BABY. You went grey in the face.

SWEETS. I knew pretty soon.

BABY. You need a drink after that don't you.

SWEETS. Telling me. You rotten git.

BABY. Drink?

SWEETS. Fuck it. Why not. Mickey comes down I'll just tell him you forgot something.

BABY. Is it a problem?

SWEETS. What? No. I'll just give him a spiel. Lovely.

BABY. Ice?

SWEETS. There's no ice.

BABY. What? There's always ice.

SWEETS. Not today.

BABY. No pills. No ice. Place is falling apart.

SWEETS. Yeah…

BABY. I turn my back for half an hour, place falls down round our heads. Let's have a look…

SWEETS. Ezra's in there actually.

BABY. What? In here.

SWEETS. Actually. Yes.

BABY. In with the ice?

SWEETS. Yeah. It was my idea. Just until further notice.

BABY. Both halves?

SWEETS. Yes. No. The legs are in the Frigidaire.

BABY. In the Frigidaire up there?

SWEETS. Pretty much.

BABY. Well, best leave him. Cheers.

SWEETS. Lovely. (Cheers.)

BABY. To Ezra.

SWEETS *has seen what is hanging in the middle of the room.*

Top-up?

SWEETS. What? No. No. Cheers.

BABY. You sure?

SWEETS. Uhhhh…

SWEETS *takes in the scene. He looks at* BABY, *at* SILVER JOHNNY, *everything is very quiet in the glow for ages. Then he bellows.*

Mickey!! Mickey!! Mickey!! Mickey!! Mickey!!

BABY. Ssssh. Quiet. Keep it down. You want to wake up all Soho.

SWEETS. Where'd that come from?

BABY. Keep it down. What?

SWEETS. Where d'you get that?

BABY. Oh, you know.

SWEETS. We thought –

BABY. Say hello to Sweets, John. You remember Sweets. The Sweets Man. Does the pills.

SWEETS. What's going on? I'm lost.

Enter POTTS *from down the stairs.*

POTTS. Sweets? You all right?

SWEETS. It's… Look.

POTTS. The fuck is all the clatter?

BABY. Sidney Potts coming down the stairs there. Bet you never thought you'd see his ugly mush again.

POTTS. Baby. We thought you'd gone.

SWEETS. He still had his keys Sid.

BABY. Sidney. We've got four of us… we can have a little party.

POTTS *has seen* SILVER JOHNNY.

POTTS. Suffering Shit.

SWEETS. Precisely.

POTTS. Sweet Georgia Brown.

BABY. Do you like it?

POTTS. Where the fuck did you dig him up from?

BABY. What do you think?

POTTS. That is him isn't it. (*Looks through his legs upside down.*) Baby, you fucking champion.

SWEETS. We thought he was in America.

POTTS. Will you look at this. Will you look what is hanging up there.

SWEETS. I don't understand.

POTTS. The one and only Johnny Shiny.

SWEETS. I'm lost.

POTTS. Okay. Okay. Baby. I'm catching up. I don't get it but so far I like it very very much.

BABY. You want a drink Sid?

POTTS. Yes. Yes. I do want a drink. I want a big drink. And I think we should talk because this makes a different story.

SWEETS. Get Sid a drink.

POTTS. My fucking… Right. Right. Back to plan one. Fish are jumping. Fish are jumping again. (*To* SILVER JOHNNY.) First things first. You little upside-down queer bastard. The shit you're in. Had us sitting around filling our pants. You little wanker, Sweets here shat his pants because of you.

SWEETS. I didn't. It was the pills.

POTTS. Right. Good. I'm waking up. I'm awake.

BABY. Do you like it?

POTTS. Yes. I like it. I like it very very much. But. But. One thing. What the fuck is going on?

BABY. He was on the telly. I went round the back, opened it, and got him out.

POTTS. Baby. Okay. Listen. This changes a couple of things. First of all, you're my hero.

Enter MICKEY *and* SKINNY. MICKEY *remains on the stairs, overlooking the scene.*

SKINNY. Fuckin' hell.

POTTS. Eh? Feast your eyes Skinny Luke. Feast your eyes.

SKINNY. Where d'you find him?

POTTS (*to* SILVER JOHNNY). You fucking little bastard, not so fucking croony now are you? You better get used to that chain because it ain't coming off chum. I'm keeping you on that from now on.

MICKEY. What the fuck have you done?

BABY. Hello Mickey. You asleep?

MICKEY. What have you done Baby?

SKINNY. I don't understand.

POTTS. Mickey. Hello. Welcome. I think you've got a couple of things to say to our friend here.

SKINNY.… Fuckin' 'ell…

POTTS. I thought... Oy... Go upstairs... Crawl back under Mickey's blanket, do something else, I'm talking to Baby.

SKINNY. Fuckin' hell. It's him. Mickey, it's him.

POTTS. Makes you think doesn't it. We're all in here crouched down Baby goes out and does a day's work. Does what he can for us. And Skinny, it's not sweeping up and it's not fixing jukeboxes. It's saving our fucking everything. A real day's work.

MICKEY. Baby, where did you find him?

BABY. Sorry, Mickey?

MICKEY. You heard me.

BABY. Ah, he was round Sam Ross's.

Pause.

'If your man ain't treatin' you right,
Come up and see you Dan,
I rock 'em roll 'em all night long
I'm a sixty-minute man.'

SKINNY. What's going on Mickey? Baby, what have you done?

BABY. Well, I left here and I walked around for a bit and then I sort of walked back up here and I saw... you know that Buick? Well it was still sitting there. Shiny Red Car. And I'm looking in it checking it out and the fucking keys are only sitting there in the hole. So I thought toodle-oo, why not? You ever driven one Mickey?

MICKEY. What?

BABY. One of those big yank motors. Like sitting on a velvet cushion. Floating past Nelson's Column, sitting on a velvet throne. Through Waterloo, down Camberwell, all the way, press a button, the roof comes off. Press another, the radio comes on. Cutlass on the back seat. I felt like General Patton.

And I parked it, right, and I asked around, and the first bloke I ask actually knows where Mr Ross lives. Belly up, knock on the door. And this bloke with yellow hair answers. And I chopped him.

SKINNY. You did what?

BABY. Yeah. I chopped him on the top of the head with my dad's old sword. And he fell down. And he never got up again.

SWEETS. Baby, you chopped him. You chopped Mr Ross?

BABY. Yeah. It's easier than you think. He just opens the door, and you chop him. (*Pause.*) So there's no one around so I step inside. First door I try, the parlour, watching telly, sandwich on his knee, the one and only Silver Johnny. Bit surprised to see his old mate Baby in such a place, so I take him outside, walk him up and down, put him in the motor brung him back here. Except coming over Vauxhall the engine packs in. And the buses have all stopped so this one paid for a cab.

Pause.

SKINNY. Baby? Did you kill him?

BABY. Well, Skinny Luke, I don't know. It's actually really difficult to tell…

POTTS. We're fucked. We're dead. I'm dead.

MICKEY, *who has heard all this, comes down the stairs.*

MICKEY. Sweets. Get upstairs.

SWEETS. Mickey –

MICKEY. Did you hear me. Do it now.

POTTS. Mickey what –

MICKEY. Fucking get up there. Do as I say. Get upstairs.

POTTS. We're going.

SKINNY. Mickey –

MICKEY. Do you want to die today? Eh? Do you want to die today.

POTTS. Oh my Sweet Life.

MICKEY. Do you want to die today. Get upstairs you fuck. Do as I say. Do as I say.

Exit SWEETS, POTTS *and* SKINNY, *upstairs. Very long pause.*

MICKEY. Are you all right?

BABY. Bearing up.

Pause.

MICKEY. You spoken to him?

BABY. We did have a natter on the way. Yes.

MICKEY. Right. What did he say?

BABY. He told me.

MICKEY. Everything?

BABY. How's your head cold Mickey? You feeling all right?

MICKEY. What did he tell you?

BABY. Why don't we ask him. He's right there. He said when him and Dad left here and went to Ross's place, that when they got there, that you was there Mickey. He said that your head cold had miraculously disappeared. He said you was feeling better. He said you all played billiards. Did you play billiards Mickey?

MICKEY. Yes.

BABY. I see. He said that he was sent out the room to listen to some records. With this bloke with all tattoos. And then he said he came back an hour later, and you weren't there no more. And Dad weren't there no more. Isn't that right Johnny?

MICKEY. Baby, I had no choice. We were going to lose everything.

BABY. He's going a very odd shade. We probably ought to help him down.

MICKEY. Yes.

BABY. Help him down Mickey. Help Johnny down.

MICKEY *ungags* SILVER JOHNNY. *He lets out a note. A moan. Lost.*

BABY. It's all right John.

MICKEY *helps him down. He unties him.*

MICKEY. Are you all right?

SILVER JOHNNY. Fuck you. Fuck you Mickey.

SILVER JOHNNY *runs upstairs*.

BABY. Let him go. (*Pause*.) Fancy. You're sitting there with the telly on and your supper and all then all that. Eh? He was in remarkably good shape after. Even tipped the cab driver. That's the young eh? They really bounce back, don't they.

MICKEY. I'm going to talk now and tell me to shut up if I'm saying the wrong thing –

BABY. Shut up Mickey. Please. (*Pause*.) Will you tell me something Mickey? Were you actually in the room when they cut him in half?

Pause. MICKEY *shakes his head*.

You wasn't?

MICKEY. No.

BABY. Where was you?

MICKEY. I'd gone by then. I was back home.

BABY. Back home?

MICKEY. Yes. They said wait. (*Pause*.) They said if I went home I'd get... we'd get the club. We could keep the club.

BABY. *We?*

MICKEY. That I could keep the club.

BABY. Did you go to them?

Pause.

MICKEY. Baby, this is a new time for both of us –

BABY. A new time. A new time. (*Pause*.) I like that Mickey. You have a very pleasant way with words.

MICKEY. Are you sure he's dead?

BABY. Who?

MICKEY. Mr Ross. Because if he isn't...

BABY. Mickey, he's got his yellow hair parted right down between his eyes. And it's a hell of a schlep. And I think if he is coming he's going to need a jolly good lie-down first.

MICKEY. Baby, I don't know what to do.

BABY (*copying*). Baby I don't know what to do.

MICKEY. I don't know what to do.

BABY. I don't know what to do.

MICKEY. *Baby I'm sorry.*

Pause. BABY *approaches* MICKEY.

BABY. Sometimes when I wake up I feel totally not there. I feel completely numb. And I think, 'Come on. Come alive. Feel it. Like you used to.' But I'm numb. I lie there, and my mind spins on nothing. I hear people next door, in the next one along, fighting or laughing and I can't feel their… pain or nothing.

Pause.

Woke up this afternoon, I just knew it was going to be one of those days. Beautiful, sunny, but one you're just not there for. Sorry Mickey. I just can't feel your pain.

Enter SWEETS *and* POTTS.

SWEETS. Mickey?

BABY. All right Sweets?

SWEETS. Mickey, we've got a problem.

BABY. What's that then?

SWEETS. Something's happened.

MICKEY (*quietly*). I'm dead. I'm dead.

BABY. What's the problem then?

SWEETS. Well, Silver Johnny said Mickey was round Mr Ross's Saturday night.

MICKEY. I'm sorry.

POTTS. Mickey, what have you done? It was you. It was you, you cunt. This whole thing. Fucking head cold. You cunt.

SWEETS. It's not true is it Mickey? It's because he's been hanging upside down so long.

BABY. They're really rocking in Boston…

Enter SKINNY.

SKINNY. Relax. It's bullcrap. I know it's bullcrap.

SWEETS. I told you.

POTTS. How?

SKINNY. Little cunt's twiced us all wants to blame someone else. It's bullcrap.

SWEETS. What happened Mickey?

SKINNY. Mickey's done nothing. Bastard's been hanging upside down for two hours he's gone back to front. And I'll prove it. I'll prove it. Because Mickey was at home and then he came here. He was ill. He was ill then he came here. Anyone listens to some little fuck ditched us all in the lurch is a sissy. I believe Mickey. (*To* BABY.) Shut your fucking mouth, Jew. You don't belong here. You've got no place here. None of us want you. You're nasty and you lie. We've all had enough. Take your lies somewhere else.

BABY *walks across the room with the Derringer, puts it to* SKINNY*'s head and fires once.*

Oww. Fuck. Fuck. Fuck. What did you do that for?

Blood pours from the side of SKINNY*'s head.*

What did you do that for? What did you do that for?

POTTS. Skinny…

SWEETS. Skinny…

SKINNY. I'm shot in the head. I've been shot in the head…

POTTS. It's only the Derringer…

SWEETS. Help him.

POTTS. It's only the Derringer.

SKINNY. I've been shot in the head. Right in the fucking head.

POTTS. It's only the Derringer.

SKINNY. What do you mean it's only the Derringer? I'm shot. Look at all this blood.

POTTS. Help him. Call a doctor.

SWEETS. We can't. We can't.

SKINNY. Call a doctor. I might die.

SWEETS. It's only the… It's only a little hole.

SKINNY. What did you do that for?

SWEETS. You'll be all right. You'll be all right.

SKINNY. I wasn't doing anything. I wasn't doing anything. I was only trying to help. You twat. You didn't have to… Look. Look at all this blood. Look at all this fucking blood.

SWEETS. We've got to get a doctor.

MICKEY. Skinny sit down.

SWEETS. Sit down.

SKINNY. Look. I've got… I've fucked up my new trousers. I've got blood on my new trousers.

MICKEY. Try to relax. Get a towel.

SWEETS. Sid take your shirt off.

SKINNY. Fucking great. Fucking great. What if I die. What if I die eh? Did you think of that? What if I die. How much blood do you have to lose before you die?

POTTS. You've got to lose pints of the stuff. You'll be fine.

SKINNY. Look, I've lost, look. Mickey. That's about a pint right there. Have I got any on my back?

POTTS. Your back's fine. Your back's fine.

SKINNY. My teeth have all gone loose. Look. Feel. He's unshipped all my fucking teeth.

MICKEY. Sit down. You're all right.

SKINNY. Feel. My teeth have gone wiggly. How much blood have I lost.

POTTS. Hardly any. Sit down.

SKINNY. I've already lost at least two pints. How much do you have to lose Mickey. How much do you have to lose Mickey. Mickey? How much blood do you have to lose before that's it?

SKINNY *dies.* POTTS *has just taken his shirt off.*

POTTS. Skinny...

Pause.

SWEETS. Is he all right? Skinny.

POTTS. I don't know.

SWEETS. Skinny. Sid, I think he's gone.

POTTS. Baby, I think he's gone.

MICKEY *falls to his knees to his knees next to* SKINNY*'s body.*

MICKEY. No. No. No! No! No! No!!!

SWEETS. Skinny? Skinny?

MICKEY. Skinny!!!

POTTS. Is he breathing.

MICKEY. No. No. No...

SWEETS. He might still be alive. Is he breathing?

POTTS. He's stopped.

SWEETS. He might still be...

SILVER JOHNNY *appears on the stairs.*

SWEETS. Skinny. For fuck's sake Skinny...

POTTS. Try to keep him warm.

SWEETS. I think he's gone.

Pause.

MICKEY. No. No. No. No. No.

Pause.

I'm sorry. I'm sorry Luke. I'm sorry. I'm really really...

Pause. MICKEY *is hunched over* SKINNY*'s body.* POTTS *stands above them. He kicks* MICKEY *in the stomach.*

POTTS. Let's get out of here.

SWEETS. Mickey. I thought you loved us. I thought you were my friend.

Exit SWEETS *and* POTTS. *Pause.* BABY *walks over to the desk and sits down.* SILVER JOHNNY *comes down the stairs.* MICKEY *lies on the floor, panting.* BABY *watches him.* SILVER JOHNNY *comes into the middle of the room. He watches* BABY.

BABY. Are you all right?

SILVER JOHNNY. Yes. Yes I am.

BABY. You sure? (*Pause.*) Are you dizzy?

SILVER JOHNNY. No. I'm fine.

BABY. That's good.

SILVER JOHNNY. I opened the windows.

BABY. I can smell the dawn. Good. Is the sun out?

SILVER JOHNNY. It's getting hot. Out in the street. There's people.

BABY. Good. Good. (*Pause.*) That's good. Do you want to go out there.

SILVER JOHNNY. What?

BABY. Out in the street. Get a nice cool drink. Walk around. It's lovely out this time. It's my favourite time of the day. Before anything happens.

SILVER JOHNNY. Okay.

BABY. Good. Good. Let's do that.

BABY *slips out of the silver jacket and leaves it on the floor. Exit* BABY *and* SILVER JOHNNY *into the light.* MICKEY *lies on the floor. Music.*

The End.

THE NIGHT HERON

For John Butterworth
1924–99

The Night Heron was first presented at the Royal Court Theatre
Downstairs, London, on 11 April 2002, with the following cast:

JESS WATTMORE	Karl Johnson
GRIFFIN	Ray Winstone
BOLLA FOGG	Jessica Stevenson
NEDDY BEAGLE	Roger Morlidge
ROYCE	Paul Ritter
DOUGAL	Geoffrey Church
BOY (JONATHAN)	Finlay Robertson

Director	Ian Rickson
Designer	Ultz
Lighting Designer	Mick Hughes
Sound Designer	Paul Arditti
Composer	Stephen Warbeck

Characters

JESS WATTMORE

GRIFFIN

BOLLA FOGG, *a woman*

NEDDY BEAGLE

ROYCE

DOUGAL

BOY (JONATHAN), *a student*

A BIRDWATCHER

SON *of the birdwatcher*

The play is set in the Cambridgeshire fens, in the New Year,
over a few short, freezing days

One

Darkness. Local fenland radio. A farm auction. A church fête. Rising seas. A poetry competition for short verse, organised by Cambridge University. The first prize is £2,000. The closing date is in two weeks. Wind. Gull and tern cry out. A man's VOICE *on a tape.*

VOICE. And the Lord God planted a garden eastward in Eden. And out of the ground made the Lord God to grow every tree that is pleasant to the sight, and good for food; the tree of life also in the midst of the garden, and the tree of knowledge of good and evil.

A penny whistle plays.

A cabin, built from ship timber a hundred years ago. Strip plastic hangs in a doorway downstage right. A door upstage left, to an offstage lean-to bedroom. Dominating the cabin is a giant frieze depicting Christ and the Saints. Photocopied onto many sheets of paper, it is pinned together with drawing pins.

A coal-burning stove. Church pews for chairs. A tallboy. On a table, a large, silver ghetto blaster.

And the Lord God took the man, and put him into the Garden of Eden to dress it and to keep it. And the Lord God commanded the man, saying: Of every tree of the garden thou mayest freely eat. But of the tree of the knowledge of good and evil, thou shalt not eat of it: for in the day that thou eatest thereof thou shalt surely die.

Sudden banging, off. Shouts. Barking. The shatter of glass. It fades. The voice continues on the tape. Enter WATTMORE. *He appears from the back room in housecoat and striped pyjamas. He has been beaten. He drinks from the galley tap, and spits and coughs, as if coughing teeth and blood. The tape continues. He lights a lantern, then sits at the table, and presses play and record. He speaks low, from memory.*

WATTMORE. And the Lord said unto Adam: Because thou hast hearkened unto the voice of thy wife, and hast eaten of the tree, of which I commanded thee, saying, Thou shalt not eat of it: cursed is the ground for thy sake; in sorrow shalt thou eat of it all the days of thy life; in the sweat of thy face shalt thou eat bread, till thou return unto the ground; for out of it wast thou taken: for dust thou art, and unto dust shalt thou return.

He removes a penny whistle from his housecoat pocket and plays a short refrain.

And the Lord God sent him forth from the Garden of Eden, to till the ground from whence he was taken. So he drove out the man; and he placed at the east of the garden Cherubims, and a flaming sword which turned every way, to keep... to keep... to keep the way of the tree of life.

Refrain.

He presses stop. It starts to rain. He turns the radio on – Gardeners' Question Time *– and starts rooting through the tallboy drawers. He finds what he is looking for: a rope. The rain falls harder as he pulls up a chair in the centre of the cabin. He stands on it. He slings the rope over a low beam. He ties it around his neck, and stands there, sweating, willing himself to take the step. Offstage, a lock turns. Someone taking his boots off in the porch.*

VOICE (*off*). Wattmore! There's a competition. For poetry at the university. It's open to all-comers. There's a prize. (*Stops.*) Dear oh dear. Dear oh dear oh dear. Wattmore? There's broken glass out here. Someone's had an accident. Dear oh dear oh dear.

WATTMORE *takes his neck out of the noose, and gets off the stool. He just manages to throw his housecoat over the ghetto blaster, before* GRIFFIN *enters, soaking, with two bags of chips.*

GRIFFIN. I say there's glass all over. The porch is knackered. Why don't you put the clicker on after you? The wind can't get round it, whip it open smash it to buggery. It's freezing in here Wattmore. It's colder than a witch's tit.

He takes off his hat.

Let's see. That's ten pound for the pane, never you mind about labour. Congratulations. That's twenty, thirty pound, down the sink.

GRIFFIN *makes straight for the stove and opens it, working the flame.*

There's nothing out there. Right up the church back to the road, nothing. Not one. I thought I had one, in the reed beds, I've got the torch on him. But he's twiced me. So I thought stuff this. Went into town got chips.

He drops a portion on the table in front of WATTMORE, *switches off the wireless, takes his coat off, sits down, closes his eyes. A whisper:*

For what we are about to receive may the Lord make us truly thankful. For Jesus Christ's sake. Amen.

Eats.

Bugle's still on about that bird. It's front-page news. They're offering a hundred pound for a photograph. *A hundred pound.* I thought I saw him, though. Thought I had him, in the reed beds. He's soared right over, low mind, low enough to touch. But it weren't him. It was a seagull. Or a crow.

Eats.

There's a story in the *Bugle* too, one of them, the newcomers, birdwatcher it was, he's out last night on the marsh, he's lost the path. He's fallen in a suckpit, he's kicked and kicked and it's dragged him under. He'd be dead, but he was with another had a mobile phone. He's in the hospital. Honestly, if that bird knew half the trouble he's causing.

Eats.

Did I say? There's a competition. You write a poem, and if you win they give you a prize. Wait for it. It's two thousand pound. Two thousand pound for one poem. Open to all-comers. What do you think to that eh? What do you think to that?

WATTMORE. He came here.

GRIFFIN. What? Who? Who came here?

Beat.

When?

WATTMORE. He was banging. And swearing. He smashed the porch.

Beat.

GRIFFIN. Swearing?

WATTMORE. Shouting. Shouting and swearing. He had a hound.

GRIFFIN. Right. See that's not him. Barking you say? See that's not him. See he doesn't have a hound. He doesn't keep one. Point of fact he can't stand 'em.

WATTMORE. How do you know?

GRIFFIN. Because.

WATTMORE. Because what?

GRIFFIN. Just Because.

WATTMORE. Because *what*?

GRIFFIN. Because he killed Black Bob's dogs.

Beat.

When Black Bob owed him that fifty pound.

WATTMORE. What?

GRIFFIN. The long version, see, if you want it, Black Bob's bitch has just had a litter and Black Bob's in the garden at The Plough selling the pups. He wants two pound a pup see. Anyway he starts drinking starts betting Floyd at boules. Now Floyd's bloody good at boules. Ten minutes Black Bob's into Floyd for twenty-five puppies. He's only got six. Floyd spends all week asking Black Bob for the twenty-five pups or the fifty pound, doesn't mind which. Black Bob starts avoiding him, starts drinking in The Earl of Great Gloucester. So Floyd goes over The Earl of Great Gloucester asks Black Bob for the fifty pound. Black Bob fobs him off starts staying in renting videos. Floyd goes round Black Bob's house asks Black Bob's wife for the fifty pound. She says Black Bob's in the bath. In the end Floyd gets hacked off. So he poisoned his puppies.

WATTMORE. Floyd poisoned Black Bob's dogs?

GRIFFIN. Yes. No. He poisoned the *puppies*. He beat the bitch stone dead with a cricket bat.

Beat.

So.

WATTMORE. So what?

GRIFFIN. So it's safe to assume that Floyd's no great dog lover. You heard barking. Ergo, it's not him. Be kids. Be kids, or the wind.

WATTMORE. It weren't the wind.

GRIFFIN. Be kids then. Shouting and barking. Kids love shouting. And kids love dogs. And dogs love barking. How's your chips?

WATTMORE. Where've you been?

GRIFFIN. I've been out on the marsh.

WATTMORE. You've been out all day. Where've you been?

GRIFFIN. Well let's see. I went over Fen Drayton say Happy New Year to Royce. Prat's still got his Christmas tree up. Then I flagged down the mobile library, on Over Road. And they had a poster up on the door. Two thousand pound it said for one poem. So I cycled over Cambridge. And it's true. It's on all the boards.

WATTMORE. You went to Cambridge.

GRIFFIN. I just said I did.

WATTMORE. Did you go into the college?

GRIFFIN. Now Wattmore –

WATTMORE. Did you go into Corpus Christi?

GRIFFIN. I may have. I'm welcome to. The college is open to visitors between nine and dusk weekdays twelve-thirty to three Saturdays and Sundays –

WATTMORE. *Did you go in the garden?*

Pause.

GRIFFIN. No. I didn't go in the garden. I'm not stupid Wattmore. Grant me *some* noodles.

Pause.

Bumped into Old Ben though. On his bike, riding over the backs. Says the frost took most of those rose bushes. And the old quince tree's died. He's off to King's College in the spring;

they're moving the Master's orchard or something. An orchard might be nice. In the spring. By the way I've been thinking about what you said, and you're right.

WATTMORE. What?

GRIFFIN. I think we should take a lodger.

WATTMORE. What? I never said we should take a lodger.

GRIFFIN. Yes you did.

WATTMORE. When.

GRIFFIN. The other day.

WATTMORE. What other day?

GRIFFIN. A month or two ago. A few months back. I think it's a good idea.

WATTMORE. But –

GRIFFIN. I do. So I put an advert in the *Bugle*.

WATTMORE. Hang on. What? Don't we discuss this? No way. Don't we discuss this? No bloody way. Where would we put them?

GRIFFIN. In there.

WATTMORE. I sleep in there.

GRIFFIN. Cushions then. A line of cushions. Over there.

WATTMORE. A line of cushions. Did you put that in the *Bugle*? 'For rent, *a line of cushions*.'

WATTMORE *winces*.

GRIFFIN. What would you miss? All this quality time on your own? You're sat here in your podgers morning noon and night, three weeks now, you don't wash, you let the stove go out. I'm out there looking for work. Searching the marsh in the pissing rain for rabbits. This isn't *Summer Holiday*, Wattmore. We need to tighten our belts. It's a New Year, and we've got no coal. (*Pause.*) Did you get your dole money?

WATTMORE *nods*.

Good. You owe me three pounds twenty.

WATTMORE. Why?

GRIFFIN. It's twenty-five pence a word for *Bugle* Classifieds. If we go Dutch, and double Dutch on the chips is three pound twenty. Call it three pound for cash. (*Puts his hand out.*)

WATTMORE. I haven't got it.

GRIFFIN. What?

WATTMORE. I haven't got it.

GRIFFIN. I thought you said you got it.

WATTMORE. I did.

GRIFFIN. Well where is it?

WATTMORE. I haven't got it. I gave it to someone.

GRIFFIN. Who?

WATTMORE. Why should I tell you?

GRIFFIN. Who did you give it to?

WATTMORE. I gave it to Dougal.

GRIFFIN. Dougal who? Dougal who? *Dougal?* You gave – Dougal? You gave it to *Dougal*?

WATTMORE. There.

GRIFFIN. I don't know what to say.

Beat.

Why did you give it to Dougal?

WATTMORE. He's a good man.

GRIFFIN. Jess. He's a mongol. His mother's a mongol.

WATTMORE. He's not. She's not.

GRIFFIN. Jess. I don't know everything, but Dougal and his entire breed are mongols. They're mongol children. All the Duggans are half-breeds. It's public knowledge. I was at school with four of them. They hiked them out of your class. They stuck them in a hut down the end of the field gave them *padded desks*.

WATTMORE. Not Dougal.

GRIFFIN. Jess… Dougal… Jess. Okay. Dougal Duggan smeared shit all over the walls of the school changing rooms.

WATTMORE. He's changed.

GRIFFIN. He's not changed. He's gone in there and smeared shit all over the shop. Jess… right. For instance… Dougal's mum. Dougal's mum came up the school and hacked her tit open. Her own tit. They're all of them circus freaks. They want to be in the circus.

WATTMORE. He's a good man.

GRIFFIN. I'm out chasing rabbits, you're giving your dole away to mongols.

WATTMORE. He's got me work.

GRIFFIN. What work?

WATTMORE. I'm not telling you. He said I'm a flagship. Yes. And I could work in his office.

GRIFFIN. What office?

WATTMORE. He's getting an office. He's rented a unit. In the business park. I'm working there.

GRIFFIN. Doing what?

WATTMORE. Number crunching.

Beat.

GRIFFIN. Number crunching.

WATTMORE. Yes.

Beat.

He's got the internet. He's building a website.

GRIFFIN. Oh very flash. Very… For your information, Wattmore, even the mobile library's got the internet. Yes. In fact I was surfing the world web this very afternoon before you have kittens. And you who's never touched it. The internet. I *am* impressed. Oh yes. Has he paid you?

WATTMORE. He'll be paying me…

GRIFFIN. What for?

WATTMORE. Lots of things.

GRIFFIN. What like?

WATTMORE. Doing his tapes.

Beat.

GRIFFIN. Bollocks.

WATTMORE. I am.

GRIFFIN. Bollocks.

WATTMORE *whips off the housecoat revealing the ghetto blaster underneath.*

Beat.

Fine. Okay Jess. For example... Just to say, he... Dougal asked me to do the tapes. Six weeks ago. At The Plough. At the Australian Night. Corks all round his hat. What happened? Eh? What happened? Nothing happened.

WATTMORE. Well it has now. It's happened.

Beat.

GRIFFIN. It sounds like quite a package.

WATTMORE. It is.

GRIFFIN. You must be very proud.

WATTMORE. I am.

Car lights go past on the road outside. WATTMORE *freezes.* GRIFFIN *stands. The noise subsides.*

GRIFFIN. Be one of them birdwatchers. See. They're going out on the marsh. See?

You jumpy clot.

Silence. WATTMORE *starts to cry.* GRIFFIN *sits watching him cry.*

WATTMORE. Forgive me *Prince.*

GRIFFIN. Eat your chips. You haven't touched them.

Beat.

Shall I get you a rabbit? Do a stew. I'll go back out there. I'll catch one no trouble.

WATTMORE. *Jesu* Light and Saviour, prince over time, heed the prayer of the bastard sinners. Light the way lamb, project to us the true path of several. Send a Guardian and light braziers… and mark the path through Disturbance. Display the dark path to everlasting Peace. Purge the reek of sin. Purge the reek of sin.

Silence.

I didn't do it Griffin. *I didn't do it.*

Silence.

GRIFFIN. Ssshhhh.

His breath mixes with the wind.

Blackout. Music.

The local radio returns: a night heron has been spotted in the area. It has never been seen in the British Isles, and birdwatchers are coming from across Europe to try to spot the rare creature. No one knows why it has come.

Two

The cabin, at dusk. The lanterns are lit. WATTMORE *and* GRIFFIN *stand in the middle of the room in silence. From the back bedroom appears a woman. She is* BOLLA FOGG. *She stands there.*

BOLLA. The mattress is damp.

GRIFFIN. Is it?

BOLLA. It's mildewy.

GRIFFIN. Needs turning I expect. Probably just needs… you know. A turn.

She closes the door.

WATTMORE. I told you to turn the mattress.

GRIFFIN. Leave it.

WATTMORE. I said. I said turn the mattress. I told you to turn it.

GRIFFIN. Jess –

WATTMORE. I told you to turn it.

GRIFFIN. I did fucking turn it.

The door reopens. BOLLA *looks at them both.*

BOLLA. It's cold.

GRIFFIN. Right. There's a little two-bar under the bed. Get both bars on it's roasting. Give the plug a good shake though.

She is staring at the enormous iconostasis on the wall.

Oh that.

Beat.

Where to start really? It's called uh…

WATTMORE. Iconostasis.

GRIFFIN. That's it. They're icons. Saints. What it is see, an iconostasis depicts the Lord and the Saints at the final judgement. And that's pretty much what's going on up there. It's Russian.

WATTMORE. Byzantine.

GRIFFIN. Byzantine. From the Kremlin. Jess blew it up. Not the Kremlin, the picture. He found it in the mobile library took it over Ely to Rymans, and blew it up. Few years back it was, now. You get used to it.

Beat.

BOLLA. Russian?

GRIFFIN. Byzantine. But we like it, don't we?

Silence. She goes back into the room.

WATTMORE. She thinks we're queer.

GRIFFIN. She does not.

WATTMORE. She does. She thinks we're homos.

GRIFFIN. She's temporary. She's a cash cow.

WATTMORE. What d'you ask for?

GRIFFIN. Guess.

WATTMORE. Twenty-five.

GRIFFIN. Forty. She's a *mug*. Here look.

He mimes milking a cow.

WATTMORE. She's in our room.

GRIFFIN. For the time being.

WATTMORE. The bog's through there.

GRIFFIN. I know where the bog is Wattmore. I have thought about this. It's short term, but for the immediate, it's going to have to be like last March.

WATTMORE. Oh for pity's sake.

GRIFFIN. What? You were the one blocked the bog. You were the one got the plunger stuck down there. I had to squat in the rain all of March. Did I complain?

WATTMORE. Yes.

GRIFFIN. Well it's the same as that... That was bloody ten days, pulling on the plunger. It was like the sword in the fucking stone.

WATTMORE. Did she give you a deposit? She'll break something.

GRIFFIN. She will not.

WATTMORE. She's bloody huge. She'll break the bog. I don't like it. I'm going in there.

GRIFFIN. She's got a car.

WATTMORE (*stops*). Where?

GRIFFIN. Outside. A Golf. 1990. Hot hatch... four new tyres. Electric windows. What are we talking? Five, six, seven hundred at least.

WATTMORE. Griffin.

GRIFFIN. It's purple mind.

WATTMORE. Griffin –

GRIFFIN. And she'll have thrashed the suspension.

WATTMORE. Griffin!

GRIFFIN. What?

WATTMORE. It's hers.

GRIFFIN. Of course it's hers. Of course it's hers. Of course it is.
Exactly. Yes. *Is it?* Is it hers? Get her relaxed, few drinks,
game of cards. Hearts. Brag. Beggar My Neighbour…

WATTMORE. Griffin!

Re-enter BOLLA.

BOLLA. I'll take it.

GRIFFIN. Lovely. We can fix that lock for you. And turn the
mattress…

She shakes GRIFFIN*'s hand.*

BOLLA. Bolla. Bolla Fogg. (*To* WATTMORE.) Bolla Fogg.

GRIFFIN. He's Jess Wattmore. I'm Griffin.

BOLLA. Jess.

She shakes his hand.

Big hands.

Beat.

WATTMORE. Yes.

BOLLA. That bog's a bit rocky.

WATTMORE (*to* GRIFFIN). What did I say?

BOLLA. Do they always do that?

WATTMORE. Who?

BOLLA. The birds.

GRIFFIN. No. It's unusual. It's the marsh. The marsh calls them.
They've been coming a thousand years. Crows mostly.

WATTMORE. It's Tern. Tern and black-backs.

GRIFFIN. It's the marsh that brings them.

BOLLA. Well it is a pretty view.

GRIFFIN. Yeah. Not for much longer mind.

BOLLA. What's happening?

GRIFFIN. The sea's coming. It's rising up. Ten years time this'll all be underwater. Past Ely, ten miles flatland that way west.

WATTMORE. They don't know.

GRIFFIN. We'd be treading water right now.

WATTMORE. They don't know. Nobody knows.

GRIFFIN. Exactly. Nobody knows. So. Bolla. I'm just making a peppermint tea.

WATTMORE. *Bloody* hell –

GRIFFIN. What? Or coffee. Or tea. Normal tea. What do you like?

BOLLA. Tea. Normal tea.

GRIFFIN. Splendid. A Normal Cup Of Tea.

BOLLA. You're black and blue.

WATTMORE. What?

BOLLA. You've got bust ribs. I can tell.

GRIFFIN. He's got two broke and six bruised.

WATTMORE. He wasn't there.

GRIFFIN. There was a doctor's report. He's got three chipped teeth, a twisted knee, a broken toe and a kick right up the arse.

BOLLA. Who duffed you up?

GRIFFIN. Gypsies.

WATTMORE. We don't know.

GRIFFIN. It was gypsies.

BOLLA. They mug you?

WATTMORE. No.

BOLLA. 'N' what did they want?

GRIFFIN. Who knows what gypsies want? Murderous bastards. I bet if you could read the mind of your average gypsy, you'd never leave the house.

BOLLA. I've had ribs. They're cruel. There's nothing you can do except wait.

WATTMORE. How'd you get yours?

BOLLA. Ribs? As a girl. And as a woman.

WATTMORE. Can I ask where are you from?

BOLLA. I've been in London.

WATTMORE. Oh really? Whereabouts?

BOLLA. I've been away.

WATTMORE. Away?

BOLLA. I've been in prison. Ta.

GRIFFIN *hands* BOLLA *a cup.*

WATTMORE. Griffin?

GRIFFIN.... and a normal tea for Jess here... yes?

WATTMORE. Can I speak to you please?

GRIFFIN. What about?

BOLLA. Didn't you tell him? Didn't he tell you? I'll go right now if it bothers you. I don't blame you. I'm very up front myself.

GRIFFIN *rolls up his sleeve.*

GRIFFIN. Here look. Look. See this. Look. See?

BOLLA. What's that?

GRIFFIN. Look. Feltham. 1976. Borstal remand for boys. Six months. Hard, hard time. I was sixteen.

BOLLA. What is it?

GRIFFIN. It's my dog. Was.

BOLLA. I was gonna say Kirk Douglas. It looks like Kirk Douglas out of *Spartacus.*

GRIFFIN. No. It's a Labrador. Was a Labrador.

BOLLA. He dead?

GRIFFIN. She. Pippa. 1978.

BOLLA. I'm sorry.

GRIFFIN. Thanks. That says Pippa but it's smudged with the years.

BOLLA. They don't live long. Dogs.

GRIFFIN. Oh. It's a different life.

BOLLA. What was you in for?

GRIFFIN. Guess. Go on. Guess. I bet you can't.

WATTMORE. Dog-fucking.

Beat.

BOLLA. I like that. What was you in for. Wham. Right in. I like you. I like you a lot. Dog-fucking.

She laughs.

GRIFFIN. So. Bolla. I see you're a Golf woman.

BOLLA. Sorry?

GRIFFIN. Your car. Hot hatch. What colour is that? Magenta? Cerise?

BOLLA. Purple.

GRIFFIN. Nice. Respray?

BOLLA. Recut.

GRIFFIN. Wise. The same effect for a fraction of the price.

BOLLA. Can I say something?

GRIFFIN. What?

BOLLA. This has got sugar in it.

GRIFFIN. Course it's got sugar in it. It's tea.

BOLLA. I don't have a sweet tooth Griffin.

GRIFFIN. You're sweet enough already Bolla.

BOLLA. Can I say something else? That bollocks won't work on me.

GRIFFIN. Right.

BOLLA. No offence. I'm not being funny. I can be sweet. I take your point. But you can't butter me up. No one can.

Beat.

I'm sorry. I really like you both. I'm just nervous. I get a rash when I'm nervous. I've got it now.

GRIFFIN. No you haven't.

BOLLA. I have. My neck goes all red and I get pins and needles in my hands. I've got it right now. If the hands go the neck goes.

GRIFFIN. The neck's fine.

BOLLA. I'm sorry. It's because I really like you and I think we could be friends. That's why I've the stingers. I'm very pleased to be here see. I'm just nervous. I'm a good friend to people.

GRIFFIN. I'm sure you are.

BOLLA. Also, if we become close friends, I promise you, I'll do anything. Anything. And if we become best friends, well that's when I'll die for you. I'll drink this.

GRIFFIN. Right. Well it's uh… it's good to chew the fat.

Beat.

BOLLA. I'm going to my room now. I've put both bars on and now I'm going to have a lie-down. I'm sorry about your dog, even though it was a long time ago. I like you. I like you a lot. And I like that. (*Iconostasis.*) It looks extremely grand.

She goes out. She comes back.

I'm turning over a new leaf.

Silence. She goes to her room. Silence.

GRIFFIN. Nice lady.

Beat.

What?

WATTMORE. I'm only going to say this once.

GRIFFIN. Jess, she's forty pounds a week.

WATTMORE. She's a villain. She's a jailbird.

GRIFFIN. She's turning over a new leaf.

WATTMORE. We don't know her.

GRIFFIN. Of course we don't know her. She's just got here.

WATTMORE. Don't play cards with her.

GRIFFIN. What? Why not? Did I say I was going to play cards with her? Why not? Oh I see. I see…

WATTMORE. She could be anyone. She could be –

GRIFFIN. Could be a what? Go on.

WATTMORE. We don't know her.

GRIFFIN. Go on say it. Say it. What? Say it. She could be a what? Go on say it.

WATTMORE. We don't know what she is…

GRIFFIN. Go on. Say it. She could be a demon. Isn't? Isn't it?

Car lights track aross the room. WATTMORE *freezes. They listen. The engine goes away. Silence.* WATTMORE *sits down.*

Be the winkle man. Coming back from the marsh. Two-stroke, see? Jumpy clot.

Silence.

So that's that. At least we can get coal now. Maybe another lamp. Brighten up the long nights. So did you read it?

WATTMORE. Did I read what? Oh.

GRIFFIN. What did you reckon?

WATTMORE. I don't know.

GRIFFIN. What do you mean?

WATTMORE. Look I said I have no idea, okay. I don't know poetry. I don't know any poetry.

GRIFFIN *takes a piece of paper out of his pocket.*

GRIFFIN. Close your eyes.

WATTMORE. No.

GRIFFIN. Just –

WATTMORE. I'm not closing my eyes.

GRIFFIN. Well just give it a chance. See what it conjures up.

WATTMORE *reads it again*.

WATTMORE. Oh I see. I see.

Beat.

I understood it better that time. It's extremely poor.

GRIFFIN. Give it here.

WATTMORE. I understood it better. It's very very poor. I'll tell you what it conjures up. Bugger all.

GRIFFIN. Give it back.

WATTMORE. I'll tell you what it doesn't conjure up. It doesn't conjure up two thousand pound.

GRIFFIN. How would you know? What the fuck do you know about poems?

WATTMORE. Nothing. Not the first thing. I know one thing.

GRIFFIN. What?

WATTMORE. It's for puffs. Desperate puffs.

GRIFFIN. I can win this. I know I can. It's twelve lines. Twelve. Are you saying I don't have twelve lines of poetry in me? I know what this is. I know what this is. It's St Ignatius.

WATTMORE. No it isn't.

GRIFFIN. Yes it is. It's St Ignatius. It's *True Gospel*. You and your fucking *True Gospel*. He's against it, you're against it.

WATTMORE. Wrong.

Beat.

Wrong. Wrong. Wrong.

GRIFFIN. St Ignatius says poetry is wrong. St Ignatius says dancing is wrong. St Ignatius says stick your head in the fire.

WATTMORE. We don't have a fire.

GRIFFIN. St Ignatius also said it's wrong to eat owls.

WATTMORE. It *is* wrong to eat owls.

GRIFFIN. It was my book, you only read it because of me, it was out on my ticket. You never even finished it. Admit it's Ignatius. Admit it. Go on. Admit it *you big Romanist pug*.

WATTMORE. Do your bloody poem.

GRIFFIN. You do your bloody tapes.

Enter NEDDY BEAGLE, *a large man.*

WATTMORE. Griffin.

GRIFFIN. What?

He turns around.

Neddy.

NEDDY. Your porch door's smashed.

GRIFFIN. Right.

Beat.

Was the wind. Raining is it?

NEDDY. Stopped. Was raining but it stopped.

WATTMORE *goes to the back of the room, where he stands by the sink.*

GRIFFIN. Right.

NEDDY. Griffin.

GRIFFIN. Neddy.

NEDDY. Jess…

Silence.

GRIFFIN. How's things over the gardens?

NEDDY. Same.

GRIFFIN. Right.

NEDDY. Fellow's garden caught the frost. Lost them rose bushes to it.

GRIFFIN. I heard that.

NEDDY. And the quince tree died.

GRIFFIN. I heard that too.

NEDDY. Shame really. Those roses was lovely in the summer. Still. To be expected I suppose. Not much you can do…

WATTMORE. Should have been covered.

Beat.

NEDDY. What's that Jess?

Beat.

WATTMORE. Anyone knows the first thing about English Summer Royals knows you need to cloche them in a frost. Cloches are in the greenhouse across the Library Garden. Someone should have fetched them and cloched the bushes. Then you need a piece of old carpet, and put it round the roots. There's loads of cuts of carpet in the garage with the mowers. You cloche them, carpet them, they'd be all right. Wouldn't be dead now.

He walks across the room.

GRIFFIN. Where you going?

WATTMORE. Get the last of the coal.

Exit WATTMORE. Silence.

NEDDY. Griffin.

GRIFFIN. Neddy.

NEDDY. Spoke to Floyd Fowler this morning. Was in the Fellows' Garden. Chopping down the old quince.

GRIFFIN. Right.

NEDDY. Aye. He was very unhappy. Agitated.

Beat.

GRIFFIN. I can tell you Neddy, this is a storm in a teacup.

NEDDY. I think it's a storm in a teacup.

GRIFFIN. It is. It's much ado all about nothing.

NEDDY. It's snowballed, really, hasn't it?

GRIFFIN. And now Jess is assaulted on the marsh road. Middle of the night. They beat him hard Neddy.

NEDDY. Aye was it? I was sorry to hear about that.

GRIFFIN. We have a grievance too Neddy Beagle. But we'll turn the other cheek to see an end of it.

NEDDY. Exactly.

GRIFFIN. There now.

NEDDY. That should be it now. That should be it. Except for what his boy's saying.

Pause.

All I know is something happened, and Floyd asked me to come by to present his terms.

GRIFFIN. His terms.

NEDDY. Was it, yes.

Pause.

GRIFFIN. How much does he want?

NEDDY. Well now. Let's see. He wants a thousand pound.

Pause. GRIFFIN *laughs.*

GRIFFIN. A thousand pound. A thousand pound. (*Laughs.*)

NEDDY. To compensate. To make recompense, if you like.

GRIFFIN. And what's your cut of this Neddy? Forty, fifty pound. A hundred?

NEDDY. Oh I'm just the go-between here. Just want everything to be back to normal.

GRIFFIN. I bet you do Neddy. I bet that's it.

Neddy. You go back to Floyd, and tell him this. Tell him he can whistle for it. Tell him to go back to sleep. It's a blackmail Neddy Beagle. Thou Shalt Not Bear False Witness. There's a man drowning here. And Floyd Fowler puts his foot on his head.

NEDDY. He wants justice Griffin.

GRIFFIN. He wants a thousand pounds. It's a lie. Broken ribs Neddy. A doctor's report. We're ready. We're ready when he wants to bring in the law.

NEDDY. Be no law. Floyd won't go to the coppers on account of the fact he hates them.

GRIFFIN. There then.

NEDDY. He says he'll go to the town.

Beat.

GRIFFIN. What?

NEDDY. He says he'll go to Fen Ditton. To the *Bugle*.

Beat.

And if the *Bugle* finds out the town finds out. And if the town finds out, well then it's in God's hands, I reckon.

Pause.

GRIFFIN. He said he was going to the *Bugle*.

NEDDY. Was it, yes. To the *Bugle*, then he's going in The Earl of Great Gloucester and tell all them with children. And The Plough. He said the town has the right to know. Way I see it, it's Floyd's boy's word against yours. And Jess so recently in public trouble.

GRIFFIN. Neddy.

Beat.

I want you to go to Floyd Fowler and tell him this. Will you remember it? Good. Tell Floyd Fowler I can give him satisfaction. Tell him I'll give him satisfaction in two days.

NEDDY. How's that?

GRIFFIN. Leave this to me. I've got something I'm selling.

NEDDY. What is it?… What you selling?

GRIFFIN. Never you mind.

NEDDY. It might help if I knew what it was.

GRIFFIN. Never you mind. I'm taking something into
Cambridge tomorrow where there's a buyer. Two days' time,
you return to this house, I'll have five, six hundred pound.

NEDDY. No offence Griffin, but what have you got that's worth
six hundred pound.

Pause.

Is it the car. One out there? I saw her. She's okay she is.
Where'd you come by her then?

GRIFFIN. This isn't your concern, Go-between. I'm taking it to
Cambridge, I've got a buyer, I'll have six hundred pound. And
within a month I'll have the balance. And that's the end of it.
And Jess is a good man. He's a good man Neddy.

NEDDY. I know you Griffin. Since I was a boy.

WATTMORE *re-enters, with the coal. Silence.*

Won't stay then. Goodnight Jess.

Silence.

What about the bird then. Heron is it?

Beat.

And there's one in the hospital already. Still, The Plough's full.
Earl of Great Gloucester. People ordering champagne in there
last night. And a Mercedes in the car park. I reckon that bird's
done Fen Ditton a favour.

Beat.

Griffin.

Beat.

Jess.

Exit NEDDY. *Silence.*

GRIFFIN. I tell you Jess. That boy went wrong in the juniors.
When he was nine he was four foot nothing and on his tenth
birthday he was six feet four. He went from treble to bass to
out the choir in a fortnight. And I'll say this of him. He's a
crap gardener. Fit to push a wheelbarrow full of horseshit and
that's about it.

WATTMORE. What did he say?

GRIFFIN. Nothing. You're a good man Jess Wattmore.
Everybody round here knows you're a good man.

WATTMORE. What does Floyd Fowler want?

GRIFFIN. Now don't you worry about that. In two days this will
all be in the past.

WATTMORE. Griffin –

GRIFFIN. Listen to me. In two days this will be past and
everything will be back like it was. We'll go into town hold
our head up. Go in The Earl of Great Gloucester stand up
straight. And by spring we'll be back in the garden. As the
Lord is my witness I swear.

WATTMORE. Griffin –

GRIFFIN. I believe you Jess Wattmore. Do you believe me? Do
you believe me as I believe you?

They look at each other, in the half-light of the cabin. Re-enter
BOLLA.

BOLLA. I hope you don't think this is presuming. I was just
thinking. Tomorrow night I could cook something. I could do a
housewarming.

GRIFFIN. What?

BOLLA. Or you could. You could for me. I don't mind which.

GRIFFIN. Fine.

BOLLA. Right.

GRIFFIN. Sorry?

BOLLA. Sorry, which? You or me?

Beat.

GRIFFIN. Me.

BOLLA. Really? Are you sure? I'm not presuming? That would
be lovely Griffin. What are we having?

Beat.

GRIFFIN. Rabbit.

BOLLA. Rabbit.

GRIFFIN. Rabbit stew. I'll catch one and you, Jess, you can
do your rabbit stew.

BOLLA. Well that's that. Jess's doing his rabbit stew. Jiminy
Cricket. Rabbit stew... Shit. I forgot. Also I've got miniatures.
I've been saving them for a special occasion. I don't want you
to think I'm gobbling down your food. I'm not a ponce.

GRIFFIN. We don't think you're a ponce do we Jess.

WATTMORE. No. We don't.

Beat.

BOLLA. I'm going to bed now. I've got both bars on. It's
roasting. You can come in but knock first. Just knock twice.
Or... I know. Jess is one knock, Griffin is two knocks. Or just
knock and say your name and I'll answer. Unless I'm asleep.
Don't come in if I'm asleep. Right. See you tonight Jess.

WATTMORE. See you tonight Bolla.

BOLLA. See you tonight Griffin.

GRIFFIN. See you tonight Bolla.

BOLLA. Rabbit stew. We're in the country!

GRIFFIN. Yes. Yes. We are.

Blackout. Music.

Three

*The cabin at night. A table has been set by the stove, which is
roaring.* BOLLA *and* GRIFFIN *have just finished eating.*
WATTMORE *stares out onto the marsh.*

BOLLA. So how do you catch one?

GRIFFIN. You set a trap. A snare. You need a steel loop and they
stick their head in. Now. If they stopped still they'd be fine.
But Nature takes over, see, and they struggle, they try to flee.

It's when you try to escape that it does for you. It just tightens
and tightens till it rings your neck. That's it.

BOLLA. Right. So weren't there none out there or what?

GRIFFIN. Loads. Hundreds. Little pricks are quick as fuck
though. How were your beans?

BOLLA. Lovely and hot. I don't mind my beans. I'm used to my
beans. And those were Heinz. I could tell. See inside you don't
get Heinz. You get some muck comes out of a sixty-gallon
drum. They bulk buy. And I can't stand a bulk-buy bean.

Car lights go past on the road. WATTMORE *freezes.*
GRIFFIN *too. Until it passes.*

BOLLA. You not eating Jess?

GRIFFIN. His mouth's sore. It's all cut inside.

BOLLA. Does he want a painkiller? I've got temazepam.

GRIFFIN. He's just a bit quiet. He's been a bit low recently. Gets
worse at night.

BOLLA. Was it the duffing up?

GRIFFIN. Yes. No. It was before the duffing up.

BOLLA. Right. That never helps though does it. Perhaps we
should take him out.

GRIFFIN. No point. Town's dead as Diana in the New Year.
There's The Earl of Great Gloucester, and The Plough.
Plough's crap, and The Earl of Great Gloucester's full of
birdwatchers.

BOLLA. Birdwatchers.

GRIFFIN. There's this bird that's come to the marsh see. It's the
bird that's brought the birdwatchers.

BOLLA. What bird?

GRIFFIN. Wait. It's called…

WATTMORE. The night *heron*.

GRIFFIN. That's the one. Caused quite a stir. Dutch. Norwegians.
Come over on the ferry with their dirty great Mercedes. If

you've got a camera, you can win a hundred pound. You haven't got a camera have you?

BOLLA. Sorry.

GRIFFIN. Anyway, The Earl's full of birdwatchers. Are you a card lady Bolla?

BOLLA. What?

GRIFFIN. I just wondered if you... if you ever played cards...

BOLLA. No.

GRIFFIN. Oh. Little flutter now and then?

BOLLA. Never. My stepdad lived in the bookies. Kept selling my toys.

GRIFFIN. I see.

BOLLA. In the end I threw him out. I was twelve.

WATTMORE. It's not for everyone is it. Betting.

BOLLA. So what do you two do?

GRIFFIN. Unemployed.

BOLLA. Oh. What was you?

GRIFFIN. Gardeners. Over at the university. But not anymore. We got sacked. Well Jess got sacked and I went on strike in sympathy. And I got sacked. It's a long story. But we met in the church.

BOLLA. You churchgoers?

GRIFFIN. Used to. We don't go to church any more. Actually we met in the Cubs.

We were Scoutmasters. Fen Ditton second firsts. It's a hut round the back of the church. He was Baloo.

BOLLA. Who?

GRIFFIN. It's from *The Jungle Book*. Scoutleaders take their names from *The Jungle Book*. Akela's a wolf. Bagheera's a tiger. Baloo's a bear. He was Baloo.

BOLLA. Who were you?

GRIFFIN. I was just Griffin. They'd run out of names by then. We were Baloo and Griffin.

WATTMORE *starts collecting up his tapes. He moves his ghetto blaster.* GRIFFIN *watches him.*

But they chucked us out.

BOLLA. Why?

WATTMORE. Drop it Griffin.

GRIFFIN. Doctrinal differences. Baloo thought the Cubs too worldly. He was always pushing for higher standards of devotion and cleanliness. He wanted late-night Bible classes with candles. It's the Cubs.

WATTMORE. Change the subject –

GRIFFIN. Asking eight-year-olds their views on Revelations. Poor little squirts couldn't sleep for weeks. Then he decides that someone in Brown six is in league with the Devil. Warren Lee. Fucking eight years old, and a sergeant of Satan. Then one day, they've just done the Grand Howl.

BOLLA. The what?

GRIFFIN. The Grand Howl. What happens is, at the end of the pack meeting, the Cubs go like this – (*He holds his arms out.*) and Bagheera or someone shouts 'PACK PACK PACK'. and the Cubs all shout 'PACK PACK PACK' back see, then 'A-KE-LA WE WILL DO OUR BEST' and then they do this – (*Crouches down.*) and Akela says, all solemn, 'Cubs, do your best' and they go 'we will do our best', which is odd seeing as they've just said they would, fucking yelled it too. So anyway, it's all passed off normal when this one starts pointing at Warren Lee saying he's the Devil's last son, what have you, then he falls on the floor starts speaking in tongues. He's frothing at the mouth. Half of the sixers shat their shorts. Baloo's gone potty. I mean, it's not exactly what Baden-Powell had in mind is it? It was the last straw. They threw us out. Then they threw us out of the church. Then Jess got his picture in the *Bugle*, and the university found out, and he got sacked. Which I thought was unfair, and I said so, and I got sacked.

BOLLA. That's terrible.

GRIFFIN. Yeah. But it's not all doom and gloom is it. Because now he's got Dougal.

BOLLA. Who's Dougal?

WATTMORE. Drop it Griffin.

BOLLA. Who's Dougal?

WATTMORE. Dougal's my friend.

GRIFFIN. Dougal's a mongol. His mother's a mongol. They won't let Dougal in the church either. So Dougal's setting up his own church. From his office. From his unit. In the business park. Listen to this, Bolla.

WATTMORE. That's enough –

GRIFFIN. Hang on. Listen to this. Dougal works for the Prince now but he used to work for the university as well. As a leaf blower. Lowest of the low. Used to blow leaves round the university backs, and round the Fellows' Garden. One day he's blowing leaves about, having a smoke, and his petrol tank on his back suddenly blows him up. He's a fireball. Burned all up his back, hideously scarred. He must look like a lizard in his birthday suit. I'll never forget him tearing across the backs on fire, like Halley's Comet he was. Anyway, he comes out of hospital and takes the university to court. He wins twenty grand. So Dougal's suddenly rich. What does he do? Visit the pyramids? Go to Disneyland? No. He started a cult. Yes. Dougal's starts a cult. The Holy Sons of... *Sons of the White Prince*.

WATTMORE. It's not called that.

GRIFFIN. Well what is it?

WATTMORE. He hasn't decided.

GRIFFIN. It's called *The Sons of the White Prince*. Meaning the Archangel Michael. He's got this logo he's had professionally done and I *swear to Christ* it looks like Dougal on a cross. It's the Cult of Dougal. Cult of the Mongol Child. This from a boy who shat in his desk at school. And Wattmore wants to join him, don't you? He's going to work in his office. Dougal wants to harness Wattmore's powers. His power to see evil and scare the living shite out of Cubs.

Dougal's told him he's a saint. He doesn't look like a saint does he, in his boots and his housecoat. That's because he's *not* a bloody saint. He's a bloody *gardener*. And he's not even that any more.

WATTMORE. Change the subject.

GRIFFIN. What? I'm just saying –

WATTMORE. Change the subject.

GRIFFIN. Change the subject. Change the subject.

GRIFFIN *gets up. He takes a roll of toilet paper out of the tallboy.*

I'll just get some more coal.

GRIFFIN *leaves, taking the coal pail on the way. They sit there in silence.*

BOLLA. Do you fancy some crème de menthe?

WATTMORE. No thanks.

Silence.

BOLLA. Any pets?

WATTMORE. What? No.

BOLLA. Me either. Had a mouse inside.

WATTMORE. Right.

BOLLA. When I was in solitary. I used to talk to it at night. And it used to talk back. You're short of company in solitary. It gets extremely lonely.

Pause.

Griffin says you've been a little 'piano' recently.

WATTMORE. What?

BOLLA. A bit low. Not yourself.

WATTMORE. Did he?

BOLLA. Anything you want to talk about?

WATTMORE. Not really.

Pause.

BOLLA. Has something happened? Apart from the Cubs.

WATTMORE. No. Nothing's happened.

Pause.

BOLLA. So is Fen Ditton nice?

WATTMORE. Few shops. Earl of Great Gloucester. That's about it.

BOLLA. Right.

WATTMORE. There's the mobile library comes Mondays and Thursdays.

BOLLA. Right.

WATTMORE. And the carnival in September. And a May Day festival. That's about it. Carnival's not bad. One year I helped pick out the Carnival Queen.

BOLLA. Really?

WATTMORE. It was Jane Livingstone.

BOLLA (*shakes her head*). Sorry.

WATTMORE. She was sixteen. She had these beautiful blue eyes. We rode on the float and they had a brass band. It was in the *Bugle*. With a picture of the Mayor, Jane Livingstone, and me.

BOLLA. That's nice.

WATTMORE. She's married now. The Mayor said I was the type of person they could use in the Town Hall. Anyway it was in the *Bugle*. The other thing in the *Bugle* was all wrong. They got the wrong end of the stick.

Pause.

BOLLA. So this boy, Warren. What made you think he was a wrong 'un.

WATTMORE. What?

BOLLA. I just wondered. What was it you saw?

WATTMORE. I'd rather not talk about it.

BOLLA. Oh. Right. But you sensed something in him. You sensed something in him was wrong. Something was bad.

WATTMORE. You can't describe it.

BOLLA. But when someone is bad, you can tell. If someone was sitting here, for instance, in your house, you think you could tell if they were bad or not. How do you do it. Do you look into their eyes. If you look into their eyes can you see it. Can you see it?

Pause.

Can you see it Jess?

Silence. WATTMORE *is frozen staring into* BOLLA*'s eyes.*

WATTMORE. What are you saying?

Pause.

BOLLA. I think it's very nice that you're showing me hospitality.

Pause.

When I first got here, I thought you and me might butt heads. But now I think different. Now I think we've got more in common than it appears initially, on the surface. Much, much more in common.

Pause.

And if you'll excuse me for a moment, Jess, I must just pop to the little girls' room.

She gets up. WATTMORE *gets up. She leaves* WATTMORE *alone. He stands there. Enter* GRIFFIN *with a pail full of coal.*

GRIFFIN. Here we go. Keep the party going. Where's she gone?

WATTMORE. We've got to get her out of here.

GRIFFIN. What? What's happened. What have you said Jess Wattmore. What have you done.

WATTMORE. I didn't do anything. What are *you* doing?

GRIFFIN. What? I'm fetching coal. What have you said to her? What did you say while I was out.

WATTMORE. Nothing.

GRIFFIN. What have you said to her?

WATTMORE. Nothing.

GRIFFIN. Wattmore…

WATTMORE. She had a familiar.

GRIFFIN. *What?*

WATTMORE. She had… she had a mouse…

GRIFFIN. When? What? When?

WATTMORE. She used to talk to it and it used to talk back. She said it used to talk back. We don't know what she is!

Silence.

GRIFFIN. I tell you what Jess. Why don't you ask her when she comes out? 'Excuse me, we were just wondering if you were by any chance a succubus? You know, just for the record, do you fornicate with Satan and suckle his imps?' Better still, why don't you go down the *Bugle* in the morning and tell them. I bet you a hundred pound they put you on the front page again.

WATTMORE. What are you doing telling her I was in the *Bugle*.

GRIFFIN. You were in the *Bugle*. If you weren't in the *Bugle* we wouldn't be sat here.

WATTMORE. I don't want everyone knowing it.

GRIFFIN. Everyone already knows it. It was in the *Bugle*. It was on the front page. Local Scoutleader Goes Batshit.

WATTMORE. Just shut up about it. And shut up about Dougal. And shut up about *The Sons*.

GRIFFIN. See. I told you it was called that.

WATTMORE. I'm warning you Griffin.

GRIFFIN. I didn't get us in this mess Wattmore. If you'd have not become so bloody *special* all of a sudden –

WATTMORE. Shut up.

GRIFFIN. If you'd not become so bloody *special*.

Pause.

WATTMORE. She did something.

GRIFFIN. What?

WATTMORE. She looked at me.

GRIFFIN. What do you mean.

Pause. Then:

WATTMORE.… her eyes…

Enter BOLLA. *She stands there, as if she may have heard. She enters the room.*

BOLLA. I see Griffin's back.

GRIFFIN. Yes. He is.

BOLLA. Drink?

GRIFFIN. Lovely.

BOLLA. Jess.

WATTMORE. No thank you.

Pause.

Yes. Please.

BOLLA. What have we got. Brandy. Bacardi. Frisky whisky. You're going to get me drunk.

GRIFFIN. Steady as she goes.

BOLLA. You all right Jess. You look pale.

GRIFFIN. He's fine.

BOLLA. Are you sure?

WATTMORE. Yes.

Pause. She looks at them both.

BOLLA. So who's the bard?

GRIFFIN. Shakespeare.

BOLLA. No. I mean who's the wordsmith? Who's writing the poems?

GRIFFIN. What?

BOLLA. There's poetry in my bathroom. On top of my bog. It must have been there from before I moved in because I never saw it.

GRIFFIN. Oh that's right.

BOLLA. Was it you Jess?

WATTMORE. I don't know poetry.

BOLLA. Was it you Griffin? Eh? Don't be shy.

WATTMORE. Yes.

BOLLA. Here you are.

She hands it to him.

I didn't read it. Just the first two lines. I thought it may be private. I think it's important to respect privacy. Don't you?

Pause.

So is it finished?

GRIFFIN. It's just begun. It's a work in progress.

BOLLA. What's it called?

Beat.

GRIFFIN. 'The Garden'.

BOLLA. 'The Garden'.

GRIFFIN. Yeah.

BOLLA. What's it about?

GRIFFIN. It's about where we worked I suppose. It's about the garden in the summer. See a few years ago Jess did a mass planting in the new flower beds, so he went all the way to King's Lynn and spent sixty pounds of his own money on two sacks of Organite. It's Organic nitrogen fertiliser. The factory's in King's Lynn. Anyway he went and got it and he spent all week turning in the two sacks, and it really did the trick because next May Day they all came into bloom at once. You had to see it. We had tulip, primrose, violet, marigold, pansies, dahlia, zinnia, daisies, cockscomb, oriental lily. We were the envy of all the colleges. It was beautiful, that summer. So yeah. Anyway. That's what it's about. It's not finished.

BOLLA. What does it represent?

GRIFFIN. What?

BOLLA. The garden. What does it represent?

GRIFFIN. Search me. It's just a garden.

BOLLA. You've got a problem.

GRIFFIN. What?

BOLLA. With the poem. With your garden.

GRIFFIN. Why?

BOLLA. It doesn't represent nothing and nothing rhymes with garden. Except harden. And pardon. That's your lot. You could try and rhyme some of the flowers, but, see the flowers are all tough rhymes. Daffodil. Begonia. Rhododendron. It's well known. The flowers are buggers to rhyme. Plus it's already been done.

GRIFFIN. When?

BOLLA. Andrew Marvell. He did the garden in 1681. It goes:

What a wondrous life I lead,
Ripe apples drop about my head,
The luscious clusters of the vine
Upon my mouth do crush their wine;
The nectarine and curious peach
Into my hands themselves do reach.
Stumbling on melons as I pass,
Ensnar'd with flowers I fall on grass.

She stands up. She speaks the rest of the poem straight to WATTMORE.

Such was that happy garden-state,
While man there walk'd without a mate;
After a place so pure and sweet,
What other help could yet be meet!
But 'twas beyond a mortal's share
To wander solitary there:
Two paradises 'twere in one
To live in paradise alone.

Blackout.

Interval.

Four

*The radio returns. It is a report about the birdwatcher in
Addenbrooke's Hospital. It says the police believe he was
attacked and robbed by a masked assailant.*

*Wind. Dry, rolling thunder. Lightning. The cabin as before, except
lit by candles. GRIFFIN sits alone in the candlelight, listening to
the thunder. The lights in the cabin flash on and off a few times,
and then come back on. GRIFFIN breathes a small sigh of relief.
Enter WATTMORE, grim-faced, with the toilet roll. He stows it
in the tallboy.*

GRIFFIN. Maybe it's a blessing.

WATTMORE. Maybe it's not.

    WATTMORE *takes off his coat.*

GRIFFIN. We prayed didn't we. We prayed for help. Maybe... I
don't know. Maybe them prayers got heard.

WATTMORE. Maybe they didn't.

    Silence.

GRIFFIN. Power's back on. That's a relief anyway.

WATTMORE. You shouldn't have told her about the Cubs.

GRIFFIN. Look just drop it, will you. It's done.

WATTMORE. You shouldn't have told her about the *Bugle*, you
shouldn't have told her about getting the sack. You shouldn't
have told her anything.

GRIFFIN. You're sat there like a sack of spuds. I was trying to
keep the party going.

WATTMORE. Why don't you just tell her the rest? Tell her all of
it. Why don't you tell her everything?

GRIFFIN. She can help us.

WATTMORE. How? Oh for pity's sake...

GRIFFIN. What? She can...

WATTMORE. Griffin –

GRIFFIN. What? She knows it. She knows poetry.

Thunder and lightning. The lights flash and fail. Complete darkness.

That's wonderful. That's all we need. Wattmore.

WATTMORE. Dear Lord, defend this place from –

GRIFFIN. Oh stop it.

WATTMORE. Defend this place from –

GRIFFIN. Stop it Wattmore. Stop it.

WATTMORE. Defend this place from evil, drive out the fetid envious fiend –

GRIFFIN. Brilliant.

WATTMORE.... and leave this house for meditation of your word. Help me Prince. Help me.

GRIFFIN *strikes a match. At that moment all the lights come on.* BOLLA *is standing right in front of him. He jumps.* WATTMORE *is on his knees.*

BOLLA. There's a storm coming.

GRIFFIN. What? Yes.

BOLLA. I was on the throne and all the lights went out.

GRIFFIN. It's the storm. I'll uh... I'll light the candles.

BOLLA. Not to worry. If it happens again, we can pretend it's the olden days.

You all right down there Jess?

WATTMORE. I'm fine thank you Bolla.

BOLLA. Good. Good.

GRIFFIN. You know, Bolla, it's very kind of you to furnish us and all. This really is a fitting evening.

BOLLA. Thank you Griffin. That's extremely touching. I was a bit worried at first, but by this point I feel very at home.

GRIFFIN. That's because you are at home Bolla.

BOLLA. Yes. I suppose in a way I am.

She smiles.

I've been looking to settle down for a while now.

Pause.

GRIFFIN. We were just wondering Bolla. How do you know about poetry?

BOLLA. What do you mean?

GRIFFIN. Well we… I just wondered… We just were saying I wonder how she knows that.

BOLLA. Why shouldn't I?

GRIFFIN. No reason. I was just…

BOLLA. I don't understand the question.

GRIFFIN. No it's just, it's unusual isn't it. We don't, I don't you know… Not many people bother with it any more.

Pause.

BOLLA. I have studied verse.

GRIFFIN. Oh right.

BOLLA. In Holloway.

GRIFFIN. Oh I see. I see. (*To* WATTMORE.) Do you see?

BOLLA. We had options. It was an option.

GRIFFIN. Right. It was an option. Right.

BOLLA. First year was Mah-Jong. Then Anatomy. Then Bench-pressing. Then the Aztecs and Incas. Then Verse. Some young girl, local poet, came in Saturday afternoons. She was all right but she was overly shy. She read her poems. And we read our poems. Then she got herself pregnant and never came back.

Beat.

I used to know hundreds. Me and this other girl learned them by heart. Then I got put in solitary. When I came out she'd gone.

GRIFFIN. There's a competition.

WATTMORE. Griffin.

GRIFFIN. What? There's a prize. You have to write one poem.

WATTMORE. Griffin –

GRIFFIN. They want one poem. That's all.

BOLLA. What's the prize?

GRIFFIN. It's one thousand pound.

BOLLA. Stone me Griffin. For verse? Who's got one thousand for verse?

GRIFFIN. The university. Cambridge University.

She falls silent.

Are you okay Bolla?

She sits there in silence.

Did I say something wrong. Bolla. Are you... is everything okay?

Silence.

BOLLA. Don't bother Griffin.

GRIFFIN. What?

BOLLA. Don't waste your time.

GRIFFIN. Why not?

BOLLA. Fucking cunts. Fucking fucking bastard fucking cunts. Excuse my French.

GRIFFIN. What is it?

BOLLA. One grand? They'll have a May Ball, spend that on ice. They'll roast one swan, that's a bottle of port. One grand? They shit it. Excuse my French.

Pause.

I'm sorry, it's just I hated the place.

GRIFFIN. Oh. I see. You... you went to Varsity?

BOLLA. What? No. My mum worked for St John's College. She was a bedder. You don't know what a bedder is do you Jess?

WATTMORE. No.

BOLLA. Griffin.

GRIFFIN. You bedder tell me.

Beat.

No, sorry I don't.

BOLLA. Bedder. It means some toff leaves his skidders in the middle of the floor, you have to pick 'em up. He leaves a rubber johnny swinging on the bedpost, you have to flush it for him. Because he's too busy to do it himself. He's busy off somewhere singing in Latin. In truth, he's swigging champagne in the back of a punt got his hand on some duchess's muff. Three and six an hour for eighteen years. I'll tell you what that is. It's degrading. Call me anything. Shave my head. No one degrades me.

GRIFFIN. Right.

BOLLA. She used to have to take me in with her, when I was a little girl. I watched toffs talk down to her. Bastard big students with their bastard big hands. Some day I'm going to go back there, and clean up for good.

Enter ROYCE, *a policeman.* BOLLA *stands straight up.*

Who are you?

ROYCE. Your porch is smashed.

WATTMORE. Royce.

GRIFFIN. Royce. Fucking hell. Don't you knock?

ROYCE. It's knackered. There's glass all over.

GRIFFIN. It was the wind. Don't you knock?

ROYCE. I was just on my way over Fen Ditton thought I'd drop in. How's your ribs Jess?

WATTMORE. On the mend.

ROYCE. That's good. I've been asking around. I think I'm getting to the bottom of it. I'm forming the strong opinion that it was mindless violence.

WATTMORE. I see. Well thanks anyway.

ROYCE. Who's this?

BOLLA. Who are you?

ROYCE. Who are you?

BOLLA. I asked first.

ROYCE. No you didn't.

GRIFFIN. Bolla this is Royce. Royce this is –

BOLLA. Fiona.

Beat.

GRIFFIN. Fiona. Royce this is Fiona.

ROYCE. Pleasure.

GRIFFIN. Fiona's stopped here. She's our lodger.

ROYCE. Treat to meet you Fiona. There's a storm coming.

BOLLA. Griffin. Can I have my forty pound back please?

GRIFFIN. What?

BOLLA. Can I have my forty pound back please.

GRIFFIN. Why?

BOLLA. I've changed my mind.

GRIFFIN. But…

BOLLA. I didn't know. That you, you know… that you had
friends. You never said you were friends with the coppers.

GRIFFIN. What? Oh. No. (*Laughs.*) No. Royce is fine.

BOLLA. He's the coppers.

GRIFFIN. No he's not. Well, yes he is.

BOLLA. Can I have my money back please?

GRIFFIN. No. No. Royce's a mate. Aren't you Royce.

ROYCE. That's right.

BOLLA. I know. That's why I want my money back.

GRIFFIN. Look it's perfectly all right.

BOLLA. Can I have my forty pound back please Griffin, and I'll be on my way.

GRIFFIN. Excuse us.

GRIFFIN *takes* BOLLA *downstage. Beat.*

Look Bolla.

BOLLA. Fiona.

GRIFFIN. Fiona.

BOLLA. He's the coppers Griffin.

GRIFFIN. Okay. First of all, he's a bit

He makes a 'he's mad' sign.

ROYCE. I saw that.

GRIFFIN. Royce please. I'll handle this. Second of all, he's not the coppers.

BOLLA. What?

GRIFFIN. He's not the coppers. He's a Special Constable. Sounds grand doesn't it. It's not. It's not even half a copper. He's a volunteer. He does it for free.

BOLLA. Hang on. He's not the coppers? Well what's he doing dressed as the law?

GRIFFIN. That is an excellent question. He's a strimmer.

BOLLA. A what?

GRIFFIN. Strimmer. He strims the lawn edges for the university. He keeps the borders neat. He's in charge of the borders.

BOLLA. He's a gardener?

GRIFFIN. No. *We're* gardeners. *He's* a strimmer.

ROYCE. By the way I'm up for promotion Jess. I'm going to be a full Constable.

WATTMORE. Are you Royce?

GRIFFIN (*shaking his head, looking into* BOLLA*'s eyes*). 'No.'

ROYCE. Aye a month or two I'm up for my stripes. Might even get moved to Ipswich.

GRIFFIN. Again 'No'.

ROYCE. Aye I'm reading for it. I'm pages off finishing the book.

GRIFFIN. He's not finished anything. The only thing I've ever seen him finish is sandwiches.

BOLLA. I don't like coppers Griffin. I just don't like them.

GRIFFIN. Listen. He's a strimmer. It's practically fancy dress. He hasn't got the brains of a bucket of frogs.

BOLLA. He's given me the stingers. Have I gone red?

GRIFFIN. You look lovely. Relax. Sit down, and finish your ginger cake.

She sits down.

ROYCE. Your rose bushes copped it in the freeze Jess.

WATTMORE. I heard.

ROYCE. All dead. And the quince tree's died. Floyd's chopped it down yesterday. Other than that, same. We're getting a new mower.

WATTMORE. That's nice.

ROYCE. Yeah.

Beat.

Students are back this week. And Floyd's taken on new staff. Two gyppos. Can barely speak the Queen's English. Come over in a lorry I reckon.

By the way Jess. Dougal says hello.

WATTMORE. Right. Say… say I say hello back.

ROYCE. He said to say he'd have come himself but he's got a meeting tonight. He was hoping you could make it.

WATTMORE. I'm still not a hundred per cent.

ROYCE. We're doing God's work here in Fen Ditton. Dougal's got vision. He's got charm. He's got charisma.

GRIFFIN. He's got twenty thousand pounds.

ROYCE. What?

Beat.

What about that bloody bird then? Folks are going spare for it.
I was lying in bed last night, and I thought I heard it.
The question is, did it come to Fen Ditton on purpose, or has it
been blown off-course, by forces beyond his control. In which
case, he's doomed isn't he? He'll never find his way back.

Beat.

So I was in the garden today, doing the borders, and I got
talking to Floyd Fowler.

WATTMORE. Oh.

ROYCE. Strange really. He don't normally talk to me. I mean
he's the gaffer. Normally he just puts two fingers up. Or gives
me a nip. But this morning, he stops and starts talking to me.

WATTMORE. What did he say?

ROYCE. Well, he's not happy see.

WATTMORE. What about?

ROYCE. He's not happy with you Jess. He was warning people
to stay away from you. And it's not about the cubs. He says he
laid you off for a different reason. And now he's telling me to
stay away from you, him that knows we're mates. He walked
past us playing shove-ha'penny a hundred times. Do you have
any idea what he's on about.

WATTMORE. No.

ROYCE. Strange. Anyway, I thought I'd mention it.

Beat.

So have you done the tapes?

WATTMORE. Not yet. I'm doing them. Have to get the time see.

ROYCE. Have you heard him Fiona? Jess does these wondrous
recorded renditions from both Old and New Testaments which
he relates entirely by heart. Wondrous they are. I find them
very soothing. And they really help me sleep.

WATTMORE. It's a hobby really.

GRIFFIN. Don't do yourself down Jess. It's a job. It's your job.

ROYCE. It is that.

GRIFFIN. It's a career. A profession. Your calling.

ROYCE. That's what it is. A calling. Hallelujah. You're a pure man Jess Wattmore.

GRIFFIN. Hallelujah.

ROYCE. Dougal loves you Jess.

GRIFFIN. Hallelujah. Did you hear that Jess? Dougal loves you.

ROYCE. He says he can't do it without you Jess. He says you're special.

GRIFFIN. He's not special. He's… Okay. Enough of the bloody love-in. Mutual bloody… What do you want Royce?

ROYCE. A quick word.

GRIFFIN. Well you've had it. Jess is very pleased to see you. Now please. Please. Just… Please. Go home.

ROYCE. Truth is I came to speak to you Griffin.

GRIFFIN. What about?

ROYCE. It's important.

GRIFFIN. What is it?

ROYCE. It's private.

Beat.

GRIFFIN. I see

Beat.

Fiona?

Sighs.

Fiona. Is it all right if Royce and I pop in your room for half a mo?

BOLLA. No.

Beat.

It's just you've caught me on the hop. It's just I've got all my things in there.

GRIFFIN. Okay. What if we leave the light off?

ROYCE. What?

BOLLA. No. It's my room. You can't just go in a lady's room. She might have got ladies' things in there. I'm extremely sorry. I'll tell you what? I'll go in there you can be private. I'm sorry Griffin. I'm getting prickly again. I've gone all red haven't I.

GRIFFIN. You're not red.

BOLLA. Are we still going into town? I need to lie-down if we're going into town. I'm blotchy.

GRIFFIN. What yes. No. Yes. We'll see.

BOLLA. I'd like to see the sights, you know. If you still fancy. And if it'll cheer Jess up. Is that okay?

GRIFFIN. Yes. Just give me a minute.

BOLLA. Okay. I'm going to wait in here.

GRIFFIN. Lovely.

BOLLA. Okay.

She goes to the door. She comes back.

Will he be gone when I get back?

GRIFFIN. He's just leaving.

BOLLA. I hate the coppers Griffin. I'm not good with the coppers, on account of things which have happened.

GRIFFIN. I promise.

BOLLA. Thank you Griffin. I'm very happy here. If we go out later, perhaps when we get back we could put our heads together.

GRIFFIN. What?

BOLLA. We could put our heads together and work on your poem. I could give you some pointers.

GRIFFIN. Oh. Right.

BOLLA. I'll be in here. I'm very happy here.

She goes towards her room.

ROYCE. Nice to meet you Fiona.

BOLLA. What?

ROYCE. Nice to meet you.

BOLLA *disappears into the back room. Pause.*

Who is she?

GRIFFIN. She's no one.

ROYCE. Is she your girlfriend? Are you… you know…

GRIFFIN. Sweet Jesus Royce.

ROYCE. Sorry. Right. Is that her car outside? Must be worth a bit. It's in pretty good nick.

WATTMORE. Would you like a drink Royce?

ROYCE. I shan't actually. I'm on duty.

WATTMORE. Right. I'm going to wash up then.

ROYCE. Right. Shall we Griffin?

They go to the front of the cabin.

How is he?

GRIFFIN. Who? Oh. He's the same.

ROYCE. He seems the same. Have you got to the bottom of it?

GRIFFIN. No. It's the New Year. He's just a bit low.

ROYCE. I bet the beating didn't help.

GRIFFIN. No it didn't.

ROYCE. Funny. I remember last New Year he was a full of beans. Organising the Cub ramble. The Sixers' and Seconders' Hike. It's like he's a different person these past few weeks. He should get out more. We're leafleting in Ely on the weekend. Dougal's hiring a minibus. Anyway…

GRIFFIN. What do you want Royce?

ROYCE. Okay, Griffin. I need your help. There's a man in the hospital. He came to grief, out on the marsh.

GRIFFIN. Oh?

ROYCE. I'll share what I've heard. There was two out there, a boy and his father, and they came across a man with a balaclava. They thought it was against the cold.

Beat.

He took the man's wallet, which didn't have much in it, and his binoculars. He even took the kiddies' packed lunch Griffin. And his Game Boy. He robbed them with a hammer. It was in the *Bugle* yesterday, and it's going to be in the *Bugle* again in the morning.

GRIFFIN. And?

ROYCE. I just wondered if you'd seen anyone strange. You're always out there Griffin.

GRIFFIN. I hunt in the reed beds. I stay off the marsh.

ROYCE. Right.

GRIFFIN. Everyone knows the rabbits are on the reed beds. Rabbits don't breed on the marsh. They don't go on the marsh.

ROYCE. I just wondered if you'd seen or heard anything out of the ordinary.

GRIFFIN. No.

ROYCE. Right.

GRIFFIN. Is that it?

ROYCE. Pretty much. He's going to live they think. But the brain is scrambled. They say he's lost his eyesight. I said down the station, I said it could be the Jack O'Lanterns, the will o'wisps, but they all laughed.

Beat.

Well goodnight Griffin. Say goodnight to Fiona for me. Goodnight Jess.

WATTMORE. Goodnight Royce.

ROYCE. Now you get on with those tapes. It's the Prince's work you do now.

Beat.

You want to get that porch fixed. There's a storm coming, and the wind's cruel tonight.

He leaves.

GRIFFIN. I don't know why you give that nicompoop the time of day. He thinks he's the law. He can't get his vest on straight.

WATTMORE. Royce said about the man. The one in the hospital.

GRIFFIN. What about him.

WATTMORE. He said he's blinded. He might die.

GRIFFIN. That's what he heard.

WATTMORE. I thought you said he fell in a suckpit.

GRIFFIN. So?

WATTMORE. You said you read it in the *Bugle*. You said he fell.

GRIFFIN. Do I work for the *Bugle* now? Am I their chief reporter? I skim-read it in the mobile library. I was busy doing... doing something else.

WATTMORE. It's just you said he fell.

GRIFFIN. What are you saying Wattmore? What are you saying? Eh? Are you saying you don't believe me. Eh? Are you saying that you don't believe me?

WATTMORE. Of course I believe you Griffin. Why wouldn't I?

Re-enter ROYCE.

ROYCE. I forgot to say. The scouts are having a Winter Wonderland in February. The Chief Constable is on the committee, I thought I could have a word in a few of the appropriate shell-likes. People forget very quickly. All can be redeemed, at any moment. It's never too late, when you think about it, is it?

Enter BOLLA. *She's wearing lots and lots of make-up, her hair is up, and she's changed into a skirt. They all stop and look at her.*

BOLLA. What?

She stops. She is embarrassed. Silence.

Are we going out Griffin? I thought we were going into town. I thought… To cheer Jess up.

They all stand there for a long time. In the end ROYCE *sniggers.*

ROYCE. What's she doing…?

Silence.

BOLLA. Is something funny?

ROYCE. What? Nothing's funny.

Pause.

Nothing's funny.

BOLLA. Then why are you laughing?

ROYCE. I'm not. Nothing's funny.

BOLLA. Is there a problem Griffin…?

GRIFFIN. What? No. He's just leaving. Aren't you Royce.

ROYCE. Yes. Goodnight. Goodnight Fiona.

Silence.

BOLLA. Royce is it.

ROYCE. Yes.

BOLLA. Royce. Have you ever done anatomy?

ROYCE. What?

BOLLA. Have you ever done anatomy?

ROYCE. No.

BOLLA. I have. I know all about anatomy. I know loads about it. I know where your arteries are, chum.

ROYCE. What?

BOLLA. I know where your arteries are. You've got one here, one here, one here and one here. Did you know that.

ROYCE. Sorry?

BOLLA. Did you know that?

ROYCE. No.

BOLLA. It's not the biggest. The biggest is actually in your thigh. It's called the *nodal maximus* and it pumps all the blood up and down your legs and to your groin and abdomen. You learn something new every day don't you?

ROYCE. Suppose you do.

BOLLA. I can do things you wouldn't believe. You could blink and I'd be on you, see. You'd swear it wasn't happening. But it was. See that dresser. There's a knife in that drawer, for skinning rabbits. It's very sharp. You could blink once, and I'd be in there, I'd fetch it, and you'd open your eyes and you'd be covered in blood. You'd bleed white inside a minute. And I'll mop you up, and I'll put your fucking corpse in the car, and drive you to the sea, and throw you away. Now what's so funny?

ROYCE. Nothing.

BOLLA. Then why was you laughing?

ROYCE. I just thought of something funny.

BOLLA. What was it.

Pause.

ROYCE. It was something funny that happened the other day.

BOLLA. What?

ROYCE. I saw something funny.

BOLLA. What was it?

Silence.

ROYCE. It was a man. It was this man with…

BOLLA. With what?

ROYCE. … with… no arms.

BOLLA. A man with no arms.

ROYCE. And a funny hat.

BOLLA. Sorry.

ROYCE. It was this man who had on a funny hat.

BOLLA. With no arms.

ROYCE. No he had arms. I was thinking of someone else.

BOLLA. So a man with a funny hat.

ROYCE. Yes.

BOLLA. Why was it funny.

Pause.

ROYCE. It had funny ear-flaps.

BOLLA. Did it?

ROYCE. Yes. It was blue. Bluey-green. With funny flaps. I just remembered it.

BOLLA. Is that true?

ROYCE. Sorry.

BOLLA. Is it true what you just said. About the funny bluey-green hat with the flaps. Is it true. And think very carefully before you answer.

Pause.

ROYCE. No.

Pause.

BOLLA. Have you got children Royce?

ROYCE. I've got two.

BOLLA That's nice. Girls or boys?

ROYCE. Girls.

BOLLA. Two girls. There's a hammer in that drawer, and some six-inch nails. Do you want me to nail their little faces to the floor? Right through their little eyes. Say sorry to Griffin for bothering him tonight.

ROYCE. I'm sorry Griffin.

BOLLA. And say sorry to Jess.

ROYCE. I'm sorry Jess.

BOLLA. Good. Now apologise to Bolla.

ROYCE. Who?

BOLLA. Bolla. Apologise to Bolla.

He looks around, and throws his voice.

ROYCE. I'm sorry Bolla.

BOLLA. Say it again.

ROYCE. I'm sorry Bolla.

BOLLA. Once more.

ROYCE. I'm sorry Bolla.

Pause.

BOLLA. You're never going to come here bothering Griffin again are you.

ROYCE. No.

BOLLA. Did you walk here?

ROYCE. I'm on the bike.

BOLLA. Well get on your bike, and ride home, strimmer. Ride home to your mum.

ROYCE. Goodnight Jess.

GRIFFIN. Royce.

WATTMORE. Royce.

GRIFFIN. I'm going to speak to Dougal.

WATTMORE. Royce…

ROYCE. Dougal must know this. There's evil in this house.

Prince be with you. Prince be with you.

He leaves. Silence.

BOLLA. Jess, if it's all right with you, I don't think I feel like going out now. I think I'm going to get an early night.

BOLLA *goes to the drawer and she removes the hammer and a six-inch nail.*

By the way, you can borrow my car, Griffin. Any time you want, if I'm not using it, just borrow the keys. All you have to do is ask.

BOLLA *takes the nail and she hammers it into a wooden support. She hangs her car keys on them.*

That's the nail the keys hang on. We'll keep them there, then any of us need to go somewhere we can just take them. If the keys are there, you can drive the car. When you've finished, they go back there. You don't have to ask.

BOLLA *starts to cry.*

I'm sorry. I should have… I've just damaged your wood. I never asked. I'm sorry. I just… I just… I thought we were going out.

Pause.

I'm sorry to both of you. I'm sorry. I'll make it up to you.

She cries.

I'm going to shut myself in there, and I'm not coming out until I've done you a poem. And you can have it as a present from me to you. And if it wins your competition, well then I don't want none of the prize. It's yours. I'm going in there now. I'll make it up to you Griffin. Goodnight. Goodnight Jess.

Exit BOLLA. GRIFFIN *and* WATTMORE *stand there in silence. The birds scream outside.*GRIFFIN *looks at the key, hanging there on the hook. He puts his coat on. He picks up his balaclava.*

WATTMORE. Where are you going? Griffin.

GRIFFIN. I… I set some traps out by the battery farm. I forgot to check them.

WATTMORE. Don't go on the marsh. Griffin. Griffin. Don't go on the marsh. Don't go on the marsh.

WATTMORE *is left alone. Thunder. It starts to rain hard on the tin roof.*

Blackout.

Five

Darkness. The storm is calmed. In the silence, the night heron passes low over the theatre, its scream-call ringing out, and fading over the black marsh.

The cabin in the dead of night. Enter GRIFFIN, *in his balaclava, in the moonlight. He is out of breath. He takes the balaclava off. His nose is bloody. He goes to the stove to get warm. The firelight flares up in the room, revealing a rabbit hanging from the central beam. He stares at it hanging there. He unhooks it. He switches on the light. A lithe figure, with shoulder-length blond hair, is lying there, wrapped in a white sheet.*

GRIFFIN (*hissing*). Wattmore. WATTMORE!

    WATTMORE *sits up.*

WATTMORE. What?

GRIFFIN. Get up.

WATTMORE. Griffin –

GRIFFIN. Get up.

WATTMORE. What's wrong? I'm on the cushions.

GRIFFIN. *Get up.*

    WATTMORE *stands up, laboriously.*

WATTMORE. What time is it? Where have you been?

    They both look at the BOY, *sleeping there.*

    Who's that?

    Silence.

GRIFFIN. Who's that? What?

WATTMORE. What?

GRIFFIN. What? I don't know. Who is it? Why did you let him in?

WATTMORE. I didn't let him in.

GRIFFIN. Well what's he doing here.

WATTMORE. How should I know?

Beat.

Is it a boy?

GRIFFIN. Okay.

Pause.

Wake him up.

WATTMORE. You wake him up. I'm not waking him up.

GRIFFIN. Wake him up Wattmore.

WATTMORE. Fuck off. I'm not waking him up.

GRIFFIN. What's he doing here? Wake him up.

WATTMORE. No.

GRIFFIN. Wake him up.

WATTMORE. No.

GRIFFIN. Wattmore.

WATTMORE. What?

Pause.

GRIFFIN. Stand back.

WATTMORE *does.*

WATTMORE. Griffin…

GRIFFIN. What?

WATTMORE. Put the rabbit down.

GRIFFIN *passes it to* WATTMORE. *He shakes the stranger once. He shakes him again.*

GRIFFIN. You.

Pause.

Boy.

WATTMORE. It might be a girl.

GRIFFIN. Shut up will you?

Beat.

You. Boy.

Beat.

Miss.

He shakes him again. He shakes him again. Harder. Very hard.

WATTMORE. Oh no.

GRIFFIN. What?

WATTMORE. Oh no. Is he… don't say… Oh Jesus. Is he cold?

GRIFFIN. Course he's cold. He's fucking starkers.

WATTMORE. Is he breathing?

GRIFFIN *listens.*

GRIFFIN. He's breathing.

Beat.

Okay Jess. What's going on?

WATTMORE. Nothing.

GRIFFIN. How did he get here.

WATTMORE. I don't know. What are you saying?

GRIFFIN. I come home there's a boy asleep on our couch.

WATTMORE. What are you saying? Where have you been Griffin. What happened to your face?

GRIFFIN. I went out. I fell over.

WATTMORE. What have you done Griffin?

GRIFFIN. I fell over.

WATTMORE. What's going on Griffin? Who is he?

GRIFFIN. Where's Bolla?

WATTMORE. She's in there. She's been in there all night.

GRIFFIN. Wake her up.

WATTMORE. No chance.

GRIFFIN. Wattmore…

WATTMORE. I'm not going in there.

GRIFFIN. I woke him up.

WATTMORE. No you didn't.

GRIFFIN. This is your fault.

WATTMORE. What. Why?

GRIFFIN. You were here. You were minding the fort.

WATTMORE. I was asleep.

They glare at one another in the moonlight.

GRIFFIN. Stand back.

He walks to the back door. He knocks on it.

Bolla.

He knocks harder. He goes in. Silence.

WATTMORE. The keys have gone. Griffin. And the tape recorder's gone. She's taken Dougal's recorder.

Re-enter GRIFFIN.

GRIFFIN. Is the car out there?

WATTMORE. She's gone out the window.

GRIFFIN. Wait here.

GRIFFIN *leaves through the strip plastic.* WATTMORE *approaches the youth. He reaches out a hand, but stops. He gasps.*

WATTMORE. Our father, who art in heaven, hallowed be thy name.

Re-enter GRIFFIN.

GRIFFIN. You can stop whispering now Jess. We're the only fuckers here. Who caught that rabbit? Jess. I didn't catch it. I've never went… I never went in the reeds. Who caught the rabbit? Jess? What are you doing. What's the matter? Jess?

Silence.

WATTMORE. It's an angel.

GRIFFIN (*simultaneous*). Angel.

Pause.

They both study him for a moment.

It's not.

Pause.

WATTMORE. How do you know? It could be.

GRIFFIN. It's not.

WATTMORE. It could be. Do you believe in angels?

WATTMORE *laughs quietly in wonder.*

Oh dear. Oh dear.

Pause.

I'm shivering. My hair's gone up my neck. (*He laughs.*) I prayed Griffin. Tonight. In here. I prayed for an angel. Look at his face. Do you... do you renounce Satan and his riddles and crimes?

GRIFFIN. Yes.

WATTMORE. Do you... do you... do you... I can't remember it. Do you renounce the fatted jackal? Do you renounce –

GRIFFIN. Yes.

WATTMORE. Do you spit his name?

GRIFFIN. I spit his name.

WATTMORE. I'm shivering. Will you kneel with me?

GRIFFIN. Yes.

WATTMORE. Will you begin.

GRIFFIN. Yes.

WATTMORE. Thank you Griffin. Grace to you. Grace to you.

They kneel in front of the iconostasis.

Do something easy.

Beat.

GRIFFIN. Behold… behold, I send an Angel before thee, to bring thee into the place which I have prepared… Beware –

WATTMORE. Beware of him, and obey his voice, provoke him not; for my name is in him. If thou shalt obey his voice, and do all that I speak; We're saved Griffin.

GRIFFIN.… then I will be an enemy unto thine enemies.

BOTH. For mine Angel shall go before thee… and I will cut them off.

WATTMORE. And ye shall serve the LORD your God, and he shall bless thy bread, and thy water; and I will take sickness away from the midst of thee.

Enter BOLLA. *She's soaked. She's holding the stereo in one hand and a dead rabbit by the feet in the other.*

GRIFFIN. Bolla.

WATTMORE. Bolla.

BOLLA. It's lashing it down.

GRIFFIN. Where have you been.

BOLLA. Catching rabbits.

GRIFFIN. What?

BOLLA. They're all over the road. Hundreds of 'em.

GRIFFIN. Wha –

BOLLA. My heart's pounding. Feel.

GRIFFIN. Bolla –

BOLLA. I got another in the car. There's hundreds out there.

GRIFFIN. Bolla. What's going on. Who is this?

BOLLA. Is he still asleep.

GRIFFIN. Do you know him?

BOLLA. I don't know him from Adam.

GRIFFIN. How did he get here?

BOLLA. I brung him.

GRIFFIN. Where from?

BOLLA. Cambridge.

GRIFFIN. Cambridge?

BOLLA. Yeah. He's a student.

GRIFFIN. A student of what?

BOLLA. I don't know. But I was hoping, of poetry.

GRIFFIN. What?

BOLLA. Yeah. But it's a bit fingers-crossed. I know he knows about it.

GRIFFIN. How?

BOLLA. Because he was at a poetry night. In Corpus Christi.

GRIFFIN. You went to Cambridge tonight?

BOLLA. It's horrible. I spent an hour in the one-way system, it's like the fucking minotaur's maze. Bet it's easier getting in to study Greek than it is to drive your car in.

GRIFFIN. How did you find him?

BOLLA. On a noticeboard. They've got the lot, plays, black-tie piss-ups, karate, late-night this, all-night that. These cunts'll do anything not to go to bed. So I went along, and sat at the back and I'm listening to them get up one after the other. And this one read out the first one I understood. And also, he looked quite small, so I followed him in the gents. And we chatted a bit. Then I asked him about what Corpus Christi meant, and before he could answer I gave him a left-hander then I stuffed him in the Golf.

WATTMORE. Oh no. Oh no.

BOLLA. I borrowed your recorder Jess. I hope you don't mind.

GRIFFIN. Why won't he wake up.

BOLLA. Right. He's had a lot of pills.

GRIFFIN. What?

BOLLA. He's had a lot of temazepam. Don't worry. He ain't going nowhere.

GRIFFIN. How many did you give him?

BOLLA. Not many.

GRIFFIN. How many?

BOLLA. Don't know really. Couple of handfuls.

GRIFFIN. Bolla. You could have killed him.

BOLLA. Come off it Griffin. He's a student. Have you seen what they get up to? You need the heart of a fucking bull. Look at him. He's having the time of his life.

GRIFFIN. Where's his clothes?

BOLLA. Right. Shortly after I got the pills down him, he had accident.

GRIFFIN. An accident.

BOLLA. Yes. He shat himself. At some point in the journey back, he shat himself in the boot of the car. Yeah. But don't worry. I burned 'em by the side of the road.

GRIFFIN. You burned his clothes.

BOLLA. I had to Griffin. They were festooned in shit. I thought you'd be pleased. I thought you were serious about this.
I thought you wanted a poem.

GRIFFIN. I did.

BOLLA. Well there then. I thought it best to bring in an expert.

He stirs.

Here we go. Okay. First. We need some strong coffee. Get a pint or two of that down him. Then we ask him about poetry. Get him to do some, maybe get him to read yours.

GRIFFIN. But we'll go to prison.

BOLLA. Who's going to prison? Who's going to prison Griffin. You think I'm a mug?

GRIFFIN. No.

BOLLA. You think I haven't planned this. One: he doesn't know us. Two: he's got no idea where he is. Three: we're in the middle of a fucking bog. And if he's not too much trouble to us

we'll have him back in a day or two. He'll wake up naked on
some lawn think it's all a hoot. Are you in or out? Are you in
or out Griffin?

The BOY *stirs.*

GRIFFIN. What do we do?

BOLLA. Switch off the light. Don't let him see us.

GRIFFIN *puts on his balaclava.*

What are you doing?

GRIFFIN. He'll see us.

BOLLA. You'll scare the shit out of him. Take it off.

GRIFFIN. He'll see me.

BOLLA. Griffin. You can't quiz him dressed like that. He won't
understand.

GRIFFIN. He's going to have a job understanding as it is. Okay.
We blindfold him.

BOLLA. How's he going to read if you blindfold him?

GRIFFIN. We read it to him. I'll read it aloud.

BOLLA. Griffin.

GRIFFIN. What?

BOLLA. Take the fucking balaclava off. Take it off.

GRIFFIN. Okay. Turn the light down.

GRIFFIN *turns all of the lights off. Pitch dark. Silence.*

I can't see a fucking thing. Wait.

He lights one lantern. The BOY *sits up. The* BOY *stands up,
naked in the half-light. He looks around him. From the
shadows, the three of them advance. They stand ten feet away.*
GRIFFIN *speaks very clearly.*

GRIFFIN. Who's your favorite poet?

BOLLA. Who in the field of poetry do you admire and why?

WATTMORE. Forgive me Jesus.

GRIFFIN. You. Who's… Who's your favorite poet? Say some poetry. Say some poetry.

BOLLA. Show him your poem.

GRIFFIN. Wait there.

He hands the poem to the BOY.

Read this. It's not finished. It's a first draft.

The BOY *reads it.*

Jess, get the boy a drink.

WATTMORE *doesn't move. He stays seated, staring ahead.*

He's thirsty Wattmore. Get the boy a drink. Get the boy a drink.

WATTMORE. I won't be part of this.

GRIFFIN. Wattmore.

WATTMORE *does.*

The BOY *looks at the page in his hand.*

Well? What do you think?

WATTMORE. Here.

He hands him the water.

GRIFFIN. Out the way Wattmore.

Silence. The BOY *stands there.*

What do you think? Say something you little bastard. Would it win? Would it win a prize. In your opinion. Could it win?

BOY. Cor…

BOLLA. Yes?

BOY. Cor…

GRIFFIN. Yes?

BOY. Corpus Christi. Corpus Christi means the body of Christ.

He passes out.

GRIFFIN. What the fuck? What the fuck was that?

BOLLA. I'll get him another miniature from the car. Hang about.

GRIFFIN. Bolla –

BOLLA. Wait there. He needs a pick-me-up.

She runs out. GRIFFIN runs into the back room to fetch a blanket. Wattmore searches the cupboard for brandy. He stops, and rises with a pair of brand-new binoculars.

GRIFFIN runs back in with the blanket. He sees WATTMORE standing there holding the binoculars.

GRIFFIN. Okay. Here's what we do. We –

He stops. They stand there in the silent room.

I found them. I found them in the reed beds.

Silence.

They're worth fifteen hundred pound Wattmore. I looked them up on the internet. In the library. You can see in the dark with them. And I found a buyer on the internet. In Cambridge. They're going to pay six hundred pound for them. He's got the money today. I'm cycling in, and he's going to pay me.

Silence.

We've got nothing Wattmore. Rabbits. We've got rabbits. And if the town finds out. And the town comes here.

WATTMORE. Jack O'Lanterns. Jack O'Lanterns.

He drops the binoculars on the floor.

GRIFFIN. What are you doing? You clot.

Griffin picks them up.

Brilliant. You've shattered the lenses. I can't see anything now. It's pitch dark.

Re-enter BOLLA.

BOLLA. Don't panic but someone's coming up the road. They got torches. There's lots of them.

GRIFFIN. Oh Jesus.

BOLLA. Who are they?

GRIFFIN. It's no one.

BOLLA. We've got to get him out of here. Quick. Give me a hand with this one.

GRIFFIN. Put him in the back. Can we use your room.

BOLLA. Just give me a hand.

They carry the BOY *into the back room.*

WATTMORE. Are you there Prince? Are you there? Please. Are you there?

BOLLA *and* GRIFFIN *reappear.*

BOLLA. Who is it?

GRIFFIN. It's gypsies. Wattmore has had a disagreement with the gypsies.

BOLLA. Well we'll see them off.

WATTMORE. It's not gypsies.

BOLLA. What?

WATTMORE. They're coming to gather me. They want me in the ground.

Silence.

Bolla, you should go now.

BOLLA. I want to help Jess. Griffin? If there's any trouble I'm staying here. I'll look after you.

WATTMORE (*shouts*). You don't belong here. This isn't your home. You've done enough. Now leave.

Silence. BOLLA *seems stunned. She looks at* WATTMORE *for a long time.*

BOLLA. I'm going to my room now. I'm going to look after the boy.

Exit BOLLA, *into her room.*

GRIFFIN. I just wanted to help. It's not too late Jess.

Noise outside. Breaking glass.

Get down. Switch off the light.

WATTMORE. I won't hide.

GRIFFIN *switches off the light. Enter a* MAN *with a torch.*
GRIFFIN *switches on the light. It is…*

GRIFFIN. Royce.

ROYCE. Griffin. Jess. I'm not to speak to you. Where is she?

GRIFFIN. What do you want? It's the middle… it's five thirty in
the morning.

ROYCE. I've brought one with me. We'll get to the bottom here.

Enter DOUGAL, *with* TWO WOMEN *and a* MAN. *They all
have torches.* DOUGAL *wears a black cloak.*

DOUGAL. Where is she?

WATTMORE. Dougal.

DOUGAL. Jess Wattmore. Where is this witch?

ROYCE. She's in there.

DOUGAL. What has happened in this house. You keep a woman
here?

WATTMORE. She's a guest. She's paying rent.

DOUGAL. And she threatens my flock. She threatens a good soul
here. She would kill his babies. What is happening here Jess
Wattmore. And Floyd Fowler came and he spoke to me. He
spoke to me yesterday. He was after money. He's telling lies
Jess Wattmore. Tell me he is telling lies.

WATTMORE. He's telling lies.

DOUGAL. It's a black thing he's saying. It's a black, black thing.
An abomination. And I know from where it comes. This
woman. These tales. Griffin Montgomery. This is all down to
you now, is it not.

Silence.

GRIFFIN. Hello Dougal.

DOUGAL. Admit that it's down to you. Admit that you have
brought evil into this house. It's you who's to blame.

GRIFFIN. Yes. Yes. it is.

ROYCE. Hallelujah.

DOUGAL. And you're leading my man to the beast here.

GRIFFIN. Yes I am. I am leading him to the beast.

ROYCE. Hallelujah Jesus be praised…

DOUGAL. And you brazen out and say it. It's Hell you worship. Satan has you on a leash.

GRIFFIN. He does. It's Hell I worship.

DOUGAL. There then. And they'll be a leaflet. And I'll highlight your name in bold. Griffin Montgomery runs with jackals. There it is.

Silence.

GRIFFIN. Dougal. Do you remember when we were at school. Do you remember that day you shat in your own desk. Do you remember when you failed your Watermanship swimming, and you cried, and we laughed at you for crying, and do you remember you smeared shit all over the swimming pool changing rooms. And your mother, when she came in the middle of country dancing and mutilated her womanly parts with a fishknife. I'm just wondering if you remember any of what I'm remembering.

DOUGAL. It's a black mind you have. And you always did have.

GRIFFIN. There are so many things to say to you, but I'm going to just say this. You fucking leafblower. Leave this man be. He's not special. He's a gardener. He belongs in a garden.

ROYCE. I think you've said enough Griffin. It's Jess we should hear from now. He has a charge to answer.

WATTMORE. I'll answer it.

GRIFFIN. You don't have to say anything Jess Wattmore.

WATTMORE. Griffin.

GRIFFIN. This is no court of law and this is no copper.

WATTMORE. No. I want to tell them.

ROYCE. Do you mind if I take some notes? I suppose we should start at the beginning. Where were you on the day in question…? The day Floyd Fowler brought his boy to Corpus Christi.

GRIFFIN. I was in the garden. I was working on the quince tree. I'd been working on it all day. I was in its branches, with a hand-saw, trying to stem the disease, you see. I had an idea that it was the left side which was sick, and that the right side could be saved, and it might grow back and in fifty, hundred years no one would know the difference. Anyway, I was up in the quince tree, when the boy walks underneath.

ROYCE. Little Peter. Little Peter Fowler.

WATTMORE. Floyd's boy. Yes.

ROYCE. Did he speak to you? Did he say anything?

WATTMORE. He asks me where his dad is. And I said he could be in the Scholars' Garden, he could be in the Chapel Garden, something like that. He could be anywhere see. So I said I don't know. I don't know where your dad is. Then the boy says he's cold, so I climbed down.

ROYCE. You climbed down.

WATTMORE. Yes. Well I could see he was shivering. His teeth were chattering.

ROYCE. So you climbed down the quince tree. Then what did you do.

WATTMORE. I took him into the potting shed.

GRIFFIN. That's enough now Wattmore.

WATTMORE. No Griffin. Let me tell it. I took him in the potting shed. I remember what time it was because I heard the bells of King's Chapel ring five times. And it was going dark, so I lit the lamp. I lit the lamp, and I turned the heater so the boy could get warm. It was dark now, I lit the lamp, and rubbed the boys hands to warm them up.

DOUGAL. And then what?

WATTMORE. And that was it. When he was warm, I buttoned up his coat, and he left me alone.

Pause.

I'm a good man.

DOUGAL. Do you swear Jess Wattmore. Do you swear this is what happened. The town will need the truth Jess. The town must know. Do you swear?

WATTMORE. On my eternal soul, and Jesus' eyes, and on the cross, I swear.

The BOY *appears from the back room, standing naked. Long pause.*

BOY. Shelley.

ROYCE. What?

Pause.

BOY. What is heaven?
  A globe of dew,
  Filling in the morning new,
  Some eyed flower whose young leaves waken,
  On an unimagined world,
  Constellated suns, unshaken
  Orbits measureless, are furled.
  In that frail and fading sphere,
  With ten million gathered there,
  To tremble, gleam and disappear.

  Shelley.

He goes back inside. Closes the door. Silence.

DOUGAL. Explain this Jess Wattmore.

Silence.

WATTMORE. I can't.

Silence.

I'm the Jack O'Lanterns. I robbed the man out on the marsh. Here.

He shows the binoculars.

I beat him and I blinded him. I went out and I robbed him and his boy, and I beat him with a hammer.

ROYCE. Is this true?

GRIFFIN. It's a lie.

DOUGAL. And Floyd Fowler's boy? Is that a falsehood too?

WATTMORE. I touched Floyd Fowler's boy. I touched him. I'm a grabber. I'm a dirty grabber, me. I'm the Jack O'Lanterns. I'm the Jack O'Lanterns. I'm the Will O'Wisp.

Silence.

DOUGAL. The town shall know. Jess Wattmore. The town shall know.

ROYCE. God rain down pity on your soul. And on this boy's.

Enter NEDDY.

DOUGAL. Leave this place Neddy Beagle. Leave this place.

Exit ROYCE, *and* DOUGAL, *and the others. Silence.*

NEDDY. Griffin.

GRIFFIN *stands there in silence.*

NEDDY. Well. I see you've found a buyer Griffin.

GRIFFIN. What?

NEDDY. I say I see you've found a buyer, for your car.

GRIFFIN. What do you mean?

NEDDY. I've just passed her on the road to Fen Ditton. A woman it was. Going fast, but I saw her all right. It's not a bad car, that. I'm glad for you too. We'll see an end to this now. Will you come now Griffin?

GRIFFIN. What?

Pause.

Yes. Yes I will.

Pause.

I'm going to Cambridge Jess.

Pause.

I'm coming with you Neddy Beagle. We'll settle this balance today.

GRIFFIN *puts his coat on. He picks up his gardening equipment. He stops and picks up his poem. He looks at it.*

I know who'll win it. Someone who doesn't need it. Some professor. Some girl. Some girl on her computer.

He burns the poem in the stove. Exit GRIFFIN. WATTMORE *is left alone. The peal of church bells is heard. Dawn touches the marsh outside the window. The distant church bells are pealing.* WATTMORE *presses play on the tape recorder. He goes into* BOLLA'*s room.*

TAPE. Then there was a war in Heaven. Michael and his angels under his command fought the dragon and his angels. And the dragon lost the battle and was forced out of Heaven.

He comes back out carrying the BOY *in his arms. He lays him on the Chesterfield. He looks at him sleeping.*

This dragon – the ancient serpent called the Satan, the one deceiving the whole world – was thrown down to Earth with all his angels.

He bends over him, and kisses his cheek. He goes to the tallboy drawer and fetches his rope. The tape continues, as he carries the rope into the back room, and closes the door.

Then I heard a loud voice shouting across the heavens, 'It has happened at last – They have defeated the Accuser by the blood of the Lamb. By the blood of the Lamb has he been thrown down. And they were not afraid to die. They were not afraid to die.'

WATTMORE'*s tin whistle is heard, playing alone on the tape. Suddenly* BOLLA'*s voice jump cuts in on the tape.*

BOLLA'S VOICE.... to explain why I came here in the first place. Anyway, I leave you my poem. I never wrote it down because as you probably guessed I'm not much of a writer. Or a reader. So I've spoke it instead, and perhaps if you think it could win, one of you could jot it down. I always liked you. It's called 'A Broken Bowl'.

Everything I touch ends up broken.
The dolls I had never had any heads.
When Good Bolla wakes up, the sun is shining,
She doth look out the window and behold the golden sun.
But when Bad Bolla wakes up,
She doth see a black sun in a black sky,

She doth see bad angels, pulling down the stars,
Burning the oxygen, she doth feel everything smashing down
Lying on its side
Like a broken bowl,
With the pieces still rocking.

We feel the moment when WATTMORE *hangs himself. The old wooden beams of the cabin bend and groan. Dust rains down from the beams in the sunlight. The birds cry out.*

The BOY *wakes up. He sits up, rubbing his eyes in the sunlight. He sits there rubbing his eyes. On the tape,* WATTMORE*'s tin whistle resumes. It stops, and the only sound is the birds out on the marsh.*

Enter a MAN *and a* BOY, *with a knapsack and binoculars, wrapped up against the cold.*

MAN. I don't mean to disturb you but the porch was open. Excuse me. Do you have a glass of water?

BOY. What? Yes.

MAN. Thank you. I see you have a view of the marsh. I am Tors. And you are?

BOY. Jonathan.

MAN. We are here on vacation. For two days. You know the night heron? We came to see him, but I think he has gone now. Do you know why he came?

BOY. No.

MAN. How to explain... aahh. I don't know the word. I can't explain... Aaahh. In short, he was lost. He will have fought to stay on course, but the winds are too strong. It is the winds, you know. The winds decide in advance. But I think we were blessed that he was once among us, no? Have you seen him?

BOY. No. I don't think... I don't think I have. Have you?

MAN. Nycticorax nycticorax. The native Indians called him the Night Angel. No. We have not seen him, no. But one day, perhaps. Maybe one day we shall see him.

They stand watching the light change across the broad marsh.

The End.

·

THE WINTERLING

For Shena Malone

The dog starv'd at its Master's gate
Predicts the ruin of the State.

William Blake

The Winterling was first performed at the Royal Court Theatre Downstairs, London, on 2 March 2006, with the following cast:

WEST   Robert Glenister
DRAYCOTT   Roger Lloyd Pack
WALLY   Jerome Flynn
PATSY   Daniel Mays
LUE   Sally Hawkins

Director   Ian Rickson
Designer   Ultz
Lighting Designer   Johanna Town
Sound Designer   Ian Dickinson
Composer   Stephen Warbeck

Characters

in order of appearance

WEST, *forties*

DRAYCOTT, *forties*

WALLY, *forties*

PATSY, *twenty-five*

LUE, *twenty-ish*

The action takes place in an abandoned farmhouse in the centre of the forest of Dartmoor.

Act One begins in the dead of winter. Act Two begins in the previous winter. Act Three is the first winter again.

ACT ONE

Darkness. Distant shelling. Small-arms fire. Closer. All at once, overhead, the deafening cacophony of war. Just when it can't get any louder it fades into

Light.

Dartmoor. The heart of the frozen forest, on clenched, sideways land. Sheep. Far off, a dog barking.

A deserted, half-derelict farmhouse. Doors off. Stairs up.

A rat-gnawed armchair. Small table, with no chairs. A large axe waits by a giant inglenook fireplace. The fireback is a red-rusty circular saw. Dark windows look onto an area beyond; a concrete-floor utility room, in which stands a mangle, a piece of red canvas protruding from its jaws like a lapping tongue.

From an overhead drier hangs a black woollen suit, waiting.

Suddenly, warplanes burst over, looming, shuddering. The full blaring cacophony of… It passes, back to a rumble in the distance.

Blackout.

Lights.

WEST *stands wearing the woollen suit.*

A brace of duck hangs in the kitchen, where the suit was.

WEST *takes a bottle of wine and pulls the cork. He places it on the table, with three glasses.*

WEST. Dolly. Din Dins. Dolly. Din Dins. (*Goes to the cupboard. Opens a tin of dog food.*) Din Dins, Dolly. Dolly! DOLLY!! DIN DINS.

Puts it in a bowl, carries it to the door.

DOLLY. DIN DINS. DIN DINS. DIN DINS.

Nothing. He cocks his head. The planes approach. As they scream over, he opens his mouth wide, as if to…

Blackout.

Lights.

WEST. *Opposite him,* DRAYCOTT.

DRAYCOTT. Sorry to bother you. (*Pause.*) I was just passing. I heard a din. A man it was. Top of his lungs. Yelling his bonce off. Did you hear it?

WEST. The dog's gone off.

Pause.

DRAYCOTT. The little fella. I seen him. Oftentimes, I'm up this way, early morn. He's gone off, you say?

WEST. She.

DRAYCOTT. I see. Bitch, is it? You had her done? You've got to watch 'em, bitches. If she's ripe. Out there looking for it, no doubt. You want to watch that one. She'll come home got.

WEST. What do you want?

DRAYCOTT. I was on my way over Okement Foot. They're gassing the badgers. It was on the radio. There's a mighty sett down Okement Foot. Been taking hens. Pheasants. All the way from here to Dolton. They got coughs too. Hacking coughs. The Government's had enough. They're sending a team in. Experts. What do you say? Eh? You want in? He's not far. Three, four mile, across the fields. He's a mighty sett. An underground city. Might be worth it. Might be something. Can I tempt you? What do you say?

WEST. I'm busy.

Pause.

DRAYCOTT. Oh. Well, that's that. If you're busy. Say no more. If a man's busy… (*Beat.*) I had a fight with a badger once. Wphew! It's a long story. Don't go there. Lost three pints of blood to it. And a nipple. By the way, you haven't got any Dettol, have you?

WEST. What?

DRAYCOTT. I fell yesterday. In the dark. I've chipped my hip. He's tightening. The skin's broke. There's a flap of sorts. I was thinking of staunching the pain. Dettol's my best bet. Itches. Stitches, palsies or gout, Dettol's the boy. You wouldn't keep a supply, would you? Any linament? Oinment, what have you…?

WEST. No.

DRAYCOTT. Sprays? Unguents?

WEST. I've got no ointments. I've got no sprays. I can't help you.

DRAYCOTT. No harm asking. I'll just have to keep him mobile.

WEST. Why don't you do that?

DRAYCOTT. Exactly. I will.

WEST. Better not stop too long. He might seize up.

DRAYCOTT. You're not wrong.

WEST. Get infected. Gangrenous. Then where would you be?

DRAYCOTT. Don't. They'll lop me to pieces. Butchers they are, with the likes of me. Before I know it I'll be in three bin bags and down the chute. By the way, is it still convenient?

WEST. Is what convenient?

DRAYCOTT. The arrangement.

WEST. What arrangement?

DRAYCOTT. Have I got this wrong? About… about the porch. I don't want to be a pain. I won't make a mess or a smell. I'll be gone at first light. Like I was never there.

WEST. Yes.

DRAYCOTT. That's awful kind. There won't be a trace. Above all, there won't be no mess nor smell. You'll never even know I was –

WEST. No. I mean Yes. Yes I do mind.

Pause.

DRAYCOTT. Oh.

WEST. It's not convenient. It's not convenient at all.

DRAYCOTT. Oh dear. I've got this wrong.

WEST. Come back tomorrow.

DRAYCOTT. I see. You're busy. Say no more. You're expecting someone. Is that a drop of brandy wine I see? I bet he's a vintage. Is he a nice drop? French, is he?

WEST. It's none of your business. (*Beat.*) Just stay back for one day. You come back tomorrow, I'll have something for you.

DRAYCOTT (*of the brace of duck*). I noticed them. They're beauties, they are. Full in the breast. Say no more. I'll stay back. You won't hear a peep. In fact, I'll start right now.

WEST. Why don't you do that?

DRAYCOTT. It's a juicy piece that. I know a recipe. I'm a good cook, me. I've cooked all over. I once cooked for fifty-six turf accountants. (*Beat.*) Well that's that. I'm off. And if I see that bitch of yours, I'll send her up the track. It's Okement Foot, if you change your mind. Those badgers don't know what they got coming. All warm in their holes. Bedding down. They don't know what's next.

Pause. He leaves. WEST *looks at his watch. He picks up the dog bowl.*

WEST. Dolly. Din Dins. Din Dins.

A plane screams over. He goes out the side door.

After some time, from the door out at the back, through the utility room, enter WALLY *in suit and winter coat. He is soaking, caked in mud from the knee down. He looks around. He looks at the wine.*

Enter PATSY, *in leather jacket. He is also caked in mud from the knee down. While* PATSY *speaks,* WALLY *regards the three chairs. The wine glasses. He goes over. Pours himself a glass. Sniffs it. Looks at it…*

PATSY. Just for the record, did I say, 'Don't rev it. (*Beat.*) Wally, don't spin the wheels. Just let her off, slowly. Let it bite.' (*Beat.*) Or. Did I say, 'Whatever you do, Wally, fuckin' floor it. Do a donut. In this boggy, soggy field. Dig me, Wally, a lovely big hole. Halfway to China.' (*Beat.*) That car's finished, mate.

It's a landmark. In fifty thousand years, they will come in their
hordes, gaze upon it and say, 'That was Wally done that. He
must have revved it.' (*Beat*.) Don't worry. I found my way up
here. Half a mile. No torch. Could have sworn I brung one.
Oh, there is it. In your hand. It's not like it's pitch black out
there. It's not like I completely lost the path after fifty yards,
ended up bumbling through brambles. Fucking stingers up to
here. It's not like I had to swim a considerable part of the way.
Quick question Wally. Do you know who Ozwald Boateng is?

WALLY (*sips the wine. Pause*). This coffee is cold.

PATSY. I'm not talking to you.

WALLY. This coffee is cold. (*Beat*.) This muffin is stale.

PATSY. I said. I'm not talk –

WALLY. This muffin's stale. It's dry.

PATSY. Did you taste it? It was like rock. Like a rock someone
sprayed brown. What do you want me to say? 'Ooh this is
lovely, Wally. Thank you for this poo muffin. Thank you for
this shit service-station coffee and rock-hard muffin. Thank
you for this delightful...' Did you bake it, mate? Did you bake
that muffin?

WALLY. The car's too hot.

PATSY. How much was it? Ninety pence? Go on. Just for a bit of
peace and quiet.

WALLY. It's too hot. My heated seat is stuck on hot.

PATSY. Is it your car? No. It's not. Try the passenger seat, mate.
It's like a fucking Turkish bath. I lost about a stone on the M4
alone.

WALLY. What *do* you like, Patsy?

PATSY. I like London, Wally. I like pavements. I like to walk out
the door and not sink up to my tits in primordial sludge. I don't
like sheep. I don't like Dartmoor. I don't like the country. It's
covered in shit.

Pause.

WALLY. You uptight, Patsy?

PATSY. Not me.

WALLY. You seem nervous.

PATSY. Why would I be nervous?

WALLY. You're not going to have one of your nosebleeds, are you? Make me look silly?

PATSY. I'm not nervous.

WALLY. You seem it.

PATSY. Well I'm not.

WALLY (*without moving*). Hello Mr West.

The light changes, behind in the utility room, revealing WEST *from the shadows. Only then, he moves forward.*

WEST. Hello Wally.

Pause.

WALLY. The door was open. There was a light on.

Pause.

WEST. The dog's run off.

WALLY. Has he?

WEST. She.

WALLY. Bitch, is it?

WEST. Muddy, was it?

WALLY. We lost the path.

WEST. You do what I say? Turn left at the hill.

WALLY. Thing is, yes. Thing is… There's loads of hills.

WEST. You turn right at the sheep.

WALLY. We did. We did. Thing is –

WEST. Turn left at the hill, right at the sheep, you can't go wrong. You want to watch that track up. It's treacherous. Each spring, when the snow clears, they find three or four down there. It's ramblers mostly. Last ones they brung up was a

couple of Welsh. Just married too. Skeletons they was.
Huddled together. He'd been Young Welsh Businessman of the
Year. What took you so long?

WALLY. The rivers are up. We got to Bridgetown, the road was
closed.

WEST. Bridgetown.

WALLY. The Bridgetown road was closed. Something to do with
the bridge.

WEST. The bridge at Bridgetown.

WALLY. It's been condemned.

WEST. The bridge at Bridgetown's been condemned? Well.
That's bad news for Bridgetown. That's a disaster for
Bridgetown, you'd have to say.

WALLY. We had to go the long way round. The car got stuck. It's
only a little two-seater.

WEST. A two-seater.

WALLY. We come up on foot from the road.

WEST. You see the fort.

WALLY. The what?

WEST. You pass by the fort? Iron Age fort. You can't miss it.
Been there since the Iron Age.

WALLY. That's just it. It was that dark –

WEST. But you can't have missed it. You go straight through it.
You must've blundered clean through it. Now you're all
muddy, you must be perishing. You want to pop yourself in
front of the fire. Don't stand on ceremony. Come in. Come in.
Make yourself at home. I see you found the wine.

WALLY. Yes.

WEST. Is she a nice drop?

WALLY. It is. It's very tasty.

WEST. He was always fond of a red. That was his tipple. Red. So
bloody hell, Wally.

WALLY. I know.

WEST. Bloody hell.

WALLY. Bloody hell.

WEST. Don't. Please.

WALLY. Three. Four years.

WEST. And the rest.

WALLY. Must be. Must be.

WEST. How've you been, son?

WALLY. Mustn't grumble.

WEST. Don't give me that.

WALLY. I toddle along.

WEST. Don't give me that. You're a picture of it. The very
picture.

WALLY. Nothing changes.

WEST. Bollocks, mate. You look ten years younger.

WALLY. Time flies.

WEST. Fuller, but younger. You're a breath of fresh air.

WALLY. Am I? Fuller though…

WEST. Bollocks. You're a fresh breeze and no mistake. That hair
lacquer? You been at the boot polish?

WALLY. Not me, Mr West.

WEST. You lacquering the mane. That Just for Men?

WALLY. Just for Ladies more like. From here down…

WEST. You dirty git. That's my Wally. That's my Wally.
Seriously, chum, you been at the cold cream. Got a stylist
now, have you? They had you in a tank? Up there in the
smoke. You're all at it. I bet you've got a dermatologist, you
gay prat.

WALLY. Cheeky sod!

WEST. That's more like it. So what is it then? Up there in the smoke. All the latest. You've had a face-peel. Admit it. You've been under the knife, you gay berk.

WALLY. You look well yourself.

WEST. Fresh air, Wally. No hokey-pokey. Hundred press-ups for breakfast. Squat thrusts for lunch. Star jumps for prayers. Pelting across fields. Come rain or snow. Not tucked up in some fucking clinic. Rigged up to some poncey piece of kit. Paying through the nose like a fucking woman. Look at you. Look at yourself. Look at yourself. I've missed you, Wally.

WALLY. I've missed you too, Len. Come here.

WEST. Where's Jerry?

Silence.

WALLY. He's not here.

WEST. I can see he's not here. Where is he?

WALLY. He couldn't make it.

WEST. Couldn't make it?

WALLY. Thing is… see. He couldn't come.

WEST. He couldn't come.

WALLY. No. So I brung Patsy.

Pause.

WEST. Who's Patsy? Who's Patsy, Wally?

WALLY. This is Patsy. Patsy, Mr West. Len, Patsy.

Beat.

WEST. Watcha, Patsy.

PATSY. Watcha, Mr West.

WEST. Who's Patsy?

PATSY. He's –

WEST. Patsy.

PATSY. Yes.

WEST. Who's Patsy, Wally? Who's Patsy?

WALLY. This is Patsy.

WEST. Is this him? Is this Patsy?

WALLY. Yes.

WEST. You're all dirty, Patsy. You're covered. You're worse than Wally.

PATSY. I'm a bit mucky.

WEST. You're a state, Patsy. You're filthy. We'll need to give you a bath. You cold, Patsy? You want to stand by the fire?

PATSY. Actually –

WEST. We spoke, Wally. We spoke on the phone.

WALLY. We did. We did.

WEST. You remember?

WALLY. You was in some phone box.

WEST. I tried to call Jerry. I couldn't get Jerry. So I called Wally. And what did I say?

WALLY. You said –

WEST. What did I say, Wally?

WALLY. You said –

WEST. I said bring Jerry.

WALLY. Len –

WEST. Jerry, Wally.

WALLY. Len –

WEST. Jerry, Wally –

WALLY. Len –

WEST. It's not pick-your-own strawberries, Wally. Come one, come all. Where's Jerry? I asked for Jerry.

WALLY. Len –

WEST. Where's Jerry, Wally? I asked for Jerry. Where's Jerry, Wally? Where's Jerry?

WALLY. Jerry's dead. (*Pause*.) He died. (*Pause*.) He's no longer with us. He passed on last March.

WEST. How?

Beat.

WALLY. He jumped in the Thames.

Pause.

WEST. He jumped in the Thames.

WALLY. Yes, Mr West. He jumped in the Thames.

Silence.

WEST. Why don't you stand in front of the fire, Patsy? Like Wally. Warm yourself. You're all mucky. That's it. (*Beat*.) It's nice and warm. Isn't it?

WALLY. It's toasty.

WEST. See? Get in there, snug next door.

PATSY. Thanks, Mr West.

WEST. That's better. Dry yourself off. You pair of twerps. That's better. Forgive me. I'm catching up. Patsy is –

WALLY. Right. Patsy's my…

WEST. Yes.

PATSY. I'm his –

WALLY. He's my stepson.

WEST. Are you his stepson? Are you his boy?

PATSY. Yes. (*Beat*.) Well no. Well yes. Sort of.

WEST. Are you or aren't you?

PATSY. Well –

WEST. Forgive me, Wally. I'm just catching up.

WALLY. See, the thing is Len…

PATSY. What Wally is –

WALLY (*interrupting*). Stay out of this, Patsy –

PATSY. What?

WALLY. What I'm trying to say is –

PATSY (*interrupting*). Wally's with my mum. He's seeing my mum. He's… you know… (*Beat.*) With my mum.

WEST. What you talking about? Wally's with Sarah.

WALLY. Well that's just it.

WEST. You're with Sarah. Lovely Sarah.

WALLY. See, that's just it, Len.

WEST. It was Wally and Sarah. Wally and Sarah.

PATSY. Not any more. Sarah left him.

WEST. Is this true, Wally? Has Patsy got this right?

WALLY. You know how it is, Len. Matters of the heart. Situations change. People drift apart. It was six of one –

PATSY. She was shagging some Turk.

WALLY. Half a dozen the other –

PATSY. She run off with some Turk. To Turkey.

WALLY. Shut it.

PATSY. Now it's Rita.

WEST. Who's Rita?

PATSY. My mum.

WEST. Since when?

WALLY. Two years March.

WEST. Why didn't you say? You're with his mum. Here I am. Eh? Here I am… He's your boy. This is your boy.

WALLY. Well –

WEST. You're his boy…

PATSY. Well see…

WEST. Why didn't somebody tell me. You'll have to forgive me. I'm catching up. Father and son. Man and boy.

WALLY. Sort of. Exactly.

PATSY. Yes and no. Not really but yes. Exactly.

WEST. Me and your old man, Patsy. Me and the old man. We go back. Has he told you? I bet he did. I bet he did. He told you, didn't he? What did he tell you? What did he tell you, Patsy? What did he tell you? Did he leave out the best bits? The dirty stuff. You don't know the half of it. I'll tell you stories'll put hair on your chest. You got hair on your chest, Patsy?

PATSY. I have as it happens.

WEST. I bet you have. So that's that. You're a hairy boy. Bloody hell, Wally. They grow up fast, don't they?

WALLY. Well see, I've only known Patsy for –

WEST. You turn your back for five minutes. It's horrifying. Hang on. You uncomfortable, Patsy? You uncomfortable in your soggy trousers?

PATSY. It's not as bad as it looks, Mr West.

WEST walks forward, stands in front of PATSY.

WEST. May I?

PATSY. What?

He kneels, maintaining eye contact. Slowly, he feels the bottom of the trouser.

WEST. Whoops-a-daisy. (*Stands.*) Someone's telling whoppers. Patsy's sopping, Wally. He's soaked to the bone.

PATSY. I'm fine actually.

WEST. Nonsense, Wally. You know what he should do? You know what you should do, Patsy? You should pop them off. Hang them in front of the fire. They'll dry in no time. Go on, Patsy. Pop your slacks off. Pop them off. (*Pause.*) Why don't you pop yours off, Wally? Show him how it's done. Pop them off, Wally.

Pause.

WALLY. They are quite muddy.

WEST. Muddy? They're caked. Come on, you prat. We'll have them dry in no time. Take your slacks off, Wally. Show him how it's done.

WALLY. Well then. That's that, isn't it?

Beat. WALLY *takes his trousers off.*

WEST. That's the way. Off they come. That's it.

WALLY *stands there, holding them.*

Now just like Dad, Patsy. Just like the old man. Follow the old man.

WALLY. Come on. Mr West is right.

WEST. There's no point stood there. We're halfway there.

PATSY *undoes his belt. He takes them off.*

That's the way. That's the way.

PATSY *tosses them to* WEST *who catches them. Pause.*

And the funny thing is, I wouldn't say you were that hairy after all. I'd say you were average. Nothing to write home about.

PATSY. Thanks, Mr West. I appreciate that.

WEST. So what do you think, Dad? Can he have a glass of wine?

WALLY. What? Oh. Yes. Of course. Sure.

WEST. Is that all right? I don't want to, you know.

WALLY. No. He likes wine. I think.

WEST. Patsy?

WALLY. Yes he does. Of course he does. He loves a drop. Don't you, Patsy?

WEST. You take after Dad, Patsy. Drop of the old red. You fancy a drop. Like the old man?

PATSY. If it's all the same, Mr West, I'll have a Scotch.

Pause.

WEST. You sure? You sure, Patsy?

PATSY. If it's all the same.

Pause.

WEST. Well that's that, isn't it? Wally's red. Patsy's a Scotch. Hang about, Patsy. I'll fetch you one. Don't you worry. I'll warm you up.

He takes WALLY*'s, and hangs up the trousers.*

So you came, Wally. You came.

WALLY. Yes we did. We did, sir. We did.

Silence. Exit WEST. *They stand there, side by side, trouserless, before the fire. A plane tears over. They both duck. Silence.*

PATSY. Nice man. What?

WALLY. 'I'll have a Scotch.'

PATSY. He's asked me a question. You said. You said in the car. If he asks you a question –

WALLY. Soda? Cherry? On the rocks?

PATSY. You said. Look him in the eye –

WALLY. Umbrella? Angostura bitters?

PATSY. – tell the truth. You said. Tell the truth. Well the truth is I fancied a Scotch.

WALLY. I've got a hairy chest.

PATSY. I can't drink wine, Wally. It gives me the hives. I go blotchy. What do you want me to do? Drink it down, have a fit on the man's carpet. How's that going to help?

WALLY. You tit.

PATSY. Wally –

WALLY. You prannock. You prannie. Keep your big mouth shut.

PATSY. It's just a Scotch.

WALLY. Keep your big gob shut.

PATSY. Okay. I'm sorry.

WALLY. You blundering tit.

PATSY. I said I'm sorry. I'm sorry. (*Beat.*) Daddy.

Beat. WALLY *glares.*

Well we sorted that out.

WALLY. What?

PATSY. I think he seems fine. I don't think he seems – (*Makes the mad sign with his finger to his head.*) at all. I mean, look at it. There's three of us here. Right now, he's the only one still got his trousers on. So go on.

WALLY. What?

PATSY. I don't want to rush you. It's just this seems a good time to ask.

WALLY. What? Ask what?

PATSY. The phone rings. 'Patsy. Ten o'clock. Outside Costcutters.' Passport. Toothbrush. Roll-on. Bam. I'm there. No questions asked.

WALLY. Patsy –

PATSY. M4. M5. Not a sausage. Not a squeak. Not a prob. Wally's in charge. The all-giving, all-seeing Wally. But now we're here, now we have this moment alone, in our pants... I don't need the blueprints. I don't need a slideshow. Just throw me a bone, Wally. What's going on? I mean, where do you want me, skipper?

WALLY. Shut your cakehole, leave this to me.

PATSY. See, that's just it, Wally. I was leaving it to you. And now I'm stood here in my pants. We both are. You look nervous, Wally. You're sweating. You are. Your top lip is shiny.

WALLY. Here we go.

PATSY. Your armpits are pouring. You've kicked right up. The glands have gone.

WALLY. Here we fucking go.

PATSY. You've done your trick. Your nervous trick. Like that barbecue. 'Oh my marinade's too salty.' You've gone up chum. You've done the Sweaty Wally.

WALLY. Fuck off.

PATSY. You have. I can smell you. Dead of winter and you're sweating like a rapist. (*Offering him a roll-on.*) You want to roll on, chum? I don't mind.

WALLY. Why don't you have a nosebleed?

PATSY. I'm not having a nosebleed, am I? But you're indisputably doing the Sweaty Wally. Anyone can see it. Mr West can see it. He can smell it. Take the roll-on, Wally. Don't be proud.

WALLY. You want to go back to washing cars. Eh? Rolling cabbies on the Great West Way? Don't bite the hand, Patsy. You're lucky to be here. There's five or six blokes –

PATSY. Here we go.

WALLY. Fuck off. There's six or seven blokes could be stood here in your shoes.

PATSY. I bet they're right jealous. Six hours in a car with Wally. Shit coffee. Poo muffin. I bet they're all crying into their pillows. Verily. For I am the chosen one.

WALLY. You watch your step –

PATSY. So what is my task, O Wally? Fight a Centaur? Steal Mr West's magic bow? What is the task I am so honoured to perform by you, O Wally? O Sweaty Wally?

WALLY. You keep it down, you bumboy. Watch your step, you squashy-headed nit. I'm watching you, bumboy. Don't bite the hand.

PATSY. Why are you sweating? Eh? Wally? What's he doing here? In the middle of nowhere. Throw me a bone, Wally. Throw me a bone.

WALLY. You want to wake up tomorrow? Get back in that car? Eh? You want to spend the rest of your life in some home doing jigsaws. Colouring things in. Wake up spread all over some field. I'll throw you a bone, Patsy. You don't know where you are. You Don't Know Where You Are.

PATSY. Please, Daddy. You're scaring us.

WALLY. Watch your step. Watch your step, son.

PATSY. You watch your step, son.

Pause.

Re-enter WEST.

WEST. Patsy, you're in luck. By chance. I keep half a bottle upstairs. Under the sink. I rub it on my tummy when I've got the flu.

PATSY. I'm sorry to be so much trouble, Mr West.

WEST. Don't be gay, Patsy. It's a pleasure. Now I warn you. It's not a malt. It's not some prim job's sat in a barrel since the First World War. It's not been filtered through six millennia of granite and peat nor sieved through Rob Roy's sporran. It's good old-fashioned, straight-up-and-down Tesco's Scottish Whisky. I like it that way. Let's see if you like it that way too.

PATSY. Let's.

He pours. Raises it.

WEST. A toast. To the newcomers.

Pause.

WALLY. To the newcomers.

WEST *regards* PATSY, *who knocks it back.*

PATSY. You know what that is, Mr West? That is extremely palatable. It don't taste cheap and nasty at all.

Beat.

WEST. So who's your mum?

WALLY. What?

PATSY. What?

WALLY. Rita.

WEST. Rita?

WALLY. You know Rita.

WEST. No I don't.

WALLY. Yes you do. Rita.

WEST. Who's Rita? (*Stops.*) Rita?

WALLY. Yes.

WEST. That Rita?

WALLY. Yeah.

WEST. I see.

Beat.

WALLY. Yes, Len.

WEST. You're with Rita.

WALLY. Yes, Len. Patsy's mum.

Pause. WEST *doesn't take his eyes off* PATSY.

Bugger.

WEST. What?

WALLY. Blast.

WEST. What's wrong, Wally? What is it?

WALLY. I've left my fags in the car.

WEST. Oh no.

WALLY. I only have.

WEST. You nit.

WALLY. I'm always doing that.

WEST. You berk.

WALLY. They're in the blessed glove compartment.

WEST. Wally…

WALLY. I am. I'm that big a tonk. (*Beat.*) I tell you what. You
want to fetch them, Patsy?

PATSY. What?

WALLY. You want to fetch my fags? My Lamberts. I've left them
in the motor. In the blessed glove compartment.

PATSY. You want a Benson? I got heaps.

WEST. Nothing doing. If I know Wally.

WALLY. I smoke Lamberts. Always have.

WEST. Always has. If I know Wally.

WALLY. Been smoking Lamberts for thirty years.

WEST. You could say he's a Lamberts man.

WALLY. They're in the glove compartment, Patsy. Failing that, there's a duty-free carton in the boot. In my bowling bag. Tucked inside my bowling bag. You want to fetch me a packet?

PATSY. It's half a mile.

WALLY. It's downhill.

PATSY. It's pitch dark.

WALLY. Take the torch. Please, Patsy. I would like it. Please, son. Fetch my fags. Fetch my fags. Fetch them. Fetch.

Pause. PATSY *fetches his trousers.*

WEST. A word of advice, Patsy. The path. It's deceptively slippy on the way back down. Off to the left is a sheer drop. It falls away to nothing. My tip: stick to the solid ground. And on the way down, keep 'em peeled. For the fort. It's very, very impressive. There's an information centre. It's got a big red button. You push it, this lady tells you all about it. She does. She fills you in. Tells you everything you need to know.

Pause.

PATSY. Well that's that. I'll just fetch your fags, Wally. And it seems what's more, I'll have an informative cultural experience on the way. (*Turns to go. Turns back.*) And Mr West? If I see your bitch out there, don't worry. Dogs love me. I've been around them all my life. I know what to do.

WEST *watches him go. Long silence.* WEST *stares at* WALLY. WALLY *breathes in deep like a pearl diver, surfacing.*

WALLY. Just smell that. Eh? Smell it. (*Pause.*) I bet you sleep like a baby out here. Eh? You watch me tonight. I'll be out like a light. I won't make the count. I'll sleep like the dead.

Silence.

What about you, Len? You sleeping well?

Pause.

WEST. You been to Dartmoor before, Wally?

WALLY. Once. Camping.

WEST. As a kid?

WALLY. It was awful. All night we've got these wild horses circling the tent. I never got a wink. All around us. Just… darkness and snorting and… hooves.

WEST. Nothing sleeps out here, Wally. All the rats. The foxes. The weasels. Knackered and starving and scared. You don't sleep out here, Wally. You fall asleep out here, something creeps up and eats you. (*Beat.*) So you came.

WALLY. I course I come.

WEST. When you was late I thought whoops. Whoops Wally. Old Wally. He's let me down. He's done this. (*Turns his back.*)

WALLY. Not Wally.

WEST. Eh? (*Turns back.*) He's done this. (*Turns again. Stays turned.*)

WALLY. Not this Wally, Len.

WEST. But you come. You did. Even after what happened.

Beat.

WALLY. What happened?

WEST. In your little tent, Wally. The hooves. (*Pause.*) Well, Wally. You must be devastated.

WALLY. Sorry?

WEST. No. You must be.

WALLY. Sorry. Len. What? Sorry. You've lost me.

WEST. Jerry.

WALLY. Oh. Tragic.

WEST. Awful.

WALLY. What a waste.

WEST. You must be devastated.

WALLY. Well, strictly speaking, Jerry was more your mate, Len.

WEST. Would you say?

WALLY. Strictly speaking.

WEST. Isn't that funny? I could have sworn it was more you and Jerry. I could have sworn it was more you and Jerry, rather than me and Jerry.

WALLY. Well we were the Three Musketeers, weren't we? You know… from… you know… from a distance…

WEST. The Three Musketeers.

WALLY. We were. We were the Three Stooges.

WEST. But you and Jerry, Wally? Eh? Always off in a corner. Giggling. Making each other laugh in the car.

WALLY. I'd say we were more the Three Stooges, Len. And I think each you know… each Stooge, for example, as it were… was equal. Not equal. I'm not saying that I was, you know… Of course not. Not equal. I'm not saying that… I mean you were, you know… you were… Groucho. Or whatever. The Marx Brothers. Except there was loads of them. The Three… you know… whatever. The Three… You know… Degrees. Not Degrees. That gives the wrong impression. Entirely wrong. Anyway. The Three. The Three… whatever. Exactly. That was us.

WEST. Not any more.

Beat.

WALLY. No, Len. No. Not any more.

Pause.

WEST. Here. Eh? You, me and Jerry? Eh? You, me and Jerry.

WALLY. Don't.

WEST. Here, do you remember…

WALLY. Yes, Len?

WEST. Talking… Do you remember – (*Starts to laugh.*)

WALLY. Yes, Mr West?

More laughter.

Yes, Len…?

WEST. Wales.

WALLY. Bloody hell.

WEST. Barry Island.

WALLY. Bloody hell.

WEST. Eh?

WALLY. Bloody hell.

WEST. Eh?

WALLY. Stone me. I'd clean forgot.

WEST. Me, you and Jerry. In those chalets.

WALLY. My honeymoon. With Sarah.

WEST. Sarah.

WALLY. Bloody hell. Barry. That was a party.

WEST. The whole bank holiday. No hold barred. Jerry brung that stripper.

WALLY. You brung that coloured bird.

WEST. What was her name?

WALLY. Bahar. Bazzar. Bazzer. Ree. Bazree. ReeBoz.

WEST. Me and Jerry shared a chalet. A thousand and one nights, Wally.

WALLY. An era. In bunks. All over. Scotland.

WEST. York. Cleethorpes.

WALLY. Cork. Amsterdam.

WEST. Bromsgrove. Chorleywood.

WALLY. Hove. That Portakabin in Hove. The three of us. For ten days. Waiting.

WEST. Shitting in a bucket. Next week, we're in Claridge's.

WALLY. All in cummerbunds. Like it's the Oscars.

WEST. Like it never happened.

WALLY. Like it never happened. The Oscars. Exactly.

WEST. Shitting in a bucket. Bang. We're in Claridge's.

WALLY. Beluga. Dom Pérignon. Birds in the room.

WEST. You know what I remember. If I had to pick one, and take it with me. (*Beat*.) Highbury.

WALLY. What a day.

WEST. That day.

WALLY. What a day, Len. What a day.

WEST. In that box. It weren't the celebrities. It weren't the personalities. It was the light.

WALLY. The light.

WEST. The light. Coming right in, across the fans, onto us.

WALLY. Champagne light. Champagne.

WEST. You're in a blue suit. Jerry's in black.

WALLY. You was in a cream three-piece. You stood up the whole game at the front of the box. Ramrod straight.

WEST. That singer.

WALLY. The singer, she put her hand on your buttocks. I saw.

WEST. You don't miss a trick.

WALLY. You dirty bastard. The birds. Tongues hanging out.

WEST. How many cream suits did I have?

WALLY. It had to be ten.

WEST. Ten suits. All of white.

WALLY. No one could touch you. A lean man. All gristle. In a room. To stand a man down. Staunch. Staunch in a pinch. A flinch. Clinical. Blink. It's happened.

WEST. New York.

WALLY. Fuck me. I taught you to skate.

WEST. In Central Park. I can see us now. You, me and Jerry.

WALLY. We're on the ice.

WEST. You'd won medals.

WALLY. I was a champion skater. As a boy.

WEST. You taught us to skate.

WALLY. It was the least I could do. I walk in one day. I'm a kid.
In the club.

WEST. You can't look left or right.

WALLY. I'm shaking.

WEST. Sweating.

WALLY. They're going to eat me alive.

WEST. Your heart's doing this…

WALLY. Sixteen years old.

WEST. Who puts out a hand.

WALLY. Who takes me under their wing. I'm not proud. Without
you, Mr West, I'm a smudge somewhere. On an apron.
Washing up in some caff. Fifty-pence bets. A cheap
gravestone.

WEST. The Three Musketeers.

WALLY. Exactly, Len. That's who we were. *That's* who we were.

WEST. Who saw him jump?

WALLY. What?

Beat.

WEST. Did you see him jump, Wally? Who pulled him out? One
word to describe Jerry what would it be? Morose? Unstable?
Haunted? Desperate? Forlorn? Who saw the body? Did you
see the body? Did you see him jump in the Thames?

WALLY. Len –

WEST. You taught him to skate.

Pause.

WALLY. It's been a hard few years, Len. Everything's changed.
London is awful. You get a day off, go to the seaside, catch a
train… you can't get away. You never can. It's dark, Len. You
don't know what's next. You don't know what next.

WEST. But *you're* still here, Wally? *You're* here. *You* never jumped in the Thames.

Beat.

WALLY. Week ago, I'm sat in the doctor's, doctor in front of me, he's holding my bollocks, I'm thinking this is it. I've got cancer. Bollock cancer. My mobile rings. What do I do? Even if I could, it's some weird code. They don't call back, it's a wrong 'un. It's a wrong number. Two days later, I'm at a confirmation, it's on vibrate. I get out, I've got seven missed calls. One number. Same number. Same weird, wrong number. But I've got this sixth sense. I go outside. Press redial. It just rings and rings. I don't know it's a fucking phone box, in some field. I'm up half the night, pressing redial, don't ask me why, I've got this sixth sense. This fucking shepherd picks up. This farmer. I'm on *The Archers*. Non capiche. Not the first word. I hang up, phone directory enquiries. It's the West Country. Somewhere on Dartmoor. My hair stands up. I just think, it must be. It must be. (*Pause.*) I've sat there for two days, by my bed, Pot Noodle, mobile charging, five chunks, just staring at it. Not moving. Two days. Waiting. Waiting. (*Pause.*) Bam. Rings once. Once. (*Beat.*) 'Hello Len.' 'Hello Wally.' 'I need help, Wally. I want to come back. I want to come home.' (*Pause.*) 'What do I do, Len? I'll do anything.' (*Pause.*) You go through Bridgetown. Two miles past. Stop. Some gate. Some red gate. Keep walking. Where? Into the darkness. Into the fucking black. (*Pause.*) You're right. I *am* here. You said come. I *came*.

Beat.

Re-enter PATSY. *Pause.*

WEST. I see Patsy's back.

WALLY. Watcha, Patsy. What happened? You're all muddy again. Look at you. It's a long way down. And in the dark. You lose your bearings?

WEST. You all right, Patsy? You find your way back all right, Patsy? You stick to the path? You do what you was told?

WALLY. How'd you get on?

WEST. You see the fort? Eh? You see it this time or did you miss it again?

WALLY. Yeah… you uh… You see the fort?

WEST. Eh? Patsy? Did you see it? Did you see the fort?

PATSY. Yes. Yes. I saw it.

WEST. It's breathtaking, isn't it? Were you impressed?

Pause.

PATSY. It's nice. It's a nice fort. It must have been an extremely impressive structure in its day. Very imposing. And very atmospheric. And, I mean, I'm no expert, Mr West. But anyone can see they've built it in the wrong place.

Beat.

WEST. What's that, Patsy?

WALLY. Patsy?

PATSY. Don't get me wrong. It's a cracking fort. It's just in the wrong place.

WEST. The wrong place…

WALLY. Here we go.

PATSY. I'm just saying. Yes. It's up high. Yes. It's on high land, overlooking the river, that's all textbook, textbook fort placement. See the enemy coming from miles. But they've bodged it. See, if it was me, I'd a have carried them rocks up another two hundred yards. Up to the top of the bluff… See, the land slopes sharp, and just above, just beyond all them sheep, there's a natural spur to the bluff. It's got a three-hundred-and-sixty-degree panorama and twenty feet of sheer granite to scramble up. If they'd asked me, if they'd brung me in, I'd've said whack it up there. It's a bollocks getting all that granite up there, but you'll thank me.

WALLY. How long's it been there, Patsy?

PATSY. Two-and-a-half millennia, Wally.

WALLY. And it's still standing. It's still up. Two thousand years later, the walls are still up.

PATSY. Don't get me wrong, Wally. I'm not knocking the build quality. Anyone can see that fort is supremely well realised using unquestionably durable material. I'm just saying they

done it in the wrong place. (*Beat*.) See, Mr West. I done what
you said, I've gone to the information centre, and I've pressed
the red button, and the talking lady told me, she was very
informative, she said her fort was overrun in 250 AD by
marauding Picts. And I can see how they done it. They've
come bundling down off that bluff. They wouldn'ta been able
to've done that if the Iron Age blokes'd listened to me. You
whack your fort up on the bluff, there's no bluff to attack
from. You're on it. They'd still be there today. But no.
They've been lazy. Cut corners. Sure enough, they've got
mullered. They're yesterday's men. The sands of time have
washed over them. The rest is history. By the way, can I say
something, Mr West? Earlier, we touched upon a subject.
Namely, the subject of my mother.

WALLY. Patsy –

PATSY. It's okay, Wally. This won't take a minute. I said her
name was Rita, whereupon, in my opinion, you clearly
expressed astonishment.

WALLY. Patsy –

PATSY. Please, Wally. If I may. When you done this, Wally
suddenly remembered he'd left his Lamberts in the car. Now
Wally, as you outlined, loves his Lamberts. He's a pig for 'em.
Can't be more than three feet from a Lambert, or he starts
sweating. I bet if we frisked Wally right now, we'd find two,
possibly three packs of Lamberts secreted about his person.
(*Turns to* WALLY.) It's all right. Don't turn out your pockets. I
know why you done it. Steady the boat. Moving right along.
Well I'd like to move back if I may. To just before Wally sent
me out to fetch his Lamberts. To the subject of Rita. Rita and
Wally. My mum.

WALLY. That's enough, Patsy –

PATSY. Please, Wally. This won't take a minute. When Wally said
he was with Rita, you raised an eyebrow. Expressed a degree
of astonishment. Astonishment I took it, that Wally here would
be emotionally or otherwise associated with someone like
Mum, like my mother. Like Rita.

WALLY. All right, Patsy. That's enough.

PATSY. Can I tell you a quick story, Mr West? The other day, I'm
back home at my old mum's. I'm in the tub, when the front
door opens and in comes Wally, with Mum. They've been out,
they're a bit tiddly, in the hall. I'm in the tub. They don't know
I'm there. (*Beat*.) Wally says, I heard him downstairs clear as a
bell, he says, 'Rita, you are a good good woman. Without you,
I'm nothing. I'm just another stupid old saggy dog that's going
to die, rot and be forgotten.'

WALLY. When was this?

PATSY. And she says, 'Bollocks, Wally, you are an amazing human
being. You are a kind, strong, many-faceted individual, who
inspires and nourishes each soul you touch.' And Wally goes up.
Big heaving sobs. He says, 'Rita, you are an angel sent to protect
me. It's cold out there. It's cold. Hold me. Please hold me.'
(*Beat*.) Now, to imagine this story, you have to bear in mind
since you last seen Rita she's got new teeth. And she don't drink
shorts no more. She's got the teeth, some eyebrow lift what never
come off. New set of Bristols. Wally stumped for 'em. Don't get
me wrong. Still, Rita emphatically does not scrub up. She's still
got the sideburns. The shoulders. The big goalie hands. Plus, no
amount of sawing and stitching and hammering is going to
change what's underneath. Time spent with Rita still often has a
nightmarish quality. Wally's had to slap her down once or twice
in public. It's worked wonders. She's made him look a right prat
once or twice. A proper clown. And you've always got to watch
her. She'll go off like a rucksack. You can't give her a yard. Turn
your back for one minute, she's in the bucket cupboard with a
broom across the door. In that Chinese restaurant. With half the
staff. About sixteen Chinamen in a broom cupboard. They should
have rung Roy Castle. But then Wally's no church picnic. Ask
the birds. Proper ogre, once the door's shut. Right bedroom bully,
once the light's off. So what I'm saying is, I understand your
reaction, Mr West. But whereas most people would agree with
us, whereas most people agree Rita's a vicious, bitter moo you
wouldn't pork with a spacesuit on, Wally here don't share the
public's qualms. And the best bit, the bonus, is I get to spend
time with Wally. And time spent with Wally is golf, mate. It's
pure golf. On the way over here, he's pulled the car over, he
looked me in the eye and he's said, 'I don't want you to think I'm
soppy. I'm not being bent or nothing but I love you, Patsy.'

WALLY. Steady.

PATSY. 'I do. And I'll look after you.'

WALLY. Steady the bus.

PATSY. 'And I'm not being bent, but I love that Mr West. That Len – ' he said. Look. He's blushing now, like a woman, like a prat, but he said it, on the M5. 'It don't matter what he's done. Why he's out in the cold. I'd go to the Moon for that man. To the Moon.' (*Beat*.) I just want to say… Thank you, Wally. Some fathers wouldn't. Some would just leave you in the dark. Not you, Wally. And also to say, and *I'm* not being bent, but ditto. I love you too. And you love Mr West. And Mr West, I don't doubt, you know, eh? Eh? I bet? Eh? You know? Eh? So here we are. Eh? Men who love each other, but who are not benders. Here's your Lamberts, Wally.

He gives them to him. Long silence.

WEST. Why don't we sit down? Eh? Patsy. Come in. Come in. Come and sit down.

PATSY sits in the armchair. The others stay standing.

You want some more wine, Wally?

WALLY. Lovely. Lovely drop.

WEST. Scotch, Patsy?

PATSY. I won't if it's all the same, Mr West.

WEST. You sure? There's plenty.

PATSY. It's extremely kind. No.

Pause.

WEST. I want to apologise.

PATSY. What?

WEST. I didn't mean to cast aspersions. I'm sorry if I seemed rude. I've been out of the loop. I'm catching up.

PATSY. I understand, Mr West.

WEST. The last thing in the world I want to do is offend you. Not when we've just met.

PATSY. Thank you, Mr West.

WEST. I hope there's no hard feelings.

PATSY. None whatsoever.

WEST. Are you sure?

PATSY. Certain.

WEST. Good. Have we cleared that up?

PATSY. I believe we have.

WEST. Good. Because I need to clear something up too. Something from earlier. Something you said.

Silence.

PATSY. Yes, Mr West.

Pause.

WEST. It's about the fort.

PATSY. The fort.

WALLY. The fort.

WEST. Yes. The fort. Earlier, I said when you're on the way down, Patsy, why don't you stop and take a look at the fort. And you said you would. And you did. And when you come back, you said in your opinion, it's in the wrong place.

Beat.

PATSY. Yes, Mr West.

WEST. It's in the wrong place.

PATSY. Yes.

WEST. That's what you think.

PATSY. Well... Yes.

WEST. You're sure?

PATSY. Well... Yes.

WEST. You're absolutely one hundred per cent certain that that fort is in the wrong place?

Pause.

PATSY. Well. Mr West. If you stood on my chest. I hope I haven't offended you. I'm sorry if I have. I certainly didn't mean to. I mean. At the end of the day. It's a fort.

Pause.

WEST. You said you went to the information centre.

PATSY. Yes, Mr West.

WEST. You pressed the big red button. You got the speaking lady.

PATSY. That's right, Mr West.

WEST. You listened to what she had to say. About the fort.

PATSY. Well yes, Mr West. You said to. So I did...

WEST. You listened to her. Like I said.

PATSY. Yes, Mr West. Like you told me to.

Pause.

WEST. What year was the fort built? (*Beat.*) When was the fort built, Patsy?

PATSY. Let's see. I think she said circa 600 BC.

WEST. 600 BC.

PATSY. Yes. Wait. No.

WEST. Yes. Wait. No.

PATSY. I'm not sure.

WEST. You're not sure.

PATSY. It depends what you mean.

WEST. It's a simple question. When was the fort built?

PATSY. Well. It's tricky actually. See, the present Iron Age fort was built in 600 BC. But the speaking lady said that fort's built on the foundations of an older fort, which dates back to Mesolithic times. That's approximately 6000 BC. So it depends.

WEST. How big was the fort? What were the fort's dimensions?

PATSY. Well. The main keep is eighty yards in diameter. So it covers roughly one acre in modern terms.

WEST. What did the fort contain?

PATSY. Lots of things.

WEST. Like what?

PATSY. A granary. A smithy. An earthwatch, the chieftain's house and the citizens' dwellings.

WEST. How many dwellings?

PATSY. Twenty-five.

WEST. How big were the dwellings?

PATSY. Each dwelling was twelve to fifteen feet in diameter.

WEST. When they dug it up. What were the main archeological finds?

PATSY. Nothing special. Usual stuff. Swords, spears, axes, fish hooks. Clay pots. Arrowheads.

WEST. Nothing special.

PATSY. What do you mean? Oh. Yes. There was one thing.

WEST. What?

PATSY. A single white-flint hand axe of Iron Age workmanship.

WEST. What's Dartmoor made out of?

PATSY. Granite. Granite on molten magma.

WEST. When did tin mining begin in the area?

PATSY. The Bronze Age. What plant covers sixty per cent of Dartmoor?

WEST. Heather.

PATSY. Which way does the entrance of the fort face?

WEST. South. Towards?

PATSY. Arrowfleet. Why?

WEST. The grazing grounds. So it overlooks the grazing grounds. What stands to the west?

PATSY. A burial mound. A megalithic graveyard.

WEST. What stands to the east…?

PATSY. To the east is a stone circle. How big is it?

WEST. Eighty feet across. How many stones?

PATSY. Sixteen granite stones. How big are the stones?

WEST. Between ten and thirteen feet high.

PATSY. How heavy are the stones?

WEST. Smallest is three tons.

PATSY. The biggest is twelve tons.

WEST. What was it used for? What was the stone circle used for? (*Pause.*) What was the stone circle used for?

PATSY. I… (*Pause.*) Hang on. (*Pause.*) Wait…

Pause.

WEST. When did you decide to come? (*Pause.*) How long did you think about it? Have you got the stomach for this, Patsy? Not just the stomach. The kidneys. The lungs. The neck. The teeth. The skill. The knowledge. In your bones. In your fingernails. In your teeth. It's not just front. Muscle and front. Nerve and bluster. What are you made of, Patsy? What are you made of?

Silence.

PATSY. Sacrifice. (*Pause.*) The stone circle was used for sacrifice. (*Beat.*) Human sacrifice.

Silence. PATSY*'s nose starts to bleed.*

WALLY. Patsy –

PATSY. It's all right.

WALLY. I'm sorry, Mr West. Patsy.

PATSY. I said… I said it's… I… I get… I got… I get these… It's nothing… I… It's…

He sits there, letting it bleed.

WEST. It's your turn, Patsy. It's your go.

PATSY *wipes his nose. He has blood on his shirt. Silence.*

PATSY. Who's the girl? (*Pause.*) The one upstairs.

WALLY. What?

Pause.

PATSY. Who is she?

WALLY. What you talking about, Patsy? You not been upstairs.

PATSY. I know. But she's up there. I saw her. Coming back up the path. She's in the window. Looking out. Not moving. Just staring down. I waved to her. Who is she? Who's the girl?

Silence.

Blackout.

End of Act One.

ACT TWO

The dead of winter. The previous year.

The farmhouse is even more desolate and derelict. Many floorboards are broken. Someone has had a bonfire in the middle of the room. Rats dart about.

WEST *stands motionless to one side. He is filthy, cold, as if he has been sleeping rough for months.*

Enter DRAYCOTT *from the back.*

DRAYCOTT. It's just like I said, mister. You're a lucky man.

> *Pause.* DRAYCOTT *removes something wrapped in greaseproof paper from his pocket. He unwraps it.*

> I've been over Chagford. They love me at that butcher's. Sniff that. Get the beauty of it. That's fresh killed, that is. That was snuffling around only this morning. You had heart? He's good gear. Good for the blood. And the other. I don't mind sharing. And you look like you could use a feed. So what do you say? Are you in? (*Breaks sachets of salt and pepper.*)

WEST. Thank you.

DRAYCOTT. Pig's the best. And this is fresh. You won't get finer in Buckingham Palace. I've cooked all over the West Country. Pubs. Rugby clubs. Newton Abbot Racecourse. I once cooked for eighty-six estate agents. A good fresh piece, get the pan hot. Onions, carrot, bit of butter. You wouldn't have an onion on your person, have you?

WEST. No.

DRAYCOTT. A carrot?

WEST. No.

DRAYCOTT. Butter? (*Beat.*) Not to worry. (*Spits in the pan, tosses the hearts in, whole.*) Oh yes, you're very lucky I was in. I'm usually out, on my rounds. Mr Darling kills on Mondays. So, I'm in there early, acting the nag. Jabber away,

touch the meat, pick up the knives. They get jumpy, Hey
Preston, they bung me a trotter. A piece of liver. A heart or two
just to piss off. I pop up all over. Princetown. Two Bridges.
Dartmeet. Fruit shops are good. There's a baker in Ashburton
who'll pay me two quid just to fuck off. Newsagents. Walk in.
Start gibbering. End of the world. That's a Yorkie. Couple bags
of crisps. Just once a fortnight, mind. You can't take the piss.
But the baker's a soft touch. Try it. Be my guest. You got to
time it, see. Watch for a hour or two, wait till they're chocker,
lunchtime's good, right when they're rushed off their feet, then
bundle in, start licking the walls. Works every time. But don't
go in Darling's. That's mine. You hear? I don't want to hear
you've been in Darling's. I hear you've been bothering Mr
Darling, I'll be on the warpath. I'm serious. You set foot near
the place, I'll have your guts. In fact I've made a decision. It's
best you steer clear of Chagford altogether. Stay back. They
know me over there. (*Beat.*) Here. Do you know what I
thought when I saw you? Can I? I said to myself, there is a
capital man. He's from up there. The capital. A mile off. They
stand different, Londoners. He's seen it. He's been around it.
He's been in airports all over the world. You wouldn't think to
look at him, but I can see it. I can see through things. And look
closer. He's got good hair, also. And teeth. It's all about the
teeth and the hair, when you get down to it. (*Pause.*) What was
I saying? What was I just saying when I come in? What was I
talking about?

WEST. Badgers.

DRAYCOTT. Was I? Really?

WEST. Yes.

DRAYCOTT. Why?

WEST. I don't know.

Pause.

DRAYCOTT. Exactly. Badgers. Bastards. Never mess with a
badger. I had a fight with a badger once. I'm coming home
from The Feathers, full moon it was, and I'm taking a shortcut
across Fletcher's Field. I stop in this clearing and there he is.
Big lad. Stripy. I've seen him before. I'm good with faces. I'm
a demon. Previous June I've lugged a tree trunk at him. Now

he's back. And he's brung two mates. Now I'm a good talker, I could talk my way out of most things, but they're not having it. Their backs are up. You can smell it coming. I got no choice. So I stand as big as I can, and I bellows, 'Right. Let's have it you stripy cunts.' Big mistake. He's on me in a flash. And his chums. I was in bed for a month. Lost five pints of blood to it. And two toes. They should stamp them out. But they better do the lot, cos I'm here to tell you, the badger bears a grudge. (*Beat.*) You get to know the ropes, you'll like it down here. But steer clear of Chagford. And Ashburton. Absolute shithole. Last June I've gone over there to see if I could get a game. Cricket this is. I know the skipper. He's an old friend. Runs Specsavers in Ashburton. All right Skip, any chance of a knockaround? Nothing doing. Full up, he says. Fair enough. Week later, I'm strolling in the park and I see they're playing. The cricketeers. So I go over and I cannot believe my fucking eyes. (*Beat.*) They've got a girl at short midwicket. Ten years old. I've marched straight out to the wicket and had it out with the skipper. I've not been rude. I've got a case. That skipper's gone out of his way to humiliate a man who could put on thirty or forty without breaking a sweat. In the end, they called the police. I had the last laugh. By the time they got me off it was chucking it down. I showed them. And I never left it at that. All season, every home game, I'm there, on the boundary, when this skipper pads up, I've got the *Telegraph* rolled up… 'Oy, you fat bender.' 'You great big goggle-eyed cunt.' Now that's not me. Normally. And whoever it was chucked a breeze block through Specsavers, that weren't me neither. I walked on that one. Get some CCTV, you bastards. Pay your fucking taxes. They're all vicious, vicious people, over Ashburton. Which is odd because it's the drier side of the moor. Here we go. Here we go.

WEST. What?

A plane tears over, shaking the walls.

DRAYCOTT. Every fifteen minutes. I went down there, to the base to complain. Turns out the bloke on the desk, he can't do nothing about it. It's a trig point, he says. Says all the planes, the RAF, choppers, fighters, bombers, they roar out over the forest and turn left over the fort. It's a landmark, see. Trig point. We're losing the war, mate, meanwhile you're back home, scaring the shit out of sheep. Are you all right? You look like you're shivering. You want to get near this warm, mate. You want to come a bit closer.

WEST. Who owns it?

DRAYCOTT. Who owns what?

WEST. This house.

DRAYCOTT. What you talking about it? That's cheek, that is. That's royal cheek. *I* own it, mate. This house is *mine*. You're my guest. You're enjoying my hospitality. What did you think this was?

WEST. I'm sorry.

DRAYCOTT. You wouldn't believe it but when I first got here this place was crammed full of filthy stinking animals. Rats. Dogs. Weasels. Vagrants. The Unemployed. Deviants. Deserters. The Depressed. I didn't hang about. I used my military training. We're getting there. This'll be a home again. Slowly slowly, catchy monkey. (*Takes the frying pan off.*) That's it. Not a moment more. Here. Get the beauty of it. Smell that. Smell that.

He does.

Nope, I've fucked it. I've burned him. He's useless he is. Absolutely pointless. You need butter. And onions. And you sorely need that carrot. Not to worry. (*Tosses it away.*) I've got back-up. (*Whips out two bags of crisps.*) Smoky Bacon or Farmhouse Cheddar? Here you go. (*Throws one.*) You know I could use a man like you.

WEST. How?

DRAYCOTT. Help me do this place up. A lick of paint here and there. Fix that chair. Put in units. Get this place back to glory. I'll strike you a bargain. I know someone with access to whitewash. And I know another fellow's got a mattress. It's practically new. You give me a hand, tarting her up, keeping the riff-raff back, it's yours. You and me could go over there and bring it back. It's about six miles. It's a two-man job. We could lick this place into shape. What do you say? You and me. Are you in?

Pause.

Enter a young girl, LUE. *Young. Small. Icicle-thin. Lipstick. A small army rucksack on her back. In a mac, with high heels, holding two old plastic shopping bags in one hand, and a hat box in the other, tied up with bailing twine.*

Pause. Another plane streaks over.

Oh here we go. Here we go. Ssh. Hang on. You'll like this. This is a good laugh. Hang about. (*Goes over.*) Well well well. How is Her Majesty? Did she pass the night pleasantly? No disturbances? No bad dreams? (*Bows low.*) May I offer my lowly salutations and enquire where we have passed this crisp, fine day? Where have you been these three days hence? And pray tell, what's the capital of Russia? Where's the English Channel? Who plays centre-half for Arsenal? What's two plus two? How many fingers am I holding up? Who wrote Beethoven's Fifth?

Silence. She doesn't react.

Here look. Look. Here look. Madam has new shoes. And handsome they are too, with fine stitching. Pray tell, hast thou been to Okehampton, for a spot of shoplifting? Or in the car park of Lidls, checking car doors. Or round the back of the sport centre on your hands and knees.

He laughs. He rounds on her.

I heard you banging about down here last night. Good folk are trying to sleep. I sent you out for firewood, you swan back in three days later with a new coat. New shoes. Where's the fuel, you dozy slut? Eh? You been over Nero's, aintch you? Stuffing your face with pills. Catching stuff, bringing it back. I tell you what, you need pills, love. Some for your head and some for downstairs. And some to open that gob. I tell you, it tries you, mister. And I'm a patient soul. But day in, day out. (*Looks to* WEST.) Watch this.

He mimics a spastic. Putting on a spastic voice.

'I've been over Okehampton. I've been shagging squaddies. They been buying me coats. I been riding with the Lord Mayor with sixteen stallions. I been to the finest parts of the world. I got ladies who run my bath.' (*Stops and laughs.*) Have a go. Ask her anything? Go on. Eh? Your Majesty. Can you do this? Follow along. Follow along.

He rubs his stomach and pats his head.

Can you do this?

He makes a fucking gesture.

I tell you… someone's dropped her on her head. Or they
bloody should.

He stands right in front of her.

Where's Mummy and Daddy? Eh? Did you get lost in the
supermarket? Where's Mummy? Where's my mummy? Last
winter it was, she shows up in the middle of the afternoon in
her scundies. I swear. It's nine below. She was blue. Been out
on the moor for days. Down the barracks no doubt. Came back
stinking like a bag of whelks. (*Winks.*) What's the capital of
Persia? (*To* WEST.) Have a go. She won't mind. But watch
your stuff. You think she bought that coat. Nothing doing.
What you got in your bag, missus? Eh? Sticky fingers. She has
a bath once in a blue moon. If you're gonna get hold of her
you've got to time it right. Then she'll suck you off for a
conker. I've never known the like.

He rounds on her again.

You better start pulling your weight or you're out of here. And
I'll see to it. Contribute. Muck in. I don't mind how. There's
more than one way to skin a cat, eh? Eh?

He laughs. He takes WEST *aside.*

Here. Are you ready? I've got half a bottle of Scotch upstairs.
She's partial. She's thirsty, if you know what I mean. What do
you say, eh? Here's the play. You keep her talking, I'll get the
juice, get it down her, Hey Preston. You won't believe it. Half
a mo. Just keep her busy. This is the one, eh? Watch this.
(*Heads off.*) I won't be a minute, princess, I'm just popping
upstairs to see to the plumbing. Talk amongst yourselves.

He goes upstairs leaving the two of them together. Silence.

WEST *sits with his crisps.* LUE *puts her bags down and goes
to the cupboard. She takes out some Ribena. She makes herself
a Ribena. She drinks it. She goes to her bag. Upwraps a
Yorkie. Eats a couple of squares. They keep catching each
other's eyes. Silence.*

Sheep. WEST *can't stand it any longer.*

LUE. Who are you?

WEST. No one.

LUE. You his friend?

WEST. I thought you never spoke.

LUE. Who said I never spoke?

WEST. He said you said…

LUE. I never said nothing.

WEST. No but… he said… he said you never spoke.

LUE. Of course I speak. I just don't speak to him.

WEST. Why not?

LUE. It goes without saying. Where'd you meet him?

WEST. Today.

LUE. Where was he?

WEST. In a field.

LUE. That's him. A word of warning. You know the way most
people have got a sweet side? He hasn't. (*Beat.*) He's all right.
He's old, in'e? He be lucky he makes it through the winter. He
cries in his sleep. And he knitted me a scarf once. He's a good
knitter. You wouldn't think it, but he can really knit.

WEST. Why don't you talk to him?

LUE. I used to. It didn't pan out. So I've sent him to Coventry.
And it's not far enough. He tell his story?

WEST. About the badger.

LUE. Not the badger. How he owns this place.

WEST. Yes.

LUE. Embarrassing, isn't it? Oh yes. He's got a dozen properties
in the area. He's got a portfolio. He commutes between here
and his private island.

A plane tears over.

That's him now. He's done one. He's gone to stink up somewhere else. Why are your hands shaking?

Beat.

You're from London, aren't you?

WEST. What?

LUE. I know you. I've seen you before. (*Beat.*) Lots of times...

WEST. Where?

LUE. Lots of times. Plymouth. Last spring. You was in the hostel. On Kerry Road. You was in front of me in the queue. They asked you who you was and you said you was from London. You said you was in business. Then over Hexworthy Bridge, first week of August... Out on the moor. You was trying to skin a rabbit. Then a week later, further up river, you was washing your feet on the bank. You had a little camp. Then in Okehampton a month ago. You were drunk out your mind. Screaming at the shoppers. Foaming at the mouth. They called the police but you ran. You ran off. That was you, that was. Then I saw you yesterday.

WEST. Where?

LUE. In the fort. You were sitting there. On the parapet. You was crying, muttering to yourself. I come close but I couldn't hear you. You looked frozen. I went off, into Okehampton. To the pictures, come back and you was still there. You'd stopped gibbering. You was just looking down at the land below as it went dark. Stock-still. Staring. And when I looked out the next morning, you was gone.

Pause.

WEST. I've seen you too.

LUE. I don't doubt it. I'm around.

WEST. About a month ago. On a bus in Ashburton. You were alone. Your face was cut. You had argument with the driver. He stopped the bus and chucked you off.

LUE. Have you been abroad?

WEST. What? Yeah. I've been abroad.

LUE. Where've you been?

WEST. Lots of places.

LUE. Have you got a passport?

WEST. Not on me.

LUE. All you've got on you's dirt, mate. I'm saying before. In London. When you was a businessman. It stands to reason. You went abroad, you had a passport. Did you have a passport?

WEST. Yes.

LUE. Did you fill out the form?

WEST. What?

LUE. What colour was it?

WEST. What?

LUE. What colour was it?

WEST. I don't remember.

LUE. Was it blue?

WEST. I don't remember what colour it was.

LUE. How big was it? How many pages? Did it fold out, like this?

WEST. I can't...

LUE. What? You can't what?

WEST. It was a long time ago. What's the matter?

LUE. I need help.

WEST. What you talking about?

LUE. Filling out forms. A form. I'm going away. I'm going abroad.

WEST. Where?

LUE. I got everything else. I've got suncream. And a hat. And sunglasses. And a towel. And a bikini. And a book. I just need to do the form. I just need to fill it out. Get someone to sign it.

Then I need to borrow forty pound. For the passport
application. Then there's the stamp. Then I need two hundred
pounds for the flight. That's the cost of the flight from Exeter
Airport. Also, I've got to get to Exeter, so I need bus fare.
What do you say?

WEST. I can't help you.

LUE. Why not?

WEST. I can't... I... I haven't got any money.

LUE. You said you was a businessman.

WEST. So what?

Beat.

LUE. Here. (*Takes out a form.*) This isn't the form. This is the
form you need to fill out the form. The form form is safe. The
form form's upstairs. This is the pre-form. The other one. The
orange one. Don't touch it. Your hands are filthy. You smudge
it, we're buggered. Here look. (*Reads.*) 'Section One. Form
C1. A. One. Please keep these Notes until you receive your
passport. Note 1a, subsection one – Birth after 31 December
1982 in the United Kingdom. Tick 'Yes' if you were born
after 31 December 1982 in the United Kingdom, or if you
entered the country on or before December 31 1989, or after
July 1 1992, unless a) you were already a temporary citizen in
which case refer to note 2a, subsection seven...' And I speak
English. That's their opener. That's their warm-up. I mean,
that's that. I'm staying put. I ain't going nowhere, am I? Wait
for it. (*Searches.*) This is the bit. Where is it? (*Reads.*) 'Note
5a, section three.' No, that's not it. Where is it? Here you go.
(*Reads.*) 'Section 12a, subsection 2ii should be signed by a
British citizen, or other Commonwealth citizen, who is a
Member of Parliament, Justice of the Peace, Minister of
Religion, Established Civil Servant, or... here we go...
professionally qualified person in the community, e.g.
Businessman, Doctor, blah blah blah, or a person of similar
standing.' See? I need someone from the community.
Someone they trust. Someone of standing. Now I was
thinking, if he was a businessman, or say, or a doctor, then he
can do it. Because I figure, he's not been out here long. They
probably don't know yet. The Government. They probably

don't know that he's gibbering in Okehampton Market. What do you reckon? What do you say?

WEST. I can't help you.

LUE. What?

WEST. I can't help you.

LUE. Why not?

WEST. I can't help you... I've...

LUE. I just need you to sign my photo. Sign the form. Read the notes. Say who you are. Vouch for me. I've got everything else. You help me, I won't forget it. You help me, that's that. I'm out of here. You can have my room. You won't freeze to death, out there in your fort. What do you say? Eh? What do you say?

WEST. I can't help you.

LUE. Why not? Why can't you?

WEST. Because I'm... I'm not the man you're looking for. I'm not from the community.

LUE. You said you was in business.

WEST. No I never...

LUE. You did. I heard you. You said you was. You said you was in business. Don't lie to me. Don't fob me off. I heard you. You said you was in business. A businessman. I need a businessman. Someone from the community. That's you. Are you from the community? Are you from the community?

WEST. I'm not a businessman. I'm not a doctor. I'm not from the community.

LUE. Well then who are you?

Beat.

WEST. I'm...

LUE. Who are you? Eh? Who are you? Who are you?

WEST (*loud*). I'M NOT FROM THE COMMUNITY! Okay? I'm not a business... I'm not a fucking businessman... I'm... I'm not... I'm not from the community... (*Pause.*) I just... I fell asleep.

LUE. What?

Pause.

WEST. I fell asleep. (*Pause.*) I… I was… I was… watching this
flat. For five days. I've not slept. For weeks. I was… I was
tired. I was… I just needed to… But I had to watch this… I'm
sat in this car… And I was so tired. I just… I just… I just… I
just…

LUE. What?

WEST. I fell asleep. I must have… I… I must. I… I… (*Pause.*) I
drove back… back to London. I drove… and… They… they…
they… shut me in a room. (*Beat.*) They gave me gin. Filled me
up with… Then these blokes come in. These two… They
snapped my thumbs. They broke my thumbs. They broke my
foot… with a sledgehammer. They burned me. Kettles of water
with… with sugar in, so it sticks. They… kicked me in the
bollocks till they… till they was pumpkins… Swallow petrol.
Bleach. Piss. Spunk. For days. 'Don't fall asleep, Len. Don't
doze off. You dozy cunt. Dozy baby.' Singing lullabies. Over
and over.

Pause.

You think that's horrible. I've done it. I've done it myself. And
worse. In rooms. To… To other people. You don't know 'em.
You just… They've… they've done… A decision's been…
you know… It's… It's… (*Pause.*) I can't help you. I'm not a
businessman. I'm not… I'm not from the community.

Silence.

LUE (*putting the form away*). I'm sorry. It wasn't you I saw.
It was someone else. I thought you was someone else.

She gathers her things and heads upstairs.

WEST. Look –

LUE. I'm sorry. I won't keep you.

WEST. Look. I'll…

LUE. I'm sorry. Forget it.

WEST. No, look –

LUE. Just forget it. I'll find someone…

WEST. Look… I'll look at… I'll look at it. I'll… your form. I'll take a look at it. You… you show me it, I might be able to… I might…

Silence.

LUE. It won't be for free. I'll give you something.

WEST. What?

LUE. I'll pay you. I haven't got money, but I'll pay you.

WEST. Look, I don't want nothing.

LUE. Listen –

WEST. I don't need nothing. I just…

LUE. Hang on –

WEST. I don'. Really. Please.

LUE. You don't know what it is yet. How do you know you don't want it if you don't know what it is?

WEST. Look –

LUE. You don't know what I'm offering. (*Holds up the hat box.*)

WEST. What's that?

Pause.

LUE. I found it. Out on the moor. If you help me, you can have it.

WEST. What is it?

LUE. You help me, it's yours. If you help me… She's yours.

WEST. She?

LUE. She's only small. Just been born. Two, three days old. You'll have to look after her. If you help me, you can have her. (*Pause.*) It's the room at the end. Overlooking the fort. Come when it's dark. Will you help me?

Pause.

Re-enter DRAYCOTT, *from upstairs.*

DRAYCOTT. Here we go. I keep for emergencies. I rub it on my chest when I've got the flu. Go on then. Cowboy-style. You not thirsty, love? Don't stand on ceremony.

LUE *drinks it down.*

There we go.

She drinks it down.

One more.

She drinks it down. She finishes the whole bottle. Gives it back to him, walks up to WEST. *Silence.*

WEST (*nods*). Yes.

LUE. Come when it's dark.

She turns. And leaves.

DRAYCOTT. What? What did she say? Oy. You talking now? Where you going, you filthy twizzler? Come back, you tart. Come back. We ain't finished.

She's gone.

She'll pay for that. That's good Scotch, that is. She owes me… the fucking neck. The brass… fuckin'… She'll pay for that. She knows 'n' all. She'll pay. When she's asleep. She'll pay sorely. (*Pause.*) What did she say, mister? Just then. What did she say? What did that little cat say?

WEST. She said…

DRAYCOTT. The minx. That little shag, what did she say?

WEST. She said she's seen me before.

DRAYCOTT. What? What's that lying tart on about? She's seen you before? Come off it. A man like you. A tart like that. Come off it.

WEST. She said she's seen me before. (*Beat.*) And I've seen you before.

DRAYCOTT. What you on about? Where?

WEST. Here. In this house.

DRAYCOTT. What you talking about? I never saw you here.

WEST. Yes you did. A few days ago. Monday it was. We sat in here. We played gin rummy.

DRAYCOTT. Gin rummy?

WEST. We played all evening. Gin. The cards are in that drawer over there.

DRAYCOTT. I never seen you before, mister. I'm a demon with faces. And I'd remember a game of gin. No danger. You owe me for the crisps. I… I show you human… I show you kindness. And the… and the… don't go into Chagford. And you can forget the mattress. And you owe me for the crisps. Go on. Get out of it. I changed my mind. I want you out of here. You hear me? Get out. Get out of it. Get out.

WEST. We sat in this room. A week ago. We played gin. We were drinking whisky. My glass. Every time it was empty. You filled it up. Just before dawn, I went outside, to piss. When I came back in, you were going through my bag. Rifling through it. You found something. I walked across the room, and took it from you. I told you who I was. I told you everything. (*Beat.*) The sun came up. It started to snow.

He regards DRAYCOTT.

Silence.

Blackout.

End of Act Two.

ACT THREE

The house as in Act One. The next morning. Sheep.

Enter PATSY *from upstairs. Freezing. He still has blood on his shirt. He looks around the place. He goes in the back and runs a tap. Comes back, wringing the shirt out. He spots the mangle. Goes over. He has no idea how to work it. He puts the shirt in. Starts winding. It gets stuck. He tries to pull it out and rips it in half. He finds a coat on the back of the door. He puts it on. He does star jumps to warm himself. Does ten press-ups. Another ten. He plays a few notes on the piano. It's out of tune. He lights a cigarette. He stops. Looks up the stairs. We can't see at what.*

PATSY. Hello there. I'm... I'm Patsy. (*Pause. Indicates the cigarette.*) I was just having my breakfast. You want one? (*Pause.*) Eh? You want a Benson then? Come on. (*Pause.*) Come on. That's it. You want one. You do, don't you? Come on then. Don't worry. I won't bite.

Enter LUE, *from upstairs.*

There we go. There we go.

He offers the packet. Slowly she takes one. She puts it in her pocket.

I saw you yesterday from the window. The one what waved. I was coming up the path last night, in the dark and I've looked up and... you saw me. Did you see me? On the path? I thought you did. Did you?

LUE. That's not your coat.

PATSY. Oh. Right. I had nosebleed. I get them sometimes... when uh... I washed my shirt and... well. You're in that end room, aren't you? Overlooks the fort. I'm next door. We're neighbours, you and me. How's your room? Is it warm? Mine's not. Mine's got no window. Someone's smashed it. And before you ask, it was a trifle. Truth is I've not slept. But

then I never slept yesterday. Or the day before. I've not slept
for weeks. Search me. When I do sleep, it's worse. But then I
don't need much, me. Never did. How's your bed? Is it warm?
I've not got a bed. I've got a pile of old rubbish. I've drawn
the short straw. (*Pause*.) We come down to visit a friend. Mr
West. Spend some time. Catch up. (*Beat*.) So are and him, you
know... So are you and him, you know...

LUE. He's my friend.

PATSY. Oh. I see.

LUE. We talk to each other. He's got this little dog I gave him.
We all sit together by that fire, or wherever, in my room.
(*Pause*.) But now the dog's run off. She's been gone for days.
So you're his friend too?

PATSY. Strictly speaking, I'm a friend of a friend. Stricter
speaking, I'm the stepson of a friend. But actually I'm not.

LUE. So why did you come?

PATSY. See, that's just it. I can't tell you. See, the way it works,
I'm in bed, my mobile rings. Someone says, 'Patsy, they'll
pick you up outside the Costcutters at ten o'clock. Don't bring
nothing.' A toothbrush. A credit card. (*Pause*.) You don't ask
questions. You don't want to put a foot wrong. Not one foot.
I'm not bothered. I'll go anywhere.

LUE. Have you been abroad?

PATSY. Once or twice.

LUE. Where have you been?

PATSY. Loads of places.

LUE. Holidays?

PATSY. Yes.

LUE. Business trips?

PATSY. One or two.

LUE. I'm going abroad. I've got my passport.

PATSY. That's nice. Where you going? Somewhere nice?
Somewhere hot.

LUE. That's right. Somewhere where it's hot all year. All summer, all winter.

PATSY. Lovely.

LUE. That's where I'm going. That's where I'm off to.

PATSY. Sounds lovely.

LUE. Yeah. But I can't go yet. See, my suitcase is broken. I bought this suitcase and it's cheap. It's a piece of crap. I put all my stuff in it, and the strap's bust. So I can't go yet. I've got to get a new suitcase. Then that's that. I'm off. Well it was nice to meet you.

PATSY. Likewise.

LUE. Goodbye.

Beat.

PATSY. Did you see me?

LUE. When?

PATSY. Last night. When you were at the window. When I waved to you. You were looking right at me. Did you see me?

Silence.

LUE. I suppose I must have.

PATSY. What do you mean?

LUE. I mean, I must have, mustn't I? Because I dreamt about you.

PATSY. What?

LUE. I dreamt about you last night. You were in my dream. It was definitely you. I can see you now.

PATSY. What happened?

LUE. I was walking down the path, down to the road. It was just getting light. And it was freezing cold, so I took the shortcut through the fort. I went into the main part. The main hall it is. The banqueting hall. Where they had the banquets. And it was freezing cold, and it was snowing. And there you was.

PATSY. What was I doing?

LUE. You was sitting on the parapet. You was staring out over the land below. You were stock-still. I went over, and when I got close, I touched your shoulder. You were frozen solid. Like a statue. Cold as stone.

PATSY. What did you do?

LUE. What could I do? I left you there.

PATSY. You left me?

LUE. Yes. But before I left you. I did something.

PATSY. What? What did you do? What did you do?

LUE. I kissed your cheek. It was frozen. But then… you opened your eyes. And you turned to me and smiled. And the next morning, I come out, and you were gone. Where you'd been there was just ripped clothes and blood. And bones.

Pause. Enter WEST.

WEST. Morning, Patsy.

PATSY. Morning, Mr West.

WEST. You sleep well?

PATSY. Not that well as it happens. We were just… we were just… you know… talking.

WEST. Oh yes. What about?

Beat.

PATSY. Holidays.

WEST. Holidays.

Pause.

PATSY. So where's this suitcase?

LUE. What?

PATSY. Your suitcase. You said it's broke. The buckle's broke. Perhaps I could take a look at it?

LUE. You sure?

PATSY. Why not?

LUE. I don't know. I can't give you nothing.

PATSY. I don't want nothing. It's just a buckle. Where is it? Where's the suitcase? I'll take a look at it.

Pause.

LUE. It's upstairs.

PATSY. We won't be a moment, Mr West.

PATSY *nods. They go upstairs.* WEST *looks up the stairs, fixed. Pause. Enter* WALLY *from outside. Behind* WEST.

WALLY. Up with the lark. Same as always. I've been for a walk. Bitter, it is. The ground's froze solid. You sleep well, Len?

WEST (*without turning*). You sleep well, Wally?

WALLY. Country air, isn't it? A right tonic. It was just like I said it would be. I've gone out sparko. I've woke up, it's like I've had a thousand nights' kip.

WEST (*up the stairs*). Where'd you walk then?

WALLY. I've just set off. I've gone for a ramble, me. The funny thing is, Len…

WEST. What's that?

WALLY. Call me a berk. Call me a tonk. I still can't find that blessed fort. I've looked everywhere. I'm thinking, 'Come on, Coker, it must be round here somewhere.' I've got completely lost. I end up down by this river. It's froze solid. I've stepped out on it and you know what's happened? Nothing. It's held my weight. I pushed off and I've slid clean across it. Did I tell you I used to skate as a kid? At Queensway. I've won medals.

WEST. Really, Wally?

WALLY. It's true. It's like riding a bicycle. I've skated clean down the river. Like a kid. Over the rocks. On my soles. By the way, there's good news.

WEST. What's that then?

WALLY. The car. Rita's car. Her little two-seater. I got Rita's two-seater out that ditch. Out that bog. See, with the freeze, with the temperature dropped, the earth's froze. I got the wheels to bite. I got traction, didn't I? I floored it, she come flying out. Now she's standing on the road. Ready to go.

WEST. You're back in business.

WALLY. We are. We are. We're ready to rock…

WEST. This time in the morning, not too much traffic.

WALLY. A following wind. We'll be home in no time. (*Pause*.) Is Patsy up?

WEST. He's upstairs.

WALLY. The dozy git. Is he asleep?

WEST. He didn't sleep.

WALLY. Did he not? That's a shame. Now he'll be grumpy all the way home. (*Pause*.) I was just thinking, Len. Can I give you a lift?

WEST. What?

WALLY. Can I give you a lift somewhere?

WEST. What do you mean?

WALLY. I just thought. The engine's running. Maybe I could give you a lift somewhere.

WEST. Where?

WALLY. Well, where do you want to go? Into town? Somewhere I can drop you. Ashburton. Exeter. Bristol. Swindon. Salisbury. Newbury. Reading. Home. (*Pause*.) It's been a while, Len. You could go up West. You could see a show. You could have dinner. Like a human. What do you say? Do you want a lift, Len?

Pause.

WEST. I thought you was a two-seater.

WALLY. We are. A two-seater. Rita's little two-seater.

Pause.

WEST. What do I have to do?

Pause.

WALLY. I said. I did. For the first year or two, mind your p's and q's. Just zip it. Watch. Clock what's going on. You know who likes jokes, I said. You know who likes that much chat. Birds.

He is. He's like a schoolgirl. An old washerwoman. Kids today. They've got no barriers. You can't teach 'em nothing. All triple-cocky. Got verbals to burn. I don't mind. I'll soak it up. But they've had a gut-full. They've had seconds. And thirds. So when I told them you'd rung, said Len's rung, they've said to me, they've said, 'Why don't you go and see him? See how he is. (*Beat.*) And when you go and see him, when you go down and see Len, why don't you take that little needler? Why don't you take that mouthy little bird.' He is. He's like a bird. A bird what you can't even shag. Although sometimes, you know. Just to shut him up. And at least now I won't have to listen to him moaning all the way home. 'My coffee's cold. My muffin's gone stale.'

Silence.

WEST. But –

WALLY. I can't make you, Len. I can't twist your arm. It's your decision. You want a lift? Back to London… Back home.

Silence.

WEST. GO AND WAIT IN THE CAR.

WALLY. You sure, Len? You don't have to…

Pause.

WEST. Go and wait in the car.

WALLY. That's the spirit. That's my Len. I'll tell you what? I'll be in the car, sunshine. And don't mention it, you prat. They'll be pleased as punch to see you. They'll be tickled pink. And you'll thank me for it. You'll see. You will, Len. You'll thank me for it.

He takes out a shiny black industrial bin liner.

Pop his head in here. They want to see it. (*Beat.*) I'll be in the car, Len. Ten minutes. Ten, then I'm off. If you want a lift… I'll be in the car. Ten minutes.

He turns. Then he turns back.

By the way, Len. This is… Look. About what happened… I just wanted to say… Well. What I'm trying to say is… (*Beat.*) Don't doze off. (*Beat.*) I know. I know. I'm just saying. This time. I know you won't. I know you'll do me proud. But don't. Eh? I know you won't. But don't. Don't... you know... Doze off. Don't make me come back up here. You've got ten minutes.

Beat.

Exit WALLY. WEST *is alone.*

PATSY (*off, upstairs. Comes downstairs*). Where's Wally? He's not in his room.

Pause.

WEST. You fix it, Patsy? You fix the suitcase?

PATSY. Where's Wally?

WEST. He's in the car.

PATSY. I see.

WEST. He's running the motor.

PATSY. Is he?

WEST. The ground froze. He's got it out. It's right as rain.

PATSY. That's good. (*Pause.*) So is he going back then? To London.

WEST. London. Yes.

PATSY. I see. Well. I better get down there then. You not coming along, Mr West?

WEST. See, that's the trouble, Patsy. It's a two-seater.

PATSY. Of course.

WEST. There's no room, see. There's only room for two.

PATSY. Of course there's not. Of course there is. I should have thought of that.

WEST. You should have, Patsy. You should have.

Pause.

PATSY. Well I better be off. Don't want to keep Mr Coker waiting.

PATSY *is shaking.*

He come in this morning. In the room. In the dark. He tells me. Why. Why he brung me. (*Beat.*) I'm their boy. They'll look after me. I'm in. I've just got to do one thing.

PATSY *takes out a black industrial bin liner.*

Silence. They stand opposite one another.

Enter LUE. *Pause.*

LUE. Look. He fixed it. He fixed my suitcase.

Silence.

What's going on? Len? What's happening?

Pause.

WEST. Well it's a very kind offer, Patsy. But as it turns out, I can't go to London today.

LUE. What? Where you going? What's going on?

WEST. That's just it. Even if there was enough room. Don't get me wrong. I'd love to, Patsy. Really I would. See, it's the pup. The pup's gone off. She's only small. (*Beat.*) So I can't up and leave her. She'd get back here, and I'd be gone. It's not fair.

PATSY. I suppose not.

WEST. The truth is, I can't, Patsy. I can't do it. (*Pause.*) Patsy is going to show you to the bus.

LUE. What do you mean?

Pause.

WEST. Who knows, maybe he'll go with you to the airport. Maybe he'll go with you. See you get there safe. He could do with the sun on his face.

Beat. PATSY *nods.*

PATSY. Maybe I could. Yes. Maybe I could.

LUE. But… but… I'm not ready to go. I've not got my maps. And I've not got an alarm clock. And I need a spare costume, and a towel and –

WEST. Just go. Just go. Now.

LUE. But –

WEST. Go out the back door. Across the field. Go across the moor.

LUE. I can't. I need –

WEST. Go. Go now. You have to go. Now.

LUE. What are you going to do?

WEST. Just. Go.

LUE. I don't have the money –

PATSY. It's all right. I'll take you there. I've… I've got it. I've got money. Let's go.

LUE *looks from one to the other. She walks up to* WEST. *She kisses his cheek.*

LUE (*to* WEST). Take care of her.

Pause.

They stand there, looking at each other. She turns and leaves. PATSY *follows.*

Silence. A plane approaches. It tears over. Then fades.

WEST *is alone.*

He goes to the kitchen. He takes out the dog food. He comes back out.

WEST. Dolly. Dolly, Din Dins. Din Dins, Dolly. Dolly. Din Dins.

WEST *picks up the axe and sits, the axe across his lap.*

He waits.

Dolly. Din Dins. Din Dins. Dolly. Din Dins.

He sits there.

Fade to black.

The End.

LEAVINGS

Leavings was first performed as part of the Ten by Twenty season at Atlantic Stage 2, the Atlantic Theater, New York, on 14 June 2006. It was performed by Peter Maloney and directed by Neil Pepe.

Characters

KEN

Sound of the sea. A bungalow. Open plan. Red-and-white chequered floor. View out over the fields. The radio is on. KEN, an old man, enters. He switches off the radio. He scrapes a few plates into a dog bowl. He puts the bowl by the door.

Dolly. Din Dins. Din Dins. Dolly! Dolly? Din Dins. Dolly Din Dins. Dinny Dins. Dinny Dins Dolly. Dolly? Dolly! Dolly Doll. Dolly Doll. Din Dins. Din. Dins. Dins Dins Dolly. Dolly.

Pause. He searches the drawers, takes out a whistle. Blows it. Stand on the doorstep, blowing it. Calls.

Dolly. Dolly Doll. Dolzy. Dolly.

Nothing. He comes back, puts the kettle on.

The dog's gone off. You hear me? The dog's... She's run off. What.

I said the dog's gone. Where's she gone. Search me. She's run off.

She'll come back. She's a pest. She's not supposed to go off.

I know she's not supposed to go off. Eighty pound to have her done and still she's off all hours. It's money down the drain.

She'll be off somewhere. Sniffing around. Sniffing after it. She's wasting her time. She's a bloody pest. She'll find her way home.

You say that. She will, she'll follow his nose. You say that. You say that. What if she doesn't. Eh? She'll wash up with the next tide. I don't want to be out walking on the beach and find her washed up. Walking on the beach? You never walk on the beach. What you talking about. I'm out there every day. When? What do you mean, when? I'm out there every bloody evening. When? When? When I'm walking the bloody dog. Well, how you going to find the dog when you're walking the bloody dog. DOLLY! DOLLY DOLL! DOLLY DOLL. DOLLY DOLLY DOLL! Reminds me of this joke. There's this man walking across the desert with his dog and he's got no food, and him and his dog, Rover was his name, they're getting hungrier and hungrier, then one morning there's nothing for it, he gets this rock and he smashes the dog's skull, and he skins him and he makes a fire and he cooks him up. And he eats him. And after, all that's left is this big pile of bones. And he looks at them, and he says, 'Rover would've loved them.' (*Laughs.*) DIN DINS. Din Dins Dolly! DIN DINS! Well, there's nothing for it. Now I'm going to have to photocopy four hundred bloody pictures, pin 'em up all over town. 'Have you see this dog.' How many did you stick up last time. Ten. Twenty. Then you went to the pub. You left a hundred of 'em in the pub. Worked, didn't it. No thanks to you. That picture looked like an indistinguishable smudge. 'Has anyone seen this blob. Fifty-pound reward for this blob. Answers to the name of Smudge.' A puppy? I don't think so. Not unless you've got a very vivid imagination. You blow the whistle. Of course I did. Bloody thing's broken, you ask me. How do you know. Eh? How do you know it's not working perfectly. How do you know that's not the finest dog whistle in the kingdom. What time did you get it? Don't you start. Dolly! Dolly Doll. Dolly Doll Din Dins. Din Dins Dolly. I'm in The Plume. This is ten, fifteen year ago. Kelly Figgis's given me a couple brace of duck. Pairs they are. Now, you know when you've got a brace of birds, they're tied together at the neck, so's you can carry them. I've chucked them on the passenger seat, driven home, bit pissed and that, and I've got inside and I've left them overnight on the seat of the truck. So anyway, I've opened the door, left it open, and there's only one brace there. Only two ducks, see. So I come back out into the yard, scratching my head, and I see this sight. What sight. There she is. This duck walking around. Alive. One of the buggers is alive. And she's dragging her mate. Who's dead as stone. Dragging him in the mud, and quacking away. Right as rain. What did you do? What could I do. I grabbed him. Her. Not hard, she's weighed down, like, can't get away. And I got a knife, and I cut it free. It didn't seem wounded, it weren't bleeding, but then a duck can be mortal and the feathers cover it. It's been shot, or what's it doing tied up in a brace in the first place. What did you do? Only thing I could do. Stamp on it? I can't. It's healthy. It's right as rain. Then what's it doing tied in a brace. It never fell out of the sky from shock. I'm telling you, there isn't a mark on it. It's an entirely, one hundred per cent viable duck. So what did you do. Only thing I could do. I went inside to get it a saucer, some water. Help it get over the shock. Because the little bugger must be parched. Anyway, I come back outside and it's gone. It's flown off.

Probably crueller, that. Probably crueller than a stamping. He's
going to die a slow death now. She. It's a her. The him's a goner.
He's passed on. *So* she flew off. At least there's a happy ending.

Yeah. Not really though. I was taking the dog the next morning,
not Dolly, the one before Dolly, she's dead now, this was before
Dolly. Anyway, I'm taking the dog before Dolly out for a walk
and I saw it. Dead on the path. Not him exactly. Just feathers.
There was just feathers all over. The fox had took him. How do
you know it was the same duck? It stands to reason.

The kettle boils.

That's a really good story, Jack. That's really cheered me up.
That's a riot, that is. A real feel-good story. You should write that
down. They could make a film of that. Fuckin'… rom-com, that
is. Fucking Christmas heartwarmer. They'll queue up round the
block to catch that. You're made, chum. You've cracked it. You
can put your feet up. Dolly. Doll. Dolly. Dolly Doll. Dolly Doll. I
went past the church earlier. They was all in there, at it. I never
got the hang of it, myself. Never felt him. Never saw more than a
flick of his tail. Talk about the afterlife. I met this man once.
Traveller, it was, and he knew his Bible backwards. He said it was
all about children. The afterlife, that is. It's children, innit. If you
think about it. Not that I know much about them either. I ain't got
none. All I got's this mangy mutt. This stupid bloody mutt, don't
even know his way home. He's lovely though. Sleeps on my feet.
Licks my toes. He's a pussycat really. I don't mean he's really a
pussycat. Do you know, I was in Edinburgh once, freezing-cold
winter, and the woman across the hall had all these cats. About
twenty pussycats in a three-room flat. Seventh floor. Howe Street.
One day, after I left, I heard she had a heart attack, and those cats,
her cats, didn't hang about. They made short work of her. They
opened that place in the spring and they'd picked her clean. You
can't blame them. They're pets, fair enough, but she don't know
the difference. If I go down and out, I don't mind if Dolly fills her
boots. It's life, innit. She's lovely, though. Sleeps on my feet. But
if she was big and I was small, I know it'd be a different story.
She wouldn't stand on ceremony either. Wait for me to keel over.
I know where… down her throat. Down her gullet. She wouldn't
hang about. She'd have me for breakfast. She'd have my tits on
toast. I'm sleeping in the afternoon now. I get up and the night's

coming. Night's coming and the dog's not in. He's out there. In the dark. Where it's blackest, that's where he'll be. I had a dream yesterday night. Yesterday afternoon. Whatever. More of a vision really. I dreamt I was in Piccadilly Circus and everywhere I looked, all I could see was teeth. Rows and rows of teeth. Thousands. On the Underground. In the shops. In the restaurants. Chatting. Smiling. Biting. Ripping. Tearing. I got up, made a sandwich. Dolly got up too. For the leavings. It was a funny old one. I'm having lots of funny ones, but this was a funny one. Seriously. It was just… all these rows of teeth. Hundreds of rows of teeth. Yellow teeth. Broken teeth. Hot breath. That's just the people. Think of them all out there. All the people. All the dogs. All of them, out there, in the dark. The hunger. All gnashing. All chomping. Claws digging. Digging up bones. I've got to get back down the doctor's. Get some tablets. Sleeping tablets. They'll set me right. I'll go to bed at the right time, normal time, I'll munch a couple of little white tablets and I'll drift off. I'll sleep like a baby. Then I'll get up in the morning. With the sun. At sunrise. I'll take Dolly out on the beach. It'll be lovely and warm. And I'll watch her run. I'll watch her run and run. (*Beat.*) Look at that. Look at her go.

Silence.

The sea.

The End.

PARLOUR SONG

Parlour Song was first performed by the Atlantic Theater Company, New York, on 15 February 2008, with the following cast:

DALE	Jonathan Cake
NED	Chris Bauer
JOY	Emily Mortimer

Director	Neil Pepe
Set Designer	Robert Brill
Costume Designer	Sarah Edwards
Lighting Designer	Kenneth Posner
Sound Designer	Obadiah Eaves
Projection Designer	Dustin O'Neil

The play received its European premiere at the Almeida Theatre, London, on 19 March 2009, with the following cast:

DALE	Andrew Lincoln
NED	Toby Jones
JOY	Amanda Drew

Director	Ian Rickson
Designer	Jeremy Herbert
Lighting Designer	Peter Mumford
Sound Designer	Paul Groothuis
Composer	Stephen Warbeck

Characters

NED, *forty*

DALE, *forty*

JOY, *forty*

*England, in the late summer/autumn. In and around the small
suburban new-built home of Ned and Joy.*

Darkness. Silence. Spotlight on:

DALE. It started small.

Blackout.

In the air, apocalyptic visions appear: buildings, towers, skyscrapers crashing to the ground; office blocks, factories, entire community projects collapsing; histories imploding, destroyed, erased for ever, disappearing in dust as the music swells to utter darkness and silence.

NED *and* JOY*'s house.* NED. DALE. *A TV.* NED *at the controls.*

DALE. Fuck me. (*Beat.*) Look at that. (*Shakes head.*) Where are we?

NED. Leeds. A cooling tower outside Leeds.

DALE. Where were you?

NED. The Buffer Zone.

DALE. The where?

NED. You got three areas. The Designated Drop Area, or DDA. That's the sector where the main body of the structure is primed to fall. Then you got the PDA. The Predicted Debris Area: namely the maximum area in which fragment equals S and/or debris can reasonably be expected. You calculate the height, weight, materials, foundations, weather conditions, crunch them, and you get a number. Then it's standard safety procedure to build an eight to ten per cent comfort zone into the number. That gives you your PDA. So you've got the DDA, the PDA, then you got a Buffer Zone. I'm in the Buffer Zone. It's the safe area. You're completely safe there. Nothing's going to hurt you in the Buffer Zone.

A surtitle appears:

'Everything is disappearing.'

NED. Anyway, that's all boring, technical stuff.

DALE. Boring?

NED. It's technical –

DALE. Do you want to swap?

NED. What? No I just –

DALE. Do you want to swap jobs, Ned?

NED. No it's just –

DALE. Okay. Please. My CV…? Just to… hang on… Since
school. Kitchen porter. Skivvy. Dogsbody –

NED. Dale –

DALE. Withering period of unemployment… Australia. Back
home. Disaster with Tanya. Back to my mum's. Little Chef
manager… Washing cars. Nowhere in all that did they give me
a thousand tons of TNT and a fucking great big plunger and
say, 'See that factory over there… Really, and I mean really,
fuck it up.' 'See that tower block? We don't want one brick left
standing on another… Don't come back till you've fully
damaged it.' Do they have a big plunger? They do, don't they.
Big comedy. (*Mimes a plunger.*) They do. I knew it. I wash
cars. Cars, Ned.

NED. Dale –

DALE. Kids' cars. Wankers' cars.

NED. How many car washes you got. Three? Four? How many
do you employ? Twenty, thirty blokes.

DALE. Kosovans, Ned. Twenty or thirty Poles. You ask for a Kit
Kat, they come back with the *Daily Mail*.

NED. You've built that business. That's a good solid local –

DALE. Cars, Ned. Wankers' cars. You have a fight with the
missus. Money worries. Whoosh. Lo the heavens shake with
thunder. What have I got, I'm feeling the pressure. A sponge,
Ned. A squeegee. A bucket of dirty water.

NED. At the end of the day –

DALE. At the end of the day, Ned, I've got pruny fingers. You've got a thousand-foot dust cloud, and a clatter you can hear ten miles away. The end of the fuckin' world.

NED. I forgot to say. I'm going to be in the paper.

DALE. When?

NED. *Advertiser*.

DALE. See?

NED. Not just me. The whole team.

DALE. See? My point exactly. What for. Is it a… (*Mimes plunger.*)

NED. Big job. Local.

DALE. You lucky sod. Tell me.

NED. It's hush-hush.

DALE. Tell me.

NED. I can't.

DALE. Tell me anyway.

NED. It's the Arndale Centre.

Pause.

DALE. You're blowing up the Arndale Centre?

NED. Yes.

DALE. Fuck me. The Arndale Centre.

NED. Six weeks Tuesday.

DALE. Why?

NED. It's obsolete.

DALE. I do all my shopping there. Everybody does.

NED. Its days are numbered, Dale. There's going to be a photograph. Of us. The team. In front of the Arndale. Then another. Of it gone. At least that's how I'd do it.

DALE. Front page?

NED. Could be. Should be.

DALE. Should be on the telly.

NED. My lips are sealed.

DALE. You bastard.

NED. No comment.

DALE. You rotter. Are you going to be on the box?

NED. It's just a bit of fun really. It's eye-candy, isn't it.
Tomorrow's fish-and-chip paper.

DALE. Well, that's that. It's going to cost a pound to talk to you.
(*Beat.*) Do you know what? I could do this all day.

NED. Where you going? We haven't finished. I was just going to
get another –

DALE. Mate –

NED. I was just going to get another one.

DALE. It's not me. You know it's not me. It's Lyn –

NED. You got time for one more. Quick one.

DALE. Lyn'll be on the warpath.

NED. Five minutes.

DALE. Oooh… He always does this…

NED. Okay? Are you… just… are you ready?

DALE. Oooh… He always does this…!

NED. Okay? Falkirk Industrial Estate, 2002. We drop this
gasworks and there's literally zero backwash.

DALE. Ned –

NED. I've got it upstairs. I know exactly where it is. I've got
them all alphabetised.

DALE. Ned –

NED. I could have found it by now.

DALE. Ned –

NED. Come on. What's five minutes? We could have watched it
by now.

DALE. Ned. I've seen it. (*Beat*.) Ned, mate, I've seen it. You
showed me it. Last week.

Pause.

NED. When?

DALE. Last week. You showed me all of these last week.

NED. No I never.

DALE. Yes you did.

NED. When?

DALE. Last week.

NED. That was Pete. From the pub.

DALE. No it wasn't.

NED. It was Pete from the pub.

DALE. Ned. Yes. Ned. You showed them to Pete from the pub.
You also showed them to me. Last week. And the week before
that. With Rodge. And Nobby. Who'd seen it the week before
that. With me. Who'd seen it three times the week before that.
Once with Nobby. Once with Rodge. Once with Pete from the
pub. What I'm saying is, what I'm getting at is, we've seen it.
I've seen it.

NED. I'm sure you haven't seen Falkirk.

DALE. Ned –

NED. In fact I'm positive you haven't seen Falkirk. You're
thinking of Kilmarnock. The block of flats in –

DALE. Not the block of flats in Kilmarnock. Although I know it
well.

NED. There's no way you've seen –

DALE. Ned –

DALE. There's no way you've seen Fal –

DALE. It's raining. There's a bagpipe band. A countdown by the local lady mayor. A Mrs Bridey McNeil. Just when she starts, a kid jumps out the crowd and gets his bum out –

NED. That shouldn't have happened –

DALE. There's the countdown. Then you blow it up. (*Pause.*) It's jaw-dropping. No one's saying it's not.

Silence.

NED. Of course. Of course. I remember. I remember now.

Pause.

DALE. Ned. Tell me to fuck off…

NED. I'm fine.

DALE. Good. Good. Excellent. Tell me to –

NED. Dale –

DALE. Good. Splendid. I was just, you know… Mates 'n' all.

NED. Hey –

DALE. You'd tell me if something was –

NED. Hey. Dale. We're mates.

DALE. Mates. Exactly. No harm done.

NED. None taken.

DALE. Well, I best be off.

NED. Yeah, I better be getting on as well.

DALE. Thanks for the… what's the word?

NED. Biscuits.

DALE. Carnage.

NED. It's a bit of fun.

DALE. Exactly.

NED. Catch you later, Dale.

DALE. Thanks for the biscuits –

NED. Everything's disappearing.

Pause.

DALE. What?

Pause.

NED. What? Nothing.

DALE. You said. (*Beat.*) You just said –

NED. You best be off.

DALE. 'Everything's disappearing.'

NED. Mind how you go.

Pause.

DALE. All right, mate. See you around.

NED. Not if I see you first.

Pause. DALE *turns to go. He turns back.*

DALE. Ned. (*Beat. Looks at watch.*) Look. (*Beat.*) Life isn't always… (*Beat.*) I mean… I'm not a doctor. Not a doctor. What's the word? Gandalf. Not Gandalf. Like Gandalf. My point is, life is like a river. Things change. For us as for the river. See, one day they may build a bridge over the river. And you know. A cycle path. There may be an industrial leak that wipes out all the fish. They didn't see it coming. How could they? They're but fish, Ned. My point is, things changeth. 'Twas ever thus. Soothsayer. Bollocks. That's the one. What?

NED. No. I mean… Everything's disappearing. From my house.

DALE. What?

NED. My stuff. My possessions… they're disappearing.

DALE. What are you talking about?

NED. I mean my belongings. My things. The things I own. My stuff. Dale, if I tell you something, do you swear you will never tell another soul?

DALE. I promise.

NED. Swear to me. Swear on your life.

DALE. Ned. What's wrong. What's the story?

Blackout.

Spotlight on:

DALE. So like I said. It started small. A pocketwatch. Old set of golf clubs. Box camera. Pair of silver-backed hairbrushes. See, Ned's a demolition expert. He goes away. On business, all the time. Up North. Wales. South East. Wherever they need something blowing up. How it worked, he'd go away for a few days, when he came back something else was missing. A set of spanners. Screwdrivers. Stuff he picked up at a car-boot sale. Tins. Old train set he had when he was a kid. Old cricket bat. Model cars. Drill bits. Drill. Knives. Now... I know Ned. My first thought was he's got his knickers in a bunch. See, Ned's a squirrel. He squirrels stuff away. Go in the man's garage. Aladdin's cave? Man goes to a house auction, buys three old sinks. Three old bog cisterns. Five old toasters. You walk in his garage, shed, his attic, you wouldn't find a Sherman tank, but he swears he's got a system. Knows where everything is. (*Beat.*) I asked him if anyone else had a set of keys. He said there was only ever two sets. His set, which he always, always kept on him. And her set. His missus. His wife. Joy.

Blackout.

A surtitle appears:

'Face it. It's a dead duck.'

NED *and* JOY's *house. Both at a table, eating.*

NED. Well, that's that. Sixty days straight without rain. That has never happened before in the entire history of here. Last day of July it was. I was in the greenhouse. Killing greenfly. Suddenly the sky turns black. 'Hello,' says I. 'So long summer. Here comes Old Jack Frost.' How wrong can you be? It better break soon because I'll tell you this much. It's not natural. It's unnatural. Mother Nature is Not a Happy Bunny. (*Beat.*) How's the bird? Is it moist enough? I rested it. That's the secret. Remove the bird. On one side, tin foil. Ten, fifteen minutes. Give it a rest. It has to relax. You can't forget you're eating muscle. Is it okay, Joy?

JOY. It's lovely.

NED. There's a leg left. Little leg? Or a wing. Little wing? You sure? It's not dry? How are the carrots? Overdone?

JOY. They're lovely.

NED. You sure you don't want more?

JOY. This is perfect.

NED. There's a leg left. Little leg. You sure. A wing? Little wing? There's more peas…

JOY. It's lovely, Ned. The bird, it's moist. The roast potatoes are crispy outside, fluffy inside. The carrots are sweet and crunchy. The gravy is lip-smacking, and the peas are perfection. And the best bit is, it's exactly the right size portion.

Pause. NED *starts to laugh.*

NED. This'll make you laugh. I'm driving over Langley Marsh, where we blew up that cement works last spring. You'll never guess what they've gone and done. They've built seventy-eight houses on that site. And every single house is the same as ours. Same layout. Same front door. So I think why not? I'll stop off. Have a nose around. Being nosey. Pop my nose in, in the kitchen and guess what? It's our kitchen. Same units. Same taps. Cloakroom. Same sink. Same fittings. Lounge-diner,

exactly the same. Same floor. Same hatch. Except for…
(*Laughs.*) Except for this bloody great rat. In the middle of the
room. Huge it was. Like a dog. Long. Sleek. Tail like a rope.
Staring at me. Not moving. Mind you, that's building sites.
You drop a biscuit, half a pork pie, that'll bring fifty. Normally
they see you and scarper. Not this chap. Blimey, he was big.
Massive, massive rodent. Makes you think, don't it.

Pause.

JOY. What about?

NED. What? Sorry?

JOY. What does it make you think about?

NED. What do you mean?

JOY. You seen this big rat. Said it makes you think. (*Pause.*)
What about?

Pause.

NED. Well, you know. About…

Pause.

JOY. Rats?

NED. No. What? No. Not just… No. (*Laughs.*) It's not about rats.
No. (*Beat.*) Well, yes. Yes. It is. It's about rats.

JOY. It is, isn't it…?

NED. I didn't explain myself. You had to be there.

JOY. I miss out on everything, me.

Silence.

NED. By the way. We got the Arndale job.

JOY. The what?

NED. The Arndale job.

JOY. What Arndale job?

NED. The Arndale Centre in town. We're knocking it down.

JOY. Why?

NED. It's being redeveloped.

JOY. Says who?

NED. The council. We got the contract.

JOY. You're knocking down the Arndale Centre.

NED. We're going to be in the paper.

JOY. But I do all my shopping there. I'm always in the Arndale Centre. The chemist is there. The newsagent's is there. Tesco's is there. That's where I go. That's where I shop.

NED. Fear not. It's being replaced.

JOY. What with?

NED. The New Arndale Centre.

JOY. What's wrong with the old one?

NED. It's obsolete.

JOY. Says who?

NED. The People. The People want bigger and better.

JOY. Which People?

NED. The People of this town, Joy. The People want flexible shopping solutions. Twenty-four-hour. A spa. Softplay. And more car parking. Ours is not to reason why, Joy. It's a relic. An eyesore. It's no longer viable.

JOY. What does that mean?

NED. It means we're knocking it down.

JOY. No you're bloody not.

NED. Joy. We're a demolition company. We don't just drive round choosing buildings to blow up. The council confers. Did you know there was a forest right here? Five years ago. Right where you're sitting. It was here for a thousand years. Now it's gone. We're here. Everything has its time, Joy. And time is up for the Arndale Centre. Face it. It's a dead duck.

JOY. Well. This calls for a celebration.

She fills his glass. Raises hers.

Congratulations, Edward.

NED. By the way, have you seen my cufflinks?

Beat.

JOY. What?

NED. My cufflinks. The gold ones. The ones you gave me.

JOY. They're in your drawer.

NED. Right. Right.

JOY. They're always in your drawer, Edward. That's where they live.

NED. Right. But you see. I had a good root around. And I couldn't find them.

JOY. Well, when did you last have them?

NED. That wedding.

JOY. What wedding?

NED. Your cousin Anne's. In Gants Hill.

JOY. That was June last year.

NED. Must be.

JOY. That was over a year ago.

NED. That was the last time I wore them. That was the last occasion I wore cufflinks.

JOY. Well, this is splendid.

NED. What?

JOY. Those are twenty-four-carat solid-gold cufflinks, Edward.

NED. I know.

JOY. Oh you know, do you? Who was it got the train into Hatton Garden and spent all day picking them out? Who got them engraved by the engraver to the Queen? Do you remember what it said on them?

NED. Joy –

JOY. I worked double shifts all spring to pay for them. This is splendid. Thank you very much, Edward. You've made my day.

NED. I'm sure they'll turn up.

JOY. I'm glad you're so confident.

NED. They'll be somewhere silly.

JOY. You've made my day.

NED. You know me. I'd lose my head if it wasn't screwed on.

Pause.

JOY. Well, that was delicious, Edward.

NED. Hang about, I've made a sweet.

JOY. I've not got the room.

NED. I've made jam roly-poly.

JOY. I couldn't possibly. I'm full up.

NED. You sure? Couldn't squeeze some in?

JOY. I'd love to but it's physically impossible. I'm stuffed. It's your fault. You've filled me up.

NED. But there's always a sweet. I always make a sweet.

JOY. I'm already in discomfort, Ned. You don't want me in more discomfort, do you.

NED. Of course not, Joy.

JOY stands up.

JOY. Compliments to the chef, Edward. I'm going to bed.

NED. It's nine o'clock.

JOY. I don't feel well.

NED. Cripes. Was it the food?

JOY. The food was fine.

NED. Was it the gravy? Was the gravy too rich?

JOY. The gravy was perfect. I need to lie down.

NED. Well, goodnight, my cuddly toy. Perhaps when I come up, we could play Scrabble. Would you like that? Little game of Scrabble?

Beat.

JOY. Goodnight, Edward.

NED. Sleep tight. (*Beat*.) My little cuddly toy.

She heads out.

Joy.

JOY. What?

NED. I remember. What it said on the cufflinks. I remember.

He watches her leave.

Blackout.

Spotlight on:

DALE. Me and Lyn, Ned and Joy, we live six feet apart. It's the
same house. But round theirs, everything's backwards. You're
in our lounge, you need a slash, come out, do a left. Do that
next door, you end up in the kitchen. It's a nice area. Young
couples. Families. You've not got to drive far to see a cow.
But like any nice area now, you've not got to drive far before
you're in the fucking Dark Ages. You can see them from the
end of the garden. Six black blocks, on the horizon. Hatfield
Towers. I know they haven't got it easy over there. And
there's some good people. Some good, hard-working folk.
And some right maggots. Their kids don't give a fuck. They
come in the car wash, some spotty little orc in a brand-new
Boxster. And the nine-year-olds. We had stinkbombs and
snappits. This lot've got crossbows. Muskets. Poison darts. So
I said to Ned, check your locks and windows, mate. Could be
a sneak thief. Someone from over there. From Middle Earth,
some twelve-year-old can inch in through a bog window.
Some four-stone kid they can grease up and feed in through
the letterbox. But Ned said, why would someone steal a stamp
collection and leave the Xbox. Walk past three tellies to nick a
box of Victorian postcards out the attic, the Collected Works
of H.G. Wells, an Edwardian clay-pipe collection, a stuffed

badger and a bronze bust of Aldous Huxley. And I had to admit it didn't add up. (*Beat.*) But you have to know Ned. What is Ned? I don't want to say paranoid. But on a good day, on the flat, he's volatile. Fragile. Sometimes, when he gets an idea, it doesn't always wash through. It plants itself. It stays there and it grows and grows and ripens. And then it starts to go off. It starts to fester. (*Beat.*) Two months back, the doorbell goes. Seven in the morning. It's Ned. Dressed for work. He looks terrible. Hasn't slept. Three, four nights on the bounce. Big bags. Shivers. He comes in the kitchen, I'm making tea, and I turn round to hand him a cuppa and he's fast asleep. On his feet. I touch him and he wakes up, takes the tea and drinks it down, boiling hot. Straight out of the kettle. Doesn't even notice. Doesn't flinch. Then he looks at me square in the eye and says, 'Dale, I am fat. I want to get fit. Tone up.' I like to keep fit. I know the ropes. So I say, 'Why not? Let's devise a program. Get you match fit. Tight. Tough. Back in shape. Can't hurt, can it?'

Blackout.

A surtitle appears:

'Each year, the birds came back.'

NED *and* JOY*'s house.* NED *and* DALE*, warming up. Stretches. They stop. Facing each other.*

DALE. How you feeling?

NED. Good. Loose.

DALE. You ready?

NED. Ready to rock, Dale.

DALE. Ready to work.

NED. Bring it on, Dale. Rock and roll.

DALE. Okay. On your back.

DALE *lies on his back.* NED *does too.*

Feet six inches off the floor. Thirty seconds. Go. (*Beat*.) How's that feel?

NED. Instantly awful. Instantly wrong.

DALE. Push on.

NED. Terribly terribly wrong. Like I'm going to puke. And possibly soil myself.

DALE. Breathe. In. Out. In. Out. Twenty more seconds.

NED. My God. Make it stop. Make it stop, Dale. Please make it stop.

DALE. And rest.

NED *collapses*.

Are you okay?

NED *is panting. He starts crying*.

NED. I'm sorry, Dale. FUCK!

DALE. Ned –

NED. Fuck it.

DALE. Ned –

NED. I tensed up. I've been building up to this all day.

DALE. Calm down.

NED. I've had a shocker there.

DALE. Okay, Ned. Stand up. Ned. Relax. Stand up. We'll take it slowly.

NED. I'm sorry, Dale.

DALE. We'll start again. We'll try something else. Just do this. On the spot. (*He starts a ropeless skipping motion*.) One foot then the next. Just copy me. Until I ask you to rest. Okay?

NED. Got it.

DALE. Keep breathing. In. Out.

He starts skipping.

How is that?

NED. Fine.

DALE. Good.

NED. Just like this?

DALE. Just like that.

NED. Cor. Feels great to blow the cobwebs out.

DALE. Tell me your goals.

NED. Basically I'm looking for core fitness. Strength. Stamina. And I want to lose the tits. I'm not worried about the legs. Fuck the legs. Ignore them. I just want to look, you know. Normal. Alive. Without tits.

DALE. So just talk normally. Okay? What were you saying before? When we came in.

NED. Where were we?

DALE. Gloucester. A five-star hotel in Gloucester.

NED. Right. Gloucester. Five-star country mansion. Michelin restaurant. Spa. Four-poster. We've just had a massage, or I've had massage, and Joy's had a facial, whatever, we're feeling well blissed out and we've got a couple of hours to kill before we go up in this balloon. (*Off* DALE's *look*.) It's the honeymoon package. You get a four-poster bed, your food, a set number of spa treatments, and a go in a balloon. Sunset balloon trip. England at sunset. Bird's eye view. Champagne and that.

DALE. And rest. That sounds regal. That is a regal package. Keep talking. Go again in thirty seconds.

NED. So we've got a couple of hours to kill before the balloon trip. I suggest a stroll. I suggest a walk round Gloucester. I've heard it's nice.

DALE. I've heard it's nice.

NED. The centre's nice. Olde worlde.

DALE. That's the Romans for you.

NED. So we park and ride, and we're walking round Gloucester, and it is nice, find the cathedral, that's nice, pop our heads in, light a candle, feeling blissed-out after the massage. Facial.

DALE. Whatever…

NED. Anyway, we're walking down the high street, and suddenly I see this thing blowing towards us down the pavement. And I bend down and pick it up and it's a fifty-pound note.

DALE. Bollocks.

NED. On my life. A nifty.

DALE. Get in!

NED. Just blowing down the street. Just blowing along the pavement.

DALE. Get in! (*Looking at watch.*) Go.

They start skipping again.

NED. So I have a shufty round and no one's looking distraught, no one's patting themselves down, having kittens, shouting for the fuzz… so I think, 'Result,' and I stick it in my pocket. So I say to Joy, you know, 'What shall we do with it?' And Joy turns to me, it's this lovely sunny day, and she turns to me, and she says this brilliant, really touching thing…

DALE. Oh no. Don't…

NED. What?

DALE *stops.*

DALE. She didn't. Tell me she didn't make you hand it in.

NED. Wait. Wait. No. She doesn't. She doesn't say that. She says… She says this fantastically romantic thing.

NED *stops.*

She says that it's a sign. From the gods. From God. Or whatever, blessing our nuptials. And she said to honour the gods, whatever, we should take half each and go and buy each other a present. Something spontaneous, you know, that we'd remember for ever, to remember this moment by. Like if you saw it in ten years' time or whatever, it would nourish us.

You know, when you think of… Just two people… in Gloucester… walking down the street…

DALE. Amazing. Magical.

NED. Just two normal people, find this money…

DALE. Get in!

NED. It's amazing. And then she says that…

DALE. It's a moment. It becomes a moment…

NED. Spontaneous –

DALE. With the money.

NED. Exactly. But it's not about the money.

DALE. Ned. Come on. Of course it's not. It's the magical…

NED. Exactly.

DALE. The magical mystery…

NED. Exactly. So we buy a Yorkie, something, Juicy Fruit, break it for change, and agree to meet back in an hour outside Argos.

DALE. I like this. I like this story.

They start skipping again.

NED. So here I am, walking around Gloucester with this big smile on my face, thinking, this is great. I am a man. On his honeymoon. I'm on my own but it's a lovely day, and I'm somewhere in this old town, and there's a woman walking around performing this magical task, on a quest to honour me. And I shall honour her.

DALE. Plus you've got the balloon ride to look forward to.

NED. Yeah, but I'm not thinking about the balloon ride at this point.

DALE. Of course not. You're lost in the moment. You're in the zone. I like this story. I like it a lot.

NED. So I start browsing. Pop in a couple of antique shops, because my first thought was get her something old. I just thought. Gloucester. Olde Worlde. Something classic. Something with soul.

DALE. With…

NED. With a past…

DALE. Character…

NED. A treasure… Exactly. I'm looking at all these bits and bobs. Trinkets, whatnot, but nothing's leaping out.

DALE. Whoops.

NED. I go from shop to shop. Nothing's leaping out.

DALE. I didn't like to say but you're going to struggle. In most antique shops with twenty-five sheets –

NED. I can't find anything…

DALE. What are we talking, realistically? Some old bottle? Some tin? 'It's filled with the patina of a bygone era.' Really. It's a piece of leather, you nit. It's a leather strap. And, you don't even know what it's off. Can I stop you, Ned? Two words. Victoria's Secrets.

NED. What?

DALE. If that was me with twenty-five sheets I'd get straight up Victoria's Secrets. Up the minty end. Get something really cheap and minty.

NED. Dale –

DALE. It's my honeymoon, Ned. There's no better time. 'There you go, love. I'll give you something to… fuckin'… nourish…' (*Beat.*) Ignore me. Please. Carry on. Please. I like this story. Ignore me.

Beat. NED sighs. Soldiers on.

NED. Now I don't know Gloucester. So I go round this one corner, and suddenly, the shops have stopped. I've run out of shops.

DALE. And rest.

DALE stops. NED too.

NED. I'm walking out of Gloucester. And I don't know why, but I didn't turn round. I just kept on walking. It's just petrol stations and roundabouts. Then the countryside. It's like I'm in a dream. But I can't stop walking. (*Beat.*) So I'm at this roundabout, fourth or fifth out of town. I come across this yard. And it's just this Portakabin, and this old bloke selling all these objects. Stone things. Things made out of stone. Wood

things. Garden seats. Benches. And I'm suddenly drawn to this
blue tarpaulin. And this is mad, but I thought, whatever it is
I'm getting her, it's under that blue tarpaulin over there, in the
rain. So I go over. And I lift the tarpaulin. And underneath,
there's this beautiful, soapstone birdbath. Really simple, but
beautiful. Not fussy, just beautifully proportioned. Simple.
Perfect. So I knock on the Portakabin and I ask the man how
much it is for the birdbath. And he says it's twenty-five
pounds. (*Beat.*) On my life. That birdbath, the one over there,
under the blue tarp, is twenty-five pound.

Pause.

DALE. Did you haggle?

Pause.

NED. What?

DALE. You didn't haggle?

NED. You're missing the point, Dale. It's twenty-five pounds.

Pause.

DALE. Of course. The fuckin'… The magical mystery twenty-
five pounds.

NED. Exactly. It's perfect. So I buy it. But now I've got ten
minutes to lug it all the way back into Gloucester. It weighs a
fucking ton.

DALE. Fuckin'… Rocky. Go on, my son.

NED. I'm telling you, Dale. It weighs A TON.

DALE. Fuck off. It's the magic birdbath. It's light as a feather.

NED. It weighs a fucking ton.

DALE. I don't care. Put your back into it.

NED. I've got to dead lift a stone birdbath half a mile back into
town. So I get back there, absolutely shagged –

DALE. Sweating like a dogger…

NED. Pouring… pouring with sweat and I show it her. And she
looks at it, and I know straight away it's perfect. She's got

tears in her eyes. And when we moved into our house, the first thing we did, we put that birdbath in the garden. And on that first morning when we woke up, there was this pair of chaffinches perched on it, drinking from it. And every single morning when we woke up, we'd go and sit by the window, before breakfast and watch the birds. Robins, finches, warblers, tits, we'd get up really early in the morning, on a spring morning, we'd watch the birds splashing in the water, watch them preening, dancing for each other, in little pairs, each pair perfect. And each year, the birds came back, and each year it was the same. (*Pause.*) Yeah. So anyway, I come out this morning, and it's gone. It's... the birthbath has gone. There's just a white patch of grass. It's disappeared.

Pause.

DALE. Ned –

NED. It's a birdbath, Dale. A twenty-five-quid birdbath. Our fence is eight foot high. The gate's padlocked. It's a soapstone birdbath. It weighs a fucking ton. I should know. I've lugged it clean across Gloucester.

Pause. DALE*'s watch alarm goes off.*

DALE. And rest. (*Pause.*) How long have you been married, Ned?

NED. Eleven years.

DALE. How are things?

NED. Things?

DALE. Things.

Beat.

NED. Things. (*Beat.*) Good.

DALE. Good.

NED. Good.

DALE. Good. I'm just kicking the tyres.

NED. Exactly. Good. (*Nods.*)

Pause.

DALE. Recently…?

Pause.

NED. Recently? Recently. (*Nods.*) Recently less good.
Recently… not so good. Recently not good.

DALE. Good.

Silence.

NED. Few years back… We used to spend all day in bed.
Drinking tea. Playing Scrabble. Then… you know… Between
games. All day long. Five, sometimes six games of Scrabble.
Sometimes we'd play Sexy Scrabble. If you could spell it, you
could have it. I once got forty-five points for 'blow-job' on a
triple-word score.

DALE *laughs.* NED *laughs. He stops laughing.*

Then we stopped. We haven't played in years. I'm not sure I'd
even remember the rules.

Pause.

DALE. Year or two back. Lyn and me. In the boudoir. Major
tumbleweed.

NED. Whoops.

DALE. Move along. Nothing to see.

NED. Whoops-a-daisy.

DALE. In the end I bought this tape. This doctor lady. New
approaches. Techniques. I used to listen to it on the way to the
car wash. I've still got it somewhere. I could dig it out.

NED. Thanks, Dale. I don't think so.

DALE. If you change your mind. But I warn you. This doctor
lady. She's dirty. She's deeply filthy. Medical website? Not a
bit of it. There's stuff on there would make a sailor blush.

NED. Thanks, Dale.

DALE. Well, if you change your mind.

Pause.

What did she get you?

NED. What?

DALE. With the magic twenty-five pound.

Beat.

NED. A tie. (*Pause.*) A tie with air balloons on.

Blackout.

Spotlight on:

DALE. Maybe it is. Maybe it isn't. Fine. Yes. At the end of the day, even if it's true… A pocketwatch? Lawnmower? A stuffed badger? That's not it. That's not the problem. That's not why he can't sleep. Shakes. When I let the dog out at four in the morning, he's out there, on his back lawn, staring out over the fence. Sometimes he goes a week, two weeks, without so much as a wink. Makes him antsy. Jumpier than a crow on roadkill. Because he doesn't sleep. He has black moods. Forgets things. Gets confused. Imagines things. And so it goes round. I said to him, I said, 'Go down the doctor, get some pills. Sort it out.' But, see, Ned's a blaster. A D-Man. He handles high explosives, week in, week out. If a D-Man's got anything more than a sniffle he can't go to his GP. They knew you was on the sleepers, or the happy pills, they wouldn't let you blow up a bouncy castle. So he's got no choice, just got to white-knuckle it. Bite down. Wait for morning. And I tell you one thing. Joy don't know. She don't know about the sleeping. (*Beat.*) Joy don't know the half of it.

Blackout.

A surtitle appears:

'An unquenchable thirst.'

NED *and* JOY*'s bedroom.* NED *is in bed, with headphones on.*

VOICE. Performing cunnilingus can be one of the most
wonderful things you can do for a woman.

Sounds of a woman getting excited. NED *listens.*

Leaving your tongue soft and your jaw relaxed, try licking
from her vaginal entrance up to her clitoris, and following the
outer edges of her vagina along both sides. This works as a
great ice-breaker. (*He frowns.*) So. Exercise one. Stick your
tongue as far out of your mouth as possible. (*He does.*) Slowly,
curl the tip up and down. And side to side. All the time focus
on your partner, and the intense pleasure only you are
delivering. Before long, she just won't be able to help herself
keep coming back for more. And don't forget, a great lover's
hands never stop moving.

He starts to move his hands.

Next, the tongue tube. Roll your tongue into a tube and slide it
back and forth. This is likely to bring any woman to a volcanic
orgasm.

NED, *tongue out, waving his hands like Al Jolson, when* JOY
enters from the bathroom. NED *deftly morphs his movement
into a dance, as if enjoying a particularly funky tune. She
watches him, lost in music.*

NED (*presses stop on the tape*). Clapton. You are a god. Timeless.
Absolutely timeless.

JOY *walks over to a chair and removes her stockings.* NED
watches.

Listen to that same dry westerly. It's raining somewhere in
America right now, and they said on the radio that that is
actually our rain. Well, it better break soon because – (*Beat.*)
What's that?

JOY. What's what?

NED. On your finger. What is it?

JOY. It's a plaster.

NED. Oh dear. You have accident? Little accident?

JOY. I cut myself.

NED. How?

JOY. Chopping lemons.

NED. Lemons? Looks nasty. I bet it bled. Did it bleed? My little
cuddly –

JOY. Ned. We need to talk.

NED. What about?

JOY. What are these?

She is holding some pills.

NED. What? I don't know.

JOY. What do you mean you don't know?

NED. I've never seen them before.

JOY. Then how did they get in your cabinet?

NED. Hang about. Oh them. They're nothing.

JOY. Where did you get these pills, Edward?

NED. Nowhere.

JOY. Nowhere.

NED. They're nothing. They're just… (*Pause.*) They're…
vitamins.

JOY. They don't look like vitamins.

NED. That's because they're special vitamins, Joy.

JOY. Where did you get them?

NED. I don't want to discuss it. They're private. Some things are
private and they're… they're private. (*Low, to himself.*) Layla.
You got me on my knees. (*To her.*) What are you doing in my
cabinet anyway?

JOY. Where did you get them, Edward?

NED. On the internet. Happy now?

JOY. Where on the internet?

NED. A website.

JOY. You're aware that it says in your contract that if you take any mood-altering drugs –

NED. Joy –

JOY. – emotional labicity stabilisers sleeping pills or prescription analgaesics –

NED. Please, Joy –

JOY. – then you have to declare them to your employers. If you don't you are liable to random testing and if you test positive you are suspended without pay. Then we default on our mortgage payments, and if we do that for three to six months then we'll lose the house. We have nothing. No money. No job. No house. Now what are these pills, Edward? And think very carefully before you answer.

NED. They're vitamins.

JOY. They're not vitamins.

NED. They are. They're a blend of vitamins and a tonic.

JOY. What type of tonic?

NED. I don't know. A pick-me-up.

JOY. Ned. What have you been taking?

NED. They're private. Okay? They're to do with me.

JOY. Ned –

NED. Leave me alone.

JOY. Edward.

NED. They're Rogaine.

Silence.

JOY. Rogaine? (*Beat.*) Hair pills.

NED. Happy now?

JOY. You're taking hair pills.

NED. Happy now, Joy?

JOY. Why are you taking hair pills?

NED. I don't know. Happy now?

JOY. Why –

NED. Look, can we… To have hair. Okay?

She laughs.

JOY. Why?

NED. I don't know. To have it. To have some. Okay?

JOY. Oh, Ned. But… You're bald.

NED. I'm aware of that.

JOY. You've never had hair.

NED. Actually. Yes I did.

JOY. Not since I've known you. On our first date you were bald. You're bald in the wedding photos. You've always been bald.

NED. I had hair. I had hair before. I did exist before. And when I did, I had hair.

JOY. But not for years.

NED. But I had it. I had it. Okay? And maybe I want some now.

She laughs.

What?

JOY. Nothing.

NED. What's so funny?

JOY. Nothing.

NED. Then why are you laughing?

JOY. How many do you take?

NED. Stop laughing at me, Joy.

JOY. How long have you been taking them?

NED. That's none of your business. Six months.

JOY. Ooh, love. You want to get your money back, love.

She laughs.

NED. Guess what? I went out to the shed this morning and guess what? The lawnmower's gone.

She stops laughing. Pause.

Someone's pinched it. Someone's pinched the lawnmower.

JOY. Don't be ridiculous. You can't get in the garden. You put a huge bloody great bike chain on the gate. Last Tuesday.

NED. I know. It's still there.

JOY. Well, how did they get in? More's the point, how the hell did they get it out?

NED. That is the question, Joy. It was there yesterday. I oiled it yesterday, after you asked me to oil it. And sharpen the blades. Said you couldn't bear me squeaking about out there every Sunday. So it was there. But now it's gone. And so have my fishing rods, my toolbox. My dad's beekeeping equipment. But they left your massage chair, your box of bone china, and your knitting machine. And they took the tandem.

JOY. The tandem's gone?

NED. Yes, Joy. Our tandem.

JOY. You bought that for our anniversary. That's a four-hundred-pound, completely unused tandem.

NED. I wanted to use it. I suggested we went on a picnic only last Sunday...

JOY. It looked like rain.

NED. It hasn't rained for seven weeks.

JOY. Hang on. There's a bloody great padlock on the shed. You put it on there only last week.

NED. They broke the padlock. They broke it off with a chisel. The chisel was broke on the floor. It had blood on it. By the way, why were you chopping lemons? (*Pause.*) I just wondered why were you chopping lemons today?

JOY. I was making lemonade.

NED. Lemonade?

JOY. Yes. I woke up this morning with an unquenchable thirst. I'd been dreaming all night about lemonade. All night long I was guzzling gallons of the stuff. I was a pig for it. Couldn't get enough. So this morning, I got up, I got the bus into town and went to the stall in the market and bought all their lemons. I bought six-dozen lemons. I brought them home, lined them up, and took a big knife and sliced the first one in half. Then I was slicing and slicing and squeezing and slicing and squeezing and slicing, and I had an accident. I thought I'd cut it off.

NED. Does it hurt? I bet it bled. Did it bleed? I bet it it stung. That explains it then. (*Pause*.) So can I have some?

JOY. Some what?

NED. Some lemonade.

JOY. You've just brushed your teeth.

NED. I can brush them again.

JOY. Don't be ridiculous.

NED. But I can. It's the work of a moment.

JOY. Don't be ridiculous, Edward. Anyway, you can't have any.

NED. Why not?

JOY. It's gone.

NED. Don't tell me you drank it, Joy. Six-dozen lemons. What's that make. Eh? Two, three gallons. Don't tell me you drank three gallons of lemonade. There must be some left. You must've saved me some. You can't have drunk it all.

JOY. Who said I drunk it?

NED. You never drunk it.

JOY. I couldn't drink it.

NED. What?

JOY. You couldn't drink it. It was too tart.

NED. Put sugar in it.

JOY. I did. Then it was too sweet. It was undrinkable. I disposed of it...

NED. You disposed of it.

JOY. I threw it away.

NED. Three gallons of lemonade.

JOY. It was too sweet.

NED. You know me, Joy. I've got a sweet tooth.

JOY. Well, it's too late now. It's down the sink.

Pause.

NED. Is it deep? The cut. What knife was it? The bread knife? The carving knife? That knife's a killer. Deep, is it? Deep gash. Bet it throbbed. I hate to think of anything hurting you.

Pause.

JOY. Why don't you kiss it better?

Pause.

NED. Can I, Joy? Can I kiss it better?

JOY. Why don't you?

She holds her hand out.

Kiss it.

He does.

NED. That's better. All better. There there. I bet it bled. Did it bleed, Joy? I bet it did.

Pause.

JOY. It bled something cruel.

Blackout.

Spotlight on:

DALE. I met my wife, Lyn, down the car wash. I'd just started out, my first place. Old burnt-out filling station. Bucket and sponge. This bird pulls up in a little clapped-out Mini. The old sponge, the old leather, splashing suds, soaping it up, wiping it off. All the time she's inside. Doing her make-up. Lipstick. Keeps catching my eye. She's short but buxom. Big. In all the right places. I'm waxing the bonnet, doors, wings, and I see she's left the window open. It's boiling hot, and we're chatting. She's shy. I'm cleaning the boot and she's got the mirror angled, looking at me, putting on bright red lipstick. I've got my shirt off, it's boiling hot. At the end, she says she's left her purse at home. She can't pay me. 'Hello,' thinks I. 'Where's this going. Where's this off to?'

Blackout.

A surtitle appears:

'I tried to grow lemons last year.'

NED *and* JOY's *house.* JOY *sitting.* DALE *standing.*

DALE. There you go.

JOY. So what was it?

DALE. Trip switch. If there's a surge in the power sometimes it trips out. We've got the same problem over the way. Have you got a torch? In case it happens again.

She flicks a lighter. Lights a cigarette.

Well, if it goes again. It's the white switch above the fusebox. Just flick it up and down three times.

JOY. Three times.

DALE. Up down. Up down. Wait a bit. Up down.

JOY. Up down. Up down. Wait a bit.

DALE. Up down.

JOY. I should be able to manage that.

DALE. I never knew you smoked, Joy.

JOY. I don't.

DALE. Right.

JOY. I used to. Not any more. Only sometimes. Now and then.

DALE. By the way, Lyn asked me to pass on a message. She was popping out, for her nightshift, she said, 'Ask Joy if she fancies a pint.'

JOY. Right.

DALE. Wednesday night. She said you two needed a catch-up. It's been ages.

And I thought, as long as this dry spell keeps up we should have a get-together. Little barbecue. Might as well make the most of it. Before winter takes hold. When's Ned back?

JOY. Friday.

DALE. Where is he this time?

JOY. It's on the fridge.

DALE. He gets around. Scotland. Wales. Yorkshire.

JOY. Tring.

DALE. Tring.

JOY. Tring.

DALE. Not far then. Just up the road...

JOY. No. Not far.

DALE. Is he stopping up that way?

JOY. A Travelodge just off the A38.

DALE. Right. Do you fancy it then? Little barbecue. When he gets back. Just the four of us.

JOY. He's blowing up a kiddies' hospital.

DALE. That should draw a crowd.

JOY. Shall we bring something?

DALE. What?

JOY. To the barbecue.

DALE. Just your good selves. And your world-famous Waldorf salad. Let's just hope the weather holds. If you have any more problems with the...

JOY. Up down. Up down.

DALE. Wait a moment. Up down. If there's any problem. I'm next door. I'll be up for a bit. I'm doing the wages. For the... the Kosovans.

JOY. Well, I shan't keep you.

DALE. Shall I tell Lyn you're on? For Wednesday. A girls' night out.

JOY. Have you got a lemon?

DALE. What? Sorry... A...

JOY. I was just going to make a gin and tonic. I've got gin. And tonic. Ice. I've not got no lemon.

DALE. Let me see. You might be in luck. Lyn went to Lidl's just this afternoon.

JOY. I don't mind replacing it.

DALE. Don't be daft.

JOY. Only if you can spare it.

DALE. Don't be daft.

JOY. Is that all right? It's just I have a craving. For a nice cool gin and tonic. I'll tell you what. If you can spare a lemon, if you give me a lemon, you'll be a lifesaver.

DALE. A lemon.

JOY. A lemon.

Silence.

DALE. Joy.

JOY. I'm thirsty, Dale. Why don't you fetch me a lemon?

Blackout on JOY. *Hold spotlight on:*

DALE. I tried to grow lemons last year. Up the allotment. I was growing the lot. Potatoes. Turnips. Runner beans. It kept getting hotter and hotter. I bought this little lemon tree from the garden centre. Went up every day to water it. Ended up with one rock-hard green bullet. Like a brussel sprout. Then the tree died. It's a desert now, with the drought. I broke my back. Now everything's gone. Just a bare patch of land with a rickety old shed.

Pause.

Spotlight up on JOY.

JOY. I never knew you had an allotment. You're full of surprises.

Well, I'd like to see it.

DALE. See what?

JOY. The allotment.

DALE. Don't be daft. There's nothing there.

JOY. Why don't you show me it?

DALE. When?

JOY. Now.

DALE. But. There's nothing there.

Blackout.

NED *appears in a spotlight. Unblinking.*

NED *and* JOY*'s living room.* NED *is alone. He skips on the spot. Does sit-ups. Ten. Pumping two dumbbells. Press-ups. Star-jumps. Picks up a barbell. Pumps out three. Four. Starts grunting. Shouting. Screaming. Six, seven, eight, nine. Puts it down.*

He puts it down and paces like a wild animal. Throwing punches. Pumped. And starts doing star-jumps. He picks up the fire poker and brandishes it like a sword. Kendo-style. He starts thrashing the sofa. Over and over, in a frenzy. He is about to smash it to pieces when he stops.

He puts the poker down. Suddenly exhausted he collapses onto his back. Breathing hard.

DALE *enters.*

DALE. Ned.

NED. Dale.

DALE. You all right?

NED. I'm good. Resting. Resting between stations.

DALE. Sorry I'm late. I had to fire a couple of Kosovans. You look warm.

NED. I'm hitting the ground running, Dale.

DALE. You've gone very red.

NED. I'm pumped. I'm in the zone.

DALE. Have you drunk any water? Sit down.

NED *removes his shirt.*

NED. Right. Don't hold back. Give it me straight.

Pause.

DALE. Ned –

NED. End-of-week report. Straight Ned. I need feedback. Tell me what you see.

Pause.

DALE. Ned –

NED. From the hip, Dale. Feedback. Hit me.

Long pause.

DALE. Ned. Listen. We're doing great.

NED. Really?

DALE. Yes. Slowly, slowly, catchy monkey.

NED. Hey – Rome wasn't –

DALE. Exactly. A journey of a thousand miles –

NED. How do the tits look?

Beat.

DALE. Great. The tits look great.

NED. Mate. Listen, I'm no fool. I know the score. But, see, last night I weighed myself. Then I checked on the charts. Last week, I was morbidly obese. This week, if my sums are correct, I'm just extremely fat. (*Beat.*) Thank you so much for this, Dale. You're a real mate. That's great feedback. Okay. I'm ready.

DALE. What for?

NED. For the test. My body-mass whatsits.

DALE. Index.

NED. Exactly. With the callipers. The pen. Crunch the numbers.

DALE. It's only been one week, Ned.

NED. Exactly. End-of-week report.

DALE. But it'll be much the same.

NED. But it won't be exactly the same. It's got to have moved a bit. Right?

DALE. Yeah but –

NED. Well, let's test it.

DALE. Ned. It just won't have moved much.

NED. But it will have moved a bit. Christ, I've been killing myself here. Please test it. I need feedback.

DALE. It's pointless, Ned.

NED. What about the chart?

DALE. The what?

NED. The chart. *Men's Monthly* says keep a chart. So fine. I have a chart at home. I drew it up on a big piece of graph paper. Like they said. I bought felt-tip pens. I'm going to chart my progress and it goes, my chart, it goes week by week. This is the end of week one. It's time to get on the chart. Now test my fat.

DALE. Slowly, slowly –

NED. Test my fat.

DALE. Catchy –

NED. Fuck off. Test my fat!

DALE. It takes time, Ned.

NED. I haven't got time, Dale. Now test my fat. Test my fat, Dale. TEST MY FUCKING FAT!

Silence.

I'm sorry.

DALE. It's all right.

NED. What is wrong with me?

DALE. Forget it. Never happened.

NED. What the fuck is wrong with me?

DALE. Shall we move on?

Silence. NED goes and fetches a book.

What's that?

NED. This. It's a diary. Have you ever kept a diary, Dale? (*Beat.*) A diary. A journal. You ever a diarist? I do. Not a diary as such. I keep a record of sorts. Every time I go away, stay in a motel, Novotel, bed and breakfast, I have to keep the receipts and they reimburse me each quarter. You've got to be thorough or you never see it back. So I keep a record. Listen to this. Here. (*Reads.*) '12th March. Newbury sevices. A bacon sandwich. Apple turnover. Two bags of cheese and onion. Can of Lilt.

Map of Berkshire. *Daily Mail*. Fifteen gallons of four star. £71.10.' (*Beat*.) Funny though. Just reading that, I remember the day perfectly. It chucked it down all day. The M4 was a nightmare. (*Reads*.) '17th March. Room at the Travelodge, Sedgemoor Services, £46. Club sandwich, £3.95. *Gladiator* on pay-per-view, £8.50. Petrol, £29. (*Beat*.) 22nd March. Lunch at The Fight Cocks in St Albans with three local councillors. The rotisserie deluxe for four people, and wine, £98.60 with a ten-pound tip.' I remember all these days. Can't remember their names or nothing. I can see their faces. I can picture them, eating. In that pub. (*Pause*.) Then it stops. After that, it changes. (*Pause. Reads*.) 'Monday, 19th April. Made Joy a cuppa. Took it through from the kitchen to the lounge. Put it on the table in front of her. She looked up and smiled. "Thanks," she said, and touched my arm. (*Pause*.) 9th June. Went out into garden. The sun was setting. Came up behind her. She was staring out, over the end fence. Put my hand on the small of her back. She didn't pull away. After ten seconds, she turned, smiled, and walked inside. (*Pause*.) 21st August. Watching telly. I laughed at something and Joy laughed too. We both laughed, together. She put her hand on my thigh as she laughed and laughed and laughed. (*Pause*.) 1st September. Woke up in middle of night to find Joy on me. Breathing hard. Sweating in the moonlight. Hot. Panting. She held me to her. "I want you," she said. "I want all of you." She ground herself into me and rode me like never before. A rhythm. A syncopation. It was like she was in a trance or... yes. Or still asleep. She never woke up. But she showed a passion like never before. As she climaxed, she gasped something. I strained close to her as she croaked out a single word. She said it once. A name. A place. I don't know. But I know one thing. It wasn't my name. It wasn't this place.'

DALE. How do you know if you didn't hear it?

NED. I didn't hear it. I felt it. Here. On my cheek. And all I knew, for sure, was that it didn't belong to me.

DALE. Ned. (*Pause*.) When did you last sleep? How long is it since you slept?

He walks over. NED *slaps himself on the forehead. There is something stuck to his forehead.*

What's that?

NED. It's a Scrabble piece. It's the blank, Dale. If you don't have
the right letter, you can use the blank. It can be anything you
want it to be. When I got up this morning, I looked in the
mirror and that was on my face. It was stuck to my forehead
when I got up this morning. Hello? What's this? Oh look. The
blank.

They look at each other.

Who plays Scrabble on their own, Dale? Who plays Scrabble
on their own?

Silence.

I love her, Dale. I love her so much. And… I don't know what
I'll do. If it's true. (*Beat.*) If it's true. She's not safe.

Blackout.

*Projection – extreme close-up on a Scrabble board. We read
words:*

SPIDER

SUNSHINE

FLYING

SHOES

FURTHER

HONEY

PLEASE

LEMONS

BOOM

GO_DNIGHT

NED *and* JOY*'s bed.* JOY *and* DALE *playing Scrabble. Pause. They both stare down at the board intensely.* JOY *puts a word down. Adds it up.*

JOY. Thirty-one.

DALE. Challenge.

JOY. Dale –

DALE. That's not a word. Challenge.

JOY. Dale.

DALE. That. Trust me. That has got an 'E' in it. That needs an 'E'. Possibly two. Challenge. (*Pause.*) How many letters are left?

JOY. None.

DALE. Bollocks. (*Beat.*) How many do I need?

JOY. A hundred and seventy-three. Give up, Dale.

DALE. Fuck off. I can do this.

JOY. Dale –

DALE. Fuck off. I feel a late surge.

JOY. With Four 'I's and a 'Y'.

DALE. Wait. Stop. How do you know my letters? How do you know what letters I've got?

JOY. I always know what letters you've got.

DALE. How do you know what letters I've got?

JOY. Because when you take them out of the bag, Dale, your lips move. You mouth the letters.

DALE. Bollocks.

JOY. You do. You pull out an 'O' you go 'Ohhh'. 'W'? (*She mouths it.*) Then if you get the blank you usually go 'Yes!' (*She punches the air.*) The trained eye can pick up on these things. The true Scrabble expert.

DALE. That's cheating.

JOY. Fifteen seconds.

DALE. You don't know my letters.

JOY. Four 'I's and a 'Y'.

DALE. I demand a rematch.

JOY. Ten. Nine. Eight.

DALE. Wait.

JOY. Six. Five. four.

DALE. Okay. Wait. I've got it.

JOY. Three. Two. One.

DALE. Oh no. Earthquake. Earthquake.

DALE shakes the board till all the letters jump up and down.
He then 'pings' the board, pinging all the letters in the air.

Pause.

What happens now? Remind me.

JOY. Now you go home.

DALE. Why? What did I do?

JOY. It's six.

DALE. I told you. She's got squash.

JOY. Dale –

DALE. She took her squash stuff. She's got squash. She's playing
Pauline. With Pauline, it always goes to the wire. It's always a
nail-biter. Lyn v Pauline. Call me biased, but Lyn's got Pauline
hands-down for flair. But Pauline has it here. (*Taps his head.*)
She wins points she shouldn't. Crazy points. Lyn calls her the
Terminator. She just keeps coming at you. With that fucking
forehand. Lyn v Pauline. It's a war.

JOY. She's dyed her hair.

DALE. Who?

JOY. Last week your wife had black hair. This week she's
strawberry blonde.

DALE. Yeah. She looks nice.

JOY. Do you think so? Younger?

DALE. I'd say it brings out her eyes.

JOY. Wouldn't you say it brings out her eyes?

DALE. I would. I'd say it brings out her eyes. Is that a new lamp?

JOY. She came round to show me yesterday morning. She looks
sweet. Don't you think she looks sweet? She's bought a new
autumn wardrobe. Blacks. Contrasting shades. And two new
pairs of shoes. She said she showed the hairdresser a picture of
Charlize Theron. Do you think she looks like Charlize Theron,
Dale? With her new hairdo. Her new strawberry-blonde hairdo
and her autumn wardrobe.

DALE *gets out of bed. Stretches.*

What are you doing?

DALE. Stretching.

He points above the window.

We've got that.

JOY. What?

DALE. That crack above the window. We've got the same crack, but
it goes the other way. But we've got that. We've got that crack.

He looks out front, out of the window.

DALE. Fuck me.

JOY. What?

DALE. You can see the motorway from here. Look at that. See,
we don't have that. Those fir trees over there are the problem.
But look at that. No fir trees. And there it is. Bang. The
motorway. (*Pause.*) All those people. Driving home. Look at
that. (*Beat.*) I'd say, on balance, yes. You've got a much better
view than us. In fact the whole neighborhood looks different
from here. You've just got a much, much more pleasing view.
(*Beat.*) By the way, why don't you ever ask me anything?

JOY. What like?

DALE. I don't know. Normally birds want chapter and verse. In two months. You haven't asked me a thing. I mean…

JOY. What's your favourite colour, Dale?

DALE. Right.

JOY. What's your favourite food, Dale?

DALE. Forget it.

JOY. If you could meet any famous person –

DALE. Forget it. Forget I said anything.

JOY. If you could come back as any animal –

DALE. What's the scariest thing you've ever done?

JOY. What's the scariest thing you've ever done? (*Pause*.) Come on. What's the scariest thing you've ever done?

Pause.

DALE. I once got my head stuck in a hole.

Pause.

JOY. What hole?

DALE. I was in the Cubs. On a sixers' camp out near North Mimms. We went looking for animal tracks. We were supposed to do plaster casts of deer prints. Badger prints. I went off on my own. Got my head stuck in a hole.

JOY. How?

DALE. I just followed these tracks. And they led to a hole. I thought I'd have a look in. See who was home. So stuck my head in. I was there for hours.

JOY. I can't bear it, Dale. What did you do?

DALE. I just waited. Waited for something to come along and tear my eyes out. Eat my little face. Pull out my tongue. I don't know. It was pitch dark.

JOY. Who found you?

DALE. The other Cubs. They got a spade and dug me out. I was eight.

JOY. What would you rather be eaten by, a shark or a lion?

DALE. Pass.

JOY. You can't pass.

DALE. A lion.

JOY. Why?

DALE. A lion is a professional. Holds you down and chokes you. You just drift off. Whereas your shark… he just keeps rushing up and taking great big bites. No one needs that.

She laughs.

If I'm going to get eaten I'd rather not be there when the actual eating part goes down. I'd rather be swiftly dispatched, then eaten. Finally, a lion shares you with its offspring. It's just more of a family occasion. Also, I've never been to Africa.

JOY. Why don't you want to be there? This is the last thing you're ever going to do, ever. There's nothing after it. I want to know what it's like to be ripped apart. To be devoured in two or three big bites. I want to be ripped limb from limb. I want to see my blood on the water. I want to be there. I want to feel it. To be devoured. Whole. Sudden. And in ten seconds, nothing. I'm gone.

DALE. What's the scariest thing you've ever done?

JOY. This.

Pause.

DALE. I better go.

JOY. She took her squash stuff. She's got squash.

DALE. Yeah but –

JOY. It's Lyn v Pauline. It's a fight to the death.

Pause.

DALE. After that first barbecue, I said to Lyn, she was brushing her teeth I said, 'Nice pair. Nice couple. He's a laugh. She don't say much. Just sits there and drinks a whole box of wine.' But Lyn weren't having it. She says to me, 'It's early days, Dale. She's shy. Trust me. That one just needs warming up.' (*Beat*.) Then the very next day, scorcher it was, I look out the window and there she is, next door, on a lounger, and she's in just a bikini. She's lying there in the all-together. And the funny thing is, as I'm looking down on her, out the window, the funny thing is, I could be wrong but it looks like she's looking straight back at me. And what if she doesn't sit up, pop her top off and lie there, in just her bikini bots. Gazing up at me. I was thinking, 'Lyn. I take it all back. I stand corrected. She's just shy. That one just needs warming up.' Did you see me, Joy?

JOY. I couldn't possibly say.

DALE. Like you're looking at me now.

JOY. Just like this.

DALE. Then you took it off.

JOY. How?

DALE. Show me.

JOY. How was it?

DALE. Show me. You slut.

JOY. Slut.

DALE. You dozy slut.

JOY. Dirty bitch.

DALE. You dirty whore. Show me.

The phone rings. Once. Twice. Three times. Four times.

NED (*on the answerphone*). Joy. Are you there? If you are there, pick up. No? It's me. I'm in the Travelodge at Cheshire Services. Had a successful day. The room isn't bad actually. I've got my own tea-making facilities. And Sky Sports. But you have to key in a code and I haven't got it. Anyway, I've got two short meetings in the morning, and then I'll hit the road. I should be back by bedtime... Well, I'm going to get some sleep now. Well, sleep well. My little cuddly toy. Night night, cuddly toy.

Silence.

JOY. If you could live anywhere in the world, where would it be?

Pause.

DALE. What?

JOY. Somewhere warm? Somewhere far away, over water? You know where I'd go? Anywhere it's spring. Early spring. Warm sunlight and cool shade.

DALE. He thinks you're nicking his stuff. He does. He thinks you're picking him clean.

JOY. Now why would I do that?

DALE. Why indeed? How did you get the birdbath out? Seriously. How did you nick his birdbath?

JOY. Strictly speaking, that was my birdbath.

Silence.

DALE. Going somewhere?

JOY. What if I was?

Pause.

DALE. Going somewhere are we, Joy? Are we going somewhere?

Pause.

JOY. I don't know, Dale. Are we?

Blackout.

Spotlight on:

DALE (*pause*). You've lived for years in the one house. For years. You know which window sticks, which floorboard creaks. Which tap drips. The cold spots. The damp patch. You know it. Like the back of your hand. You could walk round it – blindfold. Fix a lightbulb. Make a cup of tea. In your sleep. Find your way – Upstairs. To bed. Blindfold. Then one day. One day, you're in the house. Fixing a bulb. Leaky tap. Damp patch. Cup of tea. And you look round and there's… There's – a door. There's a door there. A door you never saw before. In your house. Right there. Before you. A door. A new door. Was it always there? How could you not notice it. How could you not have seen it before? Would you open it?

Blackout.

Spotlight on NED. *Watching his old tapes. Explosions on his television. Louder and louder.*

Spotlight on:

I can't sleep. I wait till Lyn's dropped off, then I'm up, pacing. If she's working nights, I'm up the allotment. Sitting in the shed. Waiting. Watching. (*Pause.*) I'm in the car in a layby. Watching the cars go by. In the car park of the Arndale. I've started smoking. For something to fucking do. Nine nights out of ten, nothing. Then on the tenth, there's her car. Pulling into the car park. I get out, go over, but she's not there. I can't see her anywhere. Joy? Joy?

Spotlight on JOY.

NED. Dale.

DALE. Jesus. Ned. You scared me.

NED. Is that you? What are you doing here? It's three o'clock.

DALE. Me? I couldn't sleep.

NED. Small world. (*Beat.*) I just thought I'd pop up here. Run through my calculations. Dot the 'I's. You can't be too careful. You've only got to overlook one tiny detail and you end up with egg on your face.

Beat.

DALE. Well, I best be off. You coming?

NED. No, you go on. I'm going to hang about for a bit. You know, it's funny. Looking at this old thing. I've always thought she was a monstrosity. But right now, in the dark, silent, she looks almost beautiful. It's always the same. Right before the big day, right before the drop, they always look… innocent. Pure. Like they're begging you not to do it.

DALE. Goodnight, mate.

NED. Give my best to Lyn.

DALE. I walk back to my car and I get in and I drive. I can see him in the mirror, standing there in the dark, still, watching me drive away. I drive home, pull in the garage and she's there. On her front lawn.

JOY. That first barbecue. I thought you were a ghost. I thought you were all ghosts. Ghouls. In the dark. Laughing. But you're the one warm thing I've touched for years. The only thing that's been there in years. I can barely look at you. (*Pause*.) Come with me…

Spotlight on DALE.

DALE. Where?

JOY. Tonight. I'm leaving tonight.

DALE. Where are you going? (*Pause*.) Where are you going? What shall I bring?

JOY. Nothing. I've got money.

DALE. Where are you going?

JOY. Meet me in the car park of the Arndale at midnight. Don't bring anything. If you're not there, you'll have lost me. You'll have missed me. Will you be there?

Blackout on DALE.

JOY *turns.* NED *is there, on the couch. He doesn't turn to look at her.*

Ned. I thought you were out.

NED. I got cold. I came back.

JOY. I thought I'd go for a walk. I can't sleep.

NED. You want to watch telly? Or we could go to bed. Come to bed, we can have a cuddle.

JOY. I need some fresh air.

NED. It's cold out there. You sure you don't want to come to bed?

JOY. I shan't be long.

Pause.

NED. Well, it'll do you good. I'll tell you what. I'll wait up. I'll be here when you get back. I'll wait for you.

Pause.

JOY. Goodnight, Ned. Sleep well.

NED. Goodnight, my love.

He watches her leave. Music. Lights fade to black.

A surtitle appears:

'It started to rain.'

Spotlight on:

DALE. It was a combination of factors. First up, do the maths. It was one summer. Add it up… Once in the shed. Once in her car. Once in the woods. Once round hers. Four times. End of the day, the whole plan was half-baked. It was full of holes. Apart from the where, what and how, I've got the business to think of. I've got responsibilities there to thirty-odd blokes. Not to mention the kids. Did I mention the kids? Me and Lyn, we've got two. One of each. I'd die for those kids. They mean, they mean the absolute world to me. In any equation, they come first. So whatever it was, whatever combination of reasons, when it came to the crunch, I never showed up. I watched her leave her front door, and walk past our house, without looking up, to the end of the close. And there she stopped, at the dark end. There she stood. Still. Looking out up the main road. Just standing there, the cars whizzing by. You couldn't help but feel for her. She stood there for thirty minutes. An hour. Then she turned round, and walked back up the street, back to her house. And went inside. And closed the door. (*Beat.*) Me, I went down to the kitchen, to make Lyn a hot-water bottle, nice cup of hot chocolate. And I walked out in the garden, while the kettle boiled. It had stopped raining. And there he was.

Lights up on NED, *looking at him.*

DALE. Ned?

NED *smiles.*

Ned, mate. Are you okay?

NED *just stares at him.*

Look, Ned... It was... Ned. Please.

NED. Help me, Dale. Help me. Please. You have to. Please help me.

DALE. What?

NED. Please. Please don't let me fall asleep. Don't let me fall asleep.

DALE. Ned –

NED. I don't know what I'll do. I... I... Please. I... I'm falling... I'm... Help me.

DALE. Ned –

NED. It's coming. It's coming for me. For me.

DALE. Oh my God.

NED. No. No. No. Please. Help me.

DALE. And then he told me. He told me his dream.

Blackout. Pause.

Spotlight on:

NED. I'm alone. In the middle of a forest. I'm surrounded by tall pines. It's freezing cold. I feel the wind. The dry, dry wind. On my face. The awful dry chill. Suddenly I see walls growing up around me. Brick by brick. Bricks growing all around. One on the other. Faster and faster. Four walls rising up. Wallpaper growing. Light switches. Fittings. Carpet growing beneath my feet.

A ceiling, closing overhead, closing out the light. I'm closed into a room. I'm in the middle of a room. I know the room. It's a bedroom. My bedroom. (*Beat.*) I'm home. I turn around. And I see it. I see it all. Everything. Everything I'd lost. Everything. It was all there.

Music. Lights up slowly as NED *turns around. The lights come up on all of the things he has lost. The room is full of clocks. Golf clubs. Stuffed badgers. Busts. Books. Lawnmowers. The tandem. The beekeeping kit. The birdbath. Everything. From out of the birdbath, he picks up the gold cufflinks. Holds them up to the light. Reads the inscription. He puts them back.*

The light catches the bed. A figure lies covered there, sleeping.

He walks over. And stands watching her sleep. Slowly he picks up the cricket bat. He holds it in his hands. He slowly raises it and brings it crashing down on the sleeper. Over and over.

Blackout.

Instant spotlight on:

JOY. I stand at the end of the street. I close my eyes and listen to the sound of the rain and the cars whizzing by. Soon the sounds fade. There's nothing but darkness. And when I open my eyes, the cars have gone. The road has gone. The houses have gone. I'm standing in a forest. After rain. I take a step forward. Another. I don't turn round. I just walk. Away. I don't look back. The wind whips up. I'm running against the wind and it's pushing me back. And suddenly the wind changes and it's behind me, pushing me along, carrying me further and further away. And I close my eyes. And I run.

Lights fade to black.

Spotlight on:

DALE. It's funny. You live six feet apart and your paths never seem to cross. Take the couple on the other side. The Harrisons. Pam and Phil. Pam and Pete. Paul. Honestly, they've lived there five years I couldn't pick him out of a line-up. Not like the other side. You'll not be surprised to hear we're still thick as thieves. Still in each other's pockets. The ladies went for a pint only last week. And I bumped into Ned on his way to work this morning. Chatted about this and that. Pencilled in a barbecue. But we never talked about that night. The night he told me his dream. (*Beat.*) Before he rushed off, I asked him if it was still happening. If his stuff was still going missing. 'You know me, Dale. I've got that much junk. That much rubbish I can't keep track of it. I'd lose my head if it wasn't screwed on. What it needs is a good spring clean.' (*Pause.*) They blew up the Arndale Centre Tuesday. Drew a crowd of over a thousand. There was hot dogs, a brass band, kids dancing with their dads and everything. The press was there. The local TV news. I bumped into Ned, but he was too busy to talk. Had this hard hat on. And a walkie-talkie. And now I think of it, yes, unless I'm mistaken, he did look better. Thinner. Less tired. Mind you, it was dark. (*Pause.*) She was there too. Joy. Standing a few rows behind us, among the crowd, in her black mac, shivering, looking up into the dark. (*Beat*.) Then suddenly, a hush fell over the crowd, there was a drum roll, and everyone joined in together, all the mums and dads, all the families what had shopped there for years, all chanting together ten, nine, eight, seven… SIX, FIVE, FOUR, THREE, TWO, ONE – and there was this rumble and the whole thing came crashing down, and when the smoke cleared there was just dust and rubble for ever. Then suddenly, the skies opened and it started to rain.

DALE *looks up*. NED *and* JOY *appear in the half-light, standing apart, still, gazing up at the dark sky.*

The End.

THE NAKED EYE

The Naked Eye was first performed as part of the 10 x 25 season at Atlantic Stage 2, the Atlantic Theater, New York, on 1 June 2011. It was performed by Zosia Mamet and directed by Neil Pepe.

The naked eye.

I was eight years old when Dad lined us up in the kitchen said he had

something important to say.

He said tonight a comet was going to pass Planet Earth. For the first

time in a hundred years, Halley's Comet was going to pass by and be

visible to the naked eye.

It was once in a lifetime, and so he and Mum had decided we were

to be allowed to stay up especially to watch it.

So we all had baths, got in our pyjamas and coats and scarves on and

sat down in the garden on deckchairs, under the stars.

Dad said we would remember this night for ever, and tell our

children about it. We had cocoa and biscuits and the radio was on

talking about the comet. It said the comet had first been spotted in

240 BC by Babylonian astronomers, how it was made of volatile

compounds, and had a tail which extended a hundred million

kilometers into space.

All day long Dad had been really excited. He kept checking the sky, changed the batteries in the

radio twice, mowed the lawn, washed the mildew off the deckchairs, put them in the sun to dry.

Then he got in the car and disappeared for two hours, and when he came back he put a box on the table and unpacked a small telescope. It was black, about two feet tall. He said he'd bought it

for the family, and it belonged to all of us. He sat at the table reading the assembly instructions,

and carefully put the thing together. He shaved, even though it was the weekend, and around

sundown I saw him ironing his pyjamas in the kitchen. I'd never seen him use an iron before. He

did it very carefully, so as not to put any creases in them, to make them perfect.

So there we were, in the dark, in pyjamas, in deckchairs, in a line, gazing up at the sky. After a

couple of hours Mum said she was tired and went inside to

bed, but the rest of us sat up waiting. My brother started dropping off and Dad suddenly stood up

out of his deckchair, picked him up and shook him. 'Wake up,' he shouted. 'You can't miss this.

It's important.' My brother looked really scared.

It got colder. I did everything I could to stay awake. I pinched

myself. Took deep breaths.

At midnight, the sky clouded over. The stars disappeared. There was

nothing we could do. The comet was up there, soaring past and we

were going to miss it. It would not be back for a hundred years. By

then, everyone, Mum, Dad, my sister, my brother, the neighbours,

everyone in our town, the whole world. Everyone would be dead.

Me and my brother and sister, we turned to Dad. And there he was,

fast asleep in his deckchair. With his hands behind his head, and sticking out of his pyjama flies, was this great big boner. Standing

up straight. Big as a milk bottle. Hard as iron.

My little sister said, 'What's that?'

And my big brother said, 'It's bedtime.'

I picked up the telescope and carefully carried it indoors. Though it was only small it was heavy,

cold, and slippery with dew. I put it on the table in the corner of the lounge, turned off the light,

and went to bed.

The radio said in olden days people thought the comet was a sign.

That it meant something wonderful or terrible was about to happen

JEZ BUTTERWORTH

Mojo (1995), *The Night Heron* (2002), *The Winterling* (2006) and *Jerusalem* (2009) were all premiered at the Royal Court Theatre, London. *Jerusalem* transferred to the Apollo Theatre in London's West End in 2010, the Music Box Theatre, New York, in 2011, and back to the Apollo later in 2011. *Parlour Song* was premiered at the Atlantic Theater, New York, in 2008, and at the Almeida Theatre, London, in 2009. *Mojo* won the George Devine Award, the Olivier Award for Best Comedy and the Writers' Guild, Critics' Circle and Evening Standard Awards for Most Promising Playwright. *Jerusalem* won the Best Play Award at the Critics' Circle, Evening Standard and WhatsOnStage.com Awards, and was nominated for the Tony Award for Best Play. Jez wrote and directed the film adaptation of *Mojo* (1998) starring Ian Hart and Harold Pinter, and *Birthday Girl* (2002) starring Nicole Kidman and Ben Chaplin, and co-wrote and produced *Fair Game* (2010) starring Sean Penn and Naomi Watts. In 2007 he was awarded the E.M. Forster Award by the American Academy of Arts and Letters.